E-GOVERNMENT IN DEVELOPING COUNTRIES

E-GOVERNMENT IN DEVELOPING COUNTRIES
THE ROLE OF PRIVACY AND DATA PROTECTION

DORCAS FADAYO

KNOWLEDGE
BAKERS

KNOWLEDGE BAKERS

Cataloging in Publication Data--DK

Courtesy: D.K. Agencies (P) Ltd. <docinfo@dkagencies.com>

Fadayo, Dorcas, author.

E-government in developing countries : the role of privacy and data protection / by Dorcas Fadayo.

pages cm

Includes bibliographical references.

ISBN 978-93-49964-06-8

1. Internet in public administration--Ghana. 2. Data protection--Ghana. I. Title.

LCC JQ1875.A55A8 2023 | DDC 352.3802854678 23

Published by : **Knowledge Bakers**
Pune, India
Email: knowledgebakers2019@gmail.com

ACKNOWLEDGEMENTS

I would first of all like to thank the almighty God, for protecting and seeing me through the study. I dedicate the thesis to the loving memory of my late father, Joseph Kwabena Bekoe and late brother, Kwame Boakye-Bekoe, through whose relentless efforts, encouragement and support, I have come this far. And to my mum, Grace Dapaah, whose prayers and love, have kept me focussed, I say thank you for providing me with love, support and inspiration.

I am most grateful to the Government of Ghana for awarding me the scholarship to pursue this PhD Programme. I would like to extend my sincere thanks to The Churches' International Student Network Hardship Fund, DMU PhD Completion Fund and DMU Hardship fund for the financial assistance when my external funding finished. I would also like to thank Prof Mike Ocquaye, the former Deputy Speaker of Parliament and other government officials of the Ghana government for their assistance during the research fieldwork. I am highly indebted to Mr Dominic Amoako for volunteering to transcribe part of the fieldwork data.

This thesis would never have been completed without the support and encouragement of my supervisors, family and friends.

I must commend my entire supervisory team for all their support and constructive criticism. I am very grateful to Professor Simon Rogerson, who gave me the opportunity to undertake this research, but had to retire before the successful completion of the research.

I must say, this research would not have seen the light of the day without Dr Ben Fairweather, my first supervisor. His support and encouragement contributed immensely to the successfully completion of the research. At a very critical period of the research when I thought everything was lost, he gave me hope to move on. To my second supervisor, Dr Richard Howley, who first introduced me to Privacy and Data Protection during my Masters Degree programme, I say thank you for showing me the way. I also appreciate your contribution and encouragement throughout the research work. Dr Catherine Flick, the later addition to the supervisory team, really made an impact to the successful completion of the thesis. Her feedback and comments have been really helpful. I am also most grateful to my examiners: Dr. Sara Wilford (Internal Examiner - De Montfort University), Dr. Kutoma Wakunuma (Internal Examiner – De Monfort University) and Dr. Penny Duquenoy (External Examiner – Middlesex University), for the suggested post viva revisions. I agree with their suggestions which helped strengthened the theoretical underpinning of the thesis. I also agree with them that the research model was complex and it was therefore reviewed to ensure that it works.

To my family, both at home and abroad, I will like to say thank you for being there for me. A special thanks to my three young lovely kids, Erica, Joseph and Sarah, who do not yet understand why I spent so much time researching and writing this thesis report instead of playing with them frequently. To the entire Bekoe family, I say thank you all for being there for me.

I am also thankful to all the interviewees who participated in the research for their time, patience, and valuable information and suggestions. Last but not the least, my appreciation goes to all members and fellow PhD students (both past and present) of the Information Society Doctoral Programme for their useful discussions, kind words and above all friendliness.

There are many people out there, whose names I cannot possibly list all here, but who have in various ways contributed to the successful completion of this PhD research. To all of you, I say 'big thanks' for everything.

CONTENTS

LIST OF FIGURES

Page

LIST OF TABLES

Page

ABBREVIATIONS

ACS	Affiliated Computer Systems
BPS	Business Process Solutions
CAC	Consumer Advocacy Centre
CHRAJ	Commission on Human Rights and Administrative Justice
CIC	Community Information Centre
DPA	Data Protection Act
ECOWAS	Economic Community Of West African States
EOCO	Economic and Organized Crime Office
EU	European Union
FARSTARS	Fair Adequate Rights Specific Transfer Accuracy Retention Security
G2B	Government to Business
G2C	Government to Citizen
G2G	Government to Government
GFA	Ghana Football Association
ICT	Information Communication Technology
ICT4AD	Information Communication Technology for Accelerated Development
IDI	ICT Development Index
IDV	Individualism
IICD	Institute for International Cooperation and Development
IS	Information Systems
IT	Information Technology
ITU	International Telecommunications Union
IVR	Indulgence Versus Restraint

KACE	Kofi Annan Centre of Excellence
LTO	Long-Term Orientation
MAS	Masculinity
NGO	Non-Governmental Organisation
NITA	National Information Technology Agency
OCED	Organisation for Economic Co-operation and Development
PDI	Power Distance Index
PDP	Privacy and Data Protection
UAI	Uncertainty Avoidance Index
UK	United Kingdom
UN	United Nations
UNESCO	United Nations Educational, Scientific and Cultural Organization
US	United States
WWW	World Wide Web

1

Research Introduction

1.1 Introduction

This study investigates the role of privacy and data protection in e-government implementation in Ghana. It explores issues that arise when e-government is introduced in developing countries[1] in Sub-Saharan Africa[2] (see table 1.1), with particular focus on Ghana.

Angola	Cote de'Ivoire	Liberia	Senegal
Benin	Djibouti	Madagascar	Sierra Leone
Botswana	Eritrea	Malawi	Somalia
Burkina Faso	Ethiopia	Mali	South Africa
Burundi	Gabon	Mauritania	Swaziland
Cameroon	Gambia	Mauritius	Tanzania
Central African Republic	Ghana	Mozambique	Togo
Chad	Guinea	Namibia	Uganda
Comoros	Guinea Bissau	Niger	Zambia
Congo	Kenya	Nigeria	Zimbabwe
Congo DR	Lesotho	Rwanda	

Table 1.1: Sub-Saharan African Countries

Source: Cagle et al. (2006)

---

[1] For the purposes of this study a developing country is a country in which the majority lives on far less money - with far fewer basic public services - than the population in highly industrialized countries. It may be one where the populace lacks education; where there is a large knowledge gap and technological innovation is scarce; where health and education systems are poor and/or lacking; and where transportation, potable water, power and communications infrastructure is also scarce. (Source: The World Bank, 2014).

[2] Sub-Saharan Africa expands the entire African continent south of the Sahara Desert. This portion of the continent differs from the North African nations in terms of culture, climate, and basic ways of life and, most importantly, its level of technological advancement (Cagle et al, 2006). Its nations are the targets of this study.

The research focuses on Ghanaian citizens' access and use of e-government services in the light of any perceived privacy risk. It looks at how privacy and data protection affects e-government implementation in a developing country like Ghana. However the findings may be generalisable to those other Sub-Saharan African countries which have sufficiently political and socio-cultural characteristics, for instance Nigeria.

It must be noted that this study does not seek to compare the role of PDP in e-government implementation in developed and developing countries. However, there may be a degree of subtle comparison between Ghana (the case study and a developing country) and UK (a developed country) in the course of the investigation. The UK was chosen among all the other developed countries due to their shared core values and principles with Ghana (Commonwealth Network, 2014).

By virtue of Britain (and for that matter UK) having colonised Ghana, both countries have a shared past. Henry Bellingham, the UK's Minister for Africa in a speech says that the strong and vibrant relationship between the UK and Ghana is "rooted in our long-standing economic, political and cultural connections, our shared values, and the deep links between our peoples" (GOV.UK, 2011). This relationship has been used to strengthen each other's development (with of course Ghana currently being more on the receiving end). Britain has influenced Ghana in so many ways, especially education and judiciary. For instance, common law is a legacy from Britain to Ghana. The recent Ghana Data Protection Act (DPA) 2012 was enacted along the lines of UK DPA 1998. The above therefore justifies the selection of UK as a developed country to compare with Ghana in the investigation of the study phenomena.

There have been quite a number of academic studies on e-government implementation in recent years, see examples in table 1.2 below. Most of these studies have been undertaken in developed countries[3] with a few taking place in developing countries.

Privacy and data protection (PDP) has also attracted research interest from the academic world. However there are only a few researchers, for example, Carter and McBride (2010) and Belanger and Hiller (2006), who focus on the combination of these two important areas in one study at the same time. Studies which focus on privacy and data protection in e-gov-

[3] A developed country is "[a] country whose per capita income is high by world standards;" and a developing country is "[a] country whose per capita income is low by world standards; same as less developed country. As usually used, it does not necessarily connote that the country's income is rising."(Source: Deardorff's Glossary of International Economics). Examples of developed countries are the UK and US.

ernment in developing countries, and for that matter sub-Saharan African country such as Ghana are rare. This research seeks to fill that knowledge gap.

Study title	Source
Implementation of e-government at the local level in underdeveloped countries. The case study of AP Vojvodina.	Paroski et al. (2013)
Critical success factors for e-government infrastructure implementation.	Janssen and Borman (2013)
Assessment of success factors of e-government project implementation: challenges for the Kosovo e-government perspective.	Rexhepi et al. (2012)
E-government implementation strategies in developed and transition economies: A comparative study.	Weerakkody et al. (2012)
Evaluation of e-government implementation at federal, state and local government levels in Malaysia	Bakar (2011)
Strategies for e-government implementation in developing countries: A case study of the Botswana government.	Moatshe and Mahmood (2011)
Emerging barriers in e-government implementation.	Angelopoulos et al. (2010)
Digital government implementation: a comparative study in USA and Russia.	Pardo (2010)

Table 1.2: Some academic studies on e-government implementation

Through a literature search it was found that a "critical obstacle in realizing e-government is the citizens' concern on privacy of their life and confidentiality of the personal data they are providing as part of obtaining government services" (Layne and Lee, 2001). Ebrahim and Irani (2005) highlight privacy as a barrier frequently cited in e-government strategy studies. This brings to the fore the important role of PDP in e-government implementation. It is therefore imperative to examine the privacy and data protection issues which arise when e-government is implemented in Ghana.

Research is sparse with regards to the role of privacy and data protection in e-government implementation in developing countries in sub-Saharan Africa, such as Ghana. To fill this gap, the study employed a case study methodology to investigate the role of PDP in e-government implementation in Ghana.

From fieldwork in Ghana, qualitative data was collected through semi-structured interviews and focus groups with the stakeholders from government departments and agencies (notably, the Ministry of Communications and the National Information Technology Agency (NITA) - the main government body in-charge of the e-government implementation), parliament, universities, private and public organisation and the general public. Guided by set criteria (see section 6.3), purposive sampling was used to select the interview participants. In total, 53 participants were interviewed (the composition is displayed in tables 6.2 and 7.2). Each individual one-to-one interview lasted in about one hour. Each focus group (six in a group) was also conducted within an average time of 3 hours.

Grounded theory approach (Straussian version) was borrowed to support the analysis of the fieldwork transcribed data. Documentation, for instance the draft copy of the Ghana Data Protection Bill 2010, and media reports, which the participants made available during the fieldwork, were also used in the analysis.

1.2 Research rationale

Ghana is a significant choice for this investigation for various reasons. It has in recent years initiated plans to implement privacy and data protection legislation as well as an electronic government (e-government) project. The Data Protection Act 2012 has been passed and the e-government implementation is at a "cataloguing stage" (Layne and Lee, 2001) where there is online presence of the government. Currently the government makes information available to the citizens on its website (www.ghana.gov.gh). The portal displays information about government day-to-day activities and its policies. It also displays links to its various ministries, departments and agencies. However, the citizens' ability to interact with government online is much more limited.

The e-government project is on-going and with time citizens will be able to apply for services such as driving licences, passports and employment online. However these online transactions with governments, as found out in previous research (Carter and McBride, 2010; Belanger and Hiller, 2006; Ebrahim and Irani, 2005; Layne and Lee, 2001) carry potential risks to the citizens. The potential for identity theft and fraud raises privacy concerns. Table 1.3 below highlights identity theft cases involving Ghanaians. Consumer Advocacy Centre, Ghana (CAC) has also expressed concern where "people used the SIM[4] card registration as an opportunity to retrieve con-

[4] The Ghana government through its agency, National Communications Au-

sumers' personal information to engage in criminal activities, which leads most of the consumers into trouble" (GraphicOnline, 2014). This is a case of some Ghanaian criminals victimising other Ghanaians by perpetrating identity theft against them.

Headlines	Source
Ghana West Africa Still A Hot Zone For Scams, Say Investigators	Birch (2012)
Man Claiming To Be From Ghana Arrested For Identity Theft at Linden Walmart, Police Say	Augenstein (2013)
Ghanaian Couple Who Stole Dead Woman's Identity to Claim False Benefits Are Jailed	WalesOnline (2013)
Catherine Kyie [A Ghanaian] Jailed over Woman's Identity Theft	BBC NEWS SOUTH EAST (2013)
Fake [Ghanaian] doctor with stolen ID saw 500 patients in South Carolina	Nikolas (2012)
Peel Police Arrest Six in Identity Theft Operation Allegedly Linked To Ghana	Wilkes (2011)
2 from Ghana Arrested in Bolingbrook on Fraud Charges	ABC EYEWITNESS NEWS (2014)

Table 1.3 Examples of identity theft cases involving Ghanaians

The Guardian (2013) newspaper report on "Snowden[5] leaks" also brings to the fore how even governments violate their citizens' personal privacy online. In spite of the examples of the potential risks aforementioned, no evidence was found of Government conducting an analysis to assess these risks.

It is in the light of this that the study seeks to investigate the role of privacy and data protection in the e-government implementation, especially in a country, which "has recently come to be recognized as a major hub for cyber-criminal activity" (Warner, 2011). Ghana has been cited as

thority, directed all telecom operators in the country to register subscribers' SIM cards starting from July 1, 2010. Mobile phone subscribers had to provide their personal details backed by an official national identity document to the service provider before they could make calls with a new SIM. Existing subscribers had up to a year get their SIM cards registered (Ghanaweb, 2010).

[5] Edward Snowden, an American citizen and a computer professional, revealed a number of mass-surveillance programs undertaking by the US government's National Security Agency (NSA), not only on American citizens but foreign nationals as well (The Guardian, 2013)

among the top ten countries in the world involved in cyber fraud (Internet Crime Complaint Center, 2010), popularly called *Sakawa*[6] in Ghanaian parlance (Boateng et al., 2011; Warner, 2011). What is unique and worth mentioning here about this Sakawa menace is perpetrators indulge in occult ritual practices to enhance their quest to defraud their online victims (Oduro-Frimpong, 2012).

Sakawa involves "manipulating evil occult powers to perform successful internet fraud. In order to gain occult powers 'Sakawa boys' are said to perform socially grotesque rituals ranging from sleeping in coffins to cannibalism. These rituals endow Sakawa boys with the power to spiritually enter the internet; possessing the mind of the foreign fraud victim to extract quick and easy money" (Armstrong, 2011).

Even though Warner (2011) states that, foreigners are the victims of Sakawa, however it must be pointed out that Ghanaians are victims as well. As reported by Armstrong (2011) in a study, the "expense [of the Sakawa] is not just paid by close kin and the local community; misfortune is inflicted on the entire nation". There is loss of life – human life is sacrificed for the ritual. This involves the sacrifice of a perpetrator's close family member, such as, mother, brother, sister or child, "who would die suddenly and inexplicably before the gains from the scam were realised" (Burrell, 2012, p.190).

Armstrong (2011) points out that "a wide range of Ghanaians condemn Sakawa as "not Ghanaian" behaviour which raises fears for Ghana's national identity and international reputation." However the activities have been gaining roots in the Ghanaian society such that certain Internet Cafes have come to "function as a de facto private clubs where customers who were not known to operators [Internet Café management] or regular users of the café were unwelcome" (Burrell, 2012, p.187).

Interestingly, the Sakawa has been ongoing and the perpetrators are not arrested for a reason that the Police "lack the technical knowledge needed to tackle the problem" (Boateng et al., 2011).

The widespread of this Internet scam and the law enforcement agencies inability to bring to justice "pose a barrier to prospective new users and to some of the broader users of the Internet café if these spaces came to be dominated physically or in the public imagination by scamming practices" (Burrell, 2012, p.187).

Guermazi and Satola (2005, p.42) write that "as a result of the FBI report [on cyber fraud activities in the country], Internet shopping was banned

[6] Sakawa is a local parlance for 'computer-assisted crime' (Wall, 2010, p. 99) in Ghana.

for Ghana, credit card holders in Ghana can no longer use their cards to buy online". The FBI report is not unexpected since some Ghanaians have been in the news recently for identity theft cases as highlighted in table 1.3.

This raises privacy concerns for potential users who will provide personal data in exchange for the e-government services. According to Layne and Lee (2001), this is a critical obstacle in realizing e-government. Also, the country's Corruption Perceptions Index score of 45 indicates a serious corruption problem (Transparency International, 2012), therefore giving credence for such a study to be undertaken to explore privacy and data protection issues in Ghana's e-government implementation project.

1.3 Ghana profile

Table 1.4 presents the profile of the country with key emphasis on information and communication technology (the main enabler of e-government) figures. Ghana is a coastal country in West Africa. It shares borders with three French-speaking countries namely: Togo (to the east), Ivory Coast (to the west) and Burkina Faso (to the north) - see figure 1.1.

Table 1.4: Ghana profile

Source: CIA-The World Factbook (2013); ITU (2013); UN (2012) and the World Bank (2012); Internet World Stats (2014)

Location	**Western Africa**
Political structure	Constitutional democracy
Population	25,199,609 (2013 est.)
Adult literacy	71.5%
E-government readiness	0.3159
Internet users (per 100 people)	14.1
Fixed broadband Internet subscribers (per 100 people)	0.25
Internet	6.56 Mbps (March 2014 est.)
Mobile cellular telephone subscribers	26.33 million[7] (ITU 2013 est.)

[7] The number of mobile phone subscriptions exceeds the national population. This suggests that some individuals subscribe to more than one mobile network. A survey conducted by Research ICT Africa confirms that most mobile phone owners have, or have had multiple SIM cards (Gillwald and Stork, 2008). The non-availability of Mobile Number Portability (MNP) in Ghana until July 2011 (NCA, 2011) may be a contributing factor. MNP is a process that allows a mobile network subscriber to switch mobile networks without the need to change their mobile number.

It gained independence from the British on 6th March 1957. The country is currently governed by a presidential system of government which has some similarities to that of United States (US). There are three branches of government:

- The Executive branch: This is headed by a President who is both the head of state and head of government and also the Commander-in-Chief of the armed forces. There is also a Vice President (who is also part of the Executive), ready to assume the presidency in the absence of the president. The position of the president is limited to two four-year terms;
- The Legislative branch consists of a single House of Parliament with 230 members from different political parties; and
- The Judiciary branch, which is overseen by the Supreme Court, has an appointed Chief Justice as its head.

Where the Executive and Legislative branches are elected by the people, members of the Judicial Branch (especially Supreme Court members) are appointed by the President and confirmed by Parliament (Government of Ghana, 2013). The 1992 constitution of Ghana encourages multiparty democracy which "has led to political culture embracing free debate" (Bowen, 2010) in Parliament.

The total land area of Ghana is 238,538 square kilometres (92,100 square miles); the southern coast line being 554 kilometres (334 miles) wide and the distance from the south to the north being 840 kilometres (522 miles). It has a population of about 25 million. English is the official language and there are about fifty-six other Ghanaian dialects. The major ones are: Akan, Dangbe, Ewe, Kasem, Gonja, Dagare, Gas, Dagbani and Nzema (CIA World Factbook, 2013; Ghana Government, 2013). "A decentralised central government administration has been fostered at local government level where there are 10 Regional Co-ordinating Councils, 170 Metropolitan, Municipal and District Assemblies which serve to involve grassroots participation in the formulation and implementation of government policies and the general development of their areas of jurisdiction" (Ghana Investors Galore, 2011).

Until the number portability was introduced in Ghana, it was not possible for Ghanaian mobile subscribers to switch networks while retaining their entire original mobile phone number. Therefore, mobile phone subscribers, in order to not lose their contacts, used their old subscription (SIM) alongside the new one, thus resulting in multiple SIMS hence the mobile phone subscriptions exceeding the total national population.

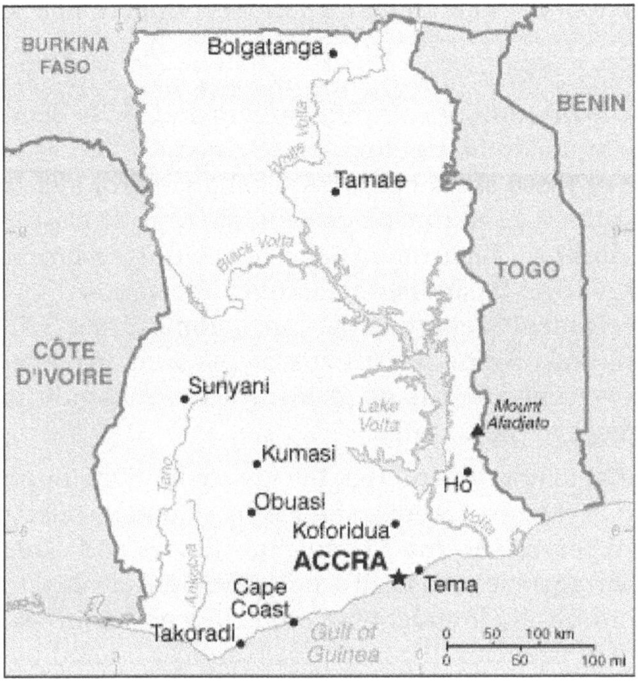

Figure 1.1: Ghana map

Source: CIA-The World Factbook (2013)

With only 14.1% of the total population having access to the internet as shown in table 1.4, Ghana is placed tenth, out of 33 African countries and 117th out of 152 countries on global ranking on the International Telecommunications Union (ITU)'s 2012 ICT Development Index (IDI) (International Telecommunication Union, 2012; Bowen, 2010). Access to broadband Internet connectivity in Ghana, as in many Sub-Sahara Africa countries, is very low. According to Internet World Stats (2014), the average internet download speed in Ghana is 5.6Mbps. Fosu (2011) in a study to exploring the potential of wireless technologies to accelerate universal Internet access in Ghana, attributes the low Internet speed to high access costs. The country's IDI of 2.23, low Internet access figure and low Internet speed pose a challenge to its e-government implementation.

1.4 Research background

The study identifies work that has been done on the research topic and the gap that exists. It bridges the gap by answering the research questions in section 1.7. There is evidence to show that Ghana has "low Internet user penetration" (International Telecommunication Union, 2012; IGF, 2011;

Bowen, 2010) and also only 6 percent of the population visit the government portal to access information (see figure 1.2), yet the country is keen on implementing e-government. Bélanger and Carter (2009) point out that "the uneven distribution of computer access and skills biases the governments' ability to make their online services equally accessible and beneficial". In spite of these challenges, the Ghana government is still keen on implementing the e-government project. There is already a government website with links to departments and agencies (Government of Ghana, 2013) for citizens and businesses to access information about government policies. Government departments can communicate with each other through emails and officials are using a *.gov.gh* domain name as their email addresses (Government of Ghana, 2013). These are all indications of e-government presence in the country.

It is essential to understand that the idea behind the implementation of e-government in countries across the world is to make electronic delivery of government services to the citizens, businesses and other government departments or agencies. Basically, e-government is about the way governments electronically interact with their citizens, businesses and various departments and agencies. It covers how services offered by governments are conducted on-line.

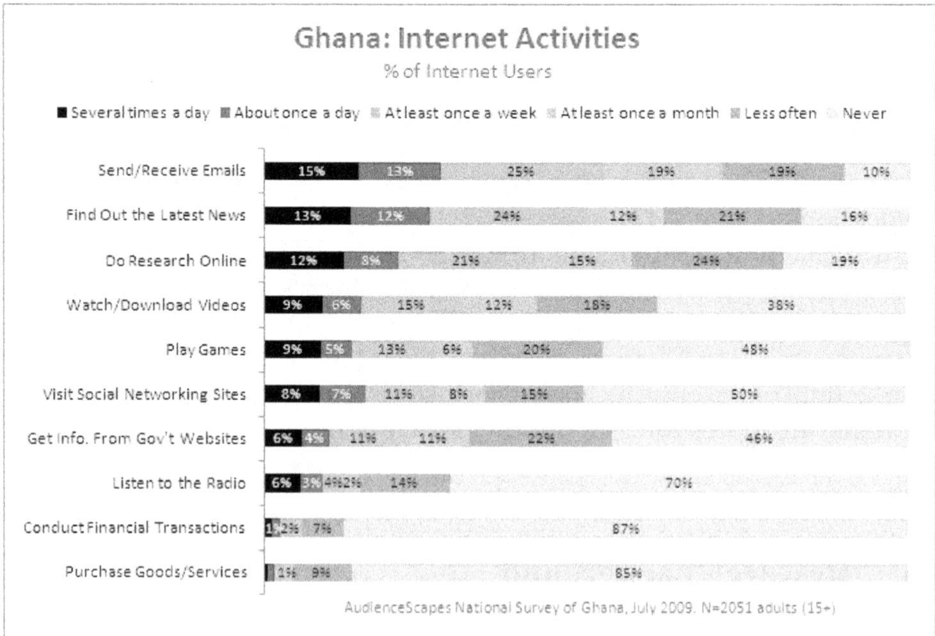

Figure 1.2: Percentage of Internet users in Ghana

Source - Bowen (2010)

Currently, in Ghana, if an individual wants to apply for a passport or driving licence he/she has to go to the appropriate department or agency in person. In an attempt to eliminate this manual way of transacting business with the public and also to cut down the paperwork, the Government of Ghana has initiated an e-government implementation project. The government's objective for this project is to improve public sector performance by eliminating the delays in offering services to citizens, businesses, departments and their subsidiary agencies (Republic of Ghana, 2003). In fact the Ghana ICT for Accelerated Development (ICT4AD) policy document highlights strategies for the implementation of e-government as well as privacy and data protection. One of its strategies is to "ensure that the development, deployment and exploitation of ICTs within the economy and society and related legal and regulatory provisions will balance and protect community and individual interests, including privacy and data protection issues" (Republic of Ghana, 2003). Following the hosting of government website, the government has initiated an e-Ghana project, which seeks to "computerise the entire Government system, by extending network connectivity of the national ICT backbone infrastructure to all Districts and providing a National Data Centre to manage its operations remotely from a central point" (Government of Ghana, 2013). This will make government abandon its reliance on paper-based, face-to-face services, and strives to conduct majority of its business electronically.

According to Chaffey (2009, p.28) it is "the application of e-commerce technologies to government and public services for citizens and businesses". It involves "using the Internet as a means to deliver services and information…[which] allows users to register for government services" (Dempsey et al, 2003) and in so doing personal data is collected. As mentioned in section 1.1, this however raises privacy concerns.

Privacy in the context of this study can be defined as "an individual's claim to control the terms under which personal [data] is acquired, disclosed, and used" (Hiller and Belanger, 2001). Dempsey et al. (2003) point out that "privacy cannot be an afterthought in the design of information systems" and for that matter e-government implementation. Fairweather and Rogerson (2006, p.173) add that "e-government should also offer a good level of data protection and security". It can thus be deduced from the aforesaid that the role of privacy cannot be overlooked in the implementation of e-government. Governments therefore may need to create and enforce the privacy and data protection legislation to protect the online personal information of users.

E-government is in part a way that Governments liaise with their various departments through the use of ICT. Furthermore, through e-government governments may be able to provide better, effective and efficient services to their citizens (Wescott, 2003). Jaeger (2003) identifies low costs, improved services and economic development as among the benefits of e-government implementation. However, the implementation carries potential risks to users. The potential for online identity theft and fraud raises privacy concerns.

Anderson (2003, p.11) points out that "countries seeking to promote e-government must protect the privacy of the information they collect". Article 12 of the Universal Declaration of Human Rights states that "no one shall be subjected to arbitrary interference with his privacy, family, home or correspondence, nor to attacks upon his honour and reputation. Everyone has the right to the protection of the law against such interference or attacks". Dix (2005) in a letter to the United Nations (UN) Chairman of the Working Group on Internet Governance stated that "Data Protection and privacy are human rights in a global information society and should be taken into account in any new setup for Internet governance". news.bbc.co.uk (2009) quotes the then EU Telecoms Commissioner Viviane Reding as also saying that "People's privacy and the integrity of their personal data in the digital world is not only an important matter, it is a fundamental right". The aforementioned therefore depicts privacy and data protection an important issue in e-governments implementation.

Having ascertained the importance of privacy and data protection in e-government implementation in the western countries through literature review, this research therefore seeks to investigate its role when e-government is implemented in Ghana. It specifically explores privacy and data protection and other related issues that arise when e-government is introduced in Ghana.

1.5 Research topic

In view of the above, the following research topic is proposed:

Empirical investigation of the role of privacy and data protection in the implementation of electronic government in Ghana.

As already mentioned in section 1.2 privacy and data protection has been studied extensively in developed countries, however fewer studies have been undertaken in developing countries such as Ghana.

Ghana, as a collectivist society[8] (Hofstede et al., 2010; Hofstede, 2014) tends to have a low privacy concern. At the same time its ranking as among top ten countries in the world involved in identity theft, with its associated

[8] Collectivist society is explained in detail in section 2.12.

Sakawa menace (as already mentioned in section 1.2) makes the country a particularly interesting case study for research. It is therefore essential to explore the extent to which privacy and data protection issues affect e-government implementation.

1.6 Research aims and objectives

The research aims to evaluate e-government, privacy and data protection issues in Ghana. As mentioned earlier in section 1.2, Ghana has been reported to be among the ten top countries in the world involved in cyber crime. There have also been news media reported cases of identity theft involving Ghanaians (see table 1.3, above); and corruption and lack of transparency remains a serious challenge across the country. These indicators make the country a prime case to investigate the role of privacy and data protection in the on-going e-government implementation.

The research aims will be achieved by reviewing the literature and also findings from analysis of data collected from stakeholders through face-to-face interviews and focus groups.

The research particularly sought to achieve the following objectives:

- To explore the role of privacy and data protection in e-government implementation;
- To identify factors which affect e-government implementation;
- To investigate empirically these factors and the relationship between them; and
- To recommend to the Ghanaian government measures that can be taken to support the implementation of e-government.

1.7 Research questions

Since issues concerning privacy and data protection are broad, the study focuses on the importance of privacy and data protection in the implementation of e-government in Ghana. It seeks to achieve the aims and objectives of the research by answering the following questions:

- *To what extent is privacy and data protection crucial to e-government?*
- *What current issues or challenges, regarding Ghana's e-government implementation, do stakeholders consider particularly significant issues?*

The research questions will be answered by analysing the views of stakeholders (that is, government officials, members of parliament, top civil servants, Information Systems (IS) staff and users) collected during fieldwork in Ghana. Having considered the various research methods (see

Chapter 4) a qualitative approach was chosen to collect the fieldwork data.

A qualitative approach is "a subjective approach which includes examining and reflecting on perceptions in order to gain understanding of social and human activities" (Hussey and Hussey, 1997, p.20). This approach, in the context of this study, allowed the researcher to answer the research questions outlined above.

Interview and focus groups were the methods used in collecting data for the analysis. These methods were chosen because of the direct access, one-to-one interaction with the stakeholders. For example, members of the Select Committee of Communications in Ghana Parliament and some other government officials agreed to face-to-face interviews. This direct access to the policy makers and government officials involved with the e-government implementation was a unique opportunity to solicit responses which were first-hand "privileged information". It facilitated an in-depth understanding of the Ghana e-government implementation process and privacy and data protection issues within it. Responses from participants were recorded and transcribed. Apart from the laborious task of transcribing there was also a large amount of data to analyse and interpret.

1.8 Thesis structure

This section presents a brief outline of each chapter of the thesis report:

Chapter 2: Literature review

The chapter reviews the literature stemming from the work that has already been done on the research topic and identifies the gap that exists. It focuses on the concept of e-government, privacy and data protection. It then takes a look at the privacy and data protection issues that arise when e-government is implemented by governments.

Chapter 3: Theoretical framework

Employing Hofstede's dimensions of national cultural model this chapter lays out the theoretical framework that examines the impact of national culture on privacy concerns of citizens in the implementation of e-government.

Chapter 4: Research methodology

This chapter gives details of the methodology employed in carrying out the research. The, philosophy, strategy, methods and design used in answering the research questions are presented. The chapter discusses the philosophical assumptions in information systems research, approaches and various qualitative research methods and the rationale for the choice of strategies. All these are explained taking into consideration the research questions outlined in section 1.6. It also describes the technique used in collecting the fieldwork data and gives reasons why interviews and focus groups were chosen over and above other available research techniques.

Chapter 5: Pilot study

The chapter discusses the pilot study that took place with a sample frame of staff from the Ghana High Commission in London, UK, before the main fieldwork was undertaken in Ghana. It highlights the reasons for conducting the pilot study; and its contribution to the adapted research methods and the overall research.

Chapter 6: Fieldwork report

The chapter presents the report of the fieldwork and a subsequent follow-up that took place in Ghana. It describes the purposive sampling method that was used to select the research participants. The interviews and the focus group processes, and the ethical considerations of the research are also highlighted in this chapter.

Chapter 7: Data analysis procedure

The strategy used in analysing the data is explained in this chapter. It discusses how the data analysis technique, borrowed the Straussian version of Grounded Theory, was employed to create the codes, categories and their associated concepts.

Chapter 8: Data analysis and findings

How the data was interpreted to arrive at the study findings is presented in this chapter. The research findings and model are discussed and the relationships among the emerged categories, concepts and attributes are presented.

Chapter 9: Research recommendations and conclusion

The research implications, contributions and limitations are presented in this chapter. A suggestion on areas for further research is highlighted. The chapter also highlights recommendations for policy makers and the Ghanaian Government.

1.9 Conclusion

The study seeks to examine the privacy and data protection issues which arise when e-government is introduced in developing countries such as Ghana. The study justifies why Ghana is chosen for the research investigation. It employs a qualitative approach, interviews and focus groups, to gain an in-depth understanding of the role of privacy and data protection in e-government implementation.

By hosting a website for information to be accessed by citizens and businesses, and departments communicating with other through emails, the Ghana government is already delivering information and services electronically to the citizens, businesses and its departments. This means there is already an initiation of an e-government project in the country. The literature search (further discussed in Chapter 2) has shown that privacy and data protection is very important in the implementation of e-government. It is related to some human rights and should therefore enjoy strong protection by governments (McRobb and Stahl, 2007).

Ghana is an ideal case for investigating the research phenomena, considering its unique position as being among the top ten countries in the world involved with cyber fraud; news media reported cases of identity theft among Ghanaians; and rampant corruption among government officials. It will be interesting to find out how privacy and data protection will affect the e-government implementation.

The next chapter which is the literature review discusses the work that has been done on the research topic and the gap that exists.

2

Literature Review

2.1 Introduction

This chapter presents a critical review of research reported in the literature that has been undertaken on e-government, privacy and data protection in the context of the research questions as stated in Chapter 1. It will be useful (considering the research topic) to highlight the impacts the implementation of e-government will have on the personal data privacy of the individuals.

Governments all over the world are implementing e-government (Grundén, 2012), they are enacting privacy and data protection laws to protect information collected about their citizens (Belanger and Hiller, 2006). Even though the Government of Ghana has not systematically implemented e-government (Government of Ghana, 2013), one can see aspects of these being practiced in the day to day activities of the people of Ghana. As mentioned in section 1.4 there is a government website presence (Government of Ghana, 2013), however, for now it is for information access only by citizens and businesses. The portal lacks online transaction capacity where for instance citizens can apply for a passport or driving licence (Government of Ghana, 2013); and businesses cannot file tax returns online or download application forms.

Government departments communicate with each other through the use of email. However one can still see major transactions, like renewing driver's license and filling tax forms being done manually. The move by the Government of Ghana to implement e-government may have serious implications on the privacy and data protection of the citizens. "Citizens may be sceptical and mistrust e-government initiatives, believing that these initiatives result in invasion of citizen privacy by government" (Belanger and Hiller, 2006). This is due to the fact that e-government involves using ICT to provide services to the people; and in so doing governments will have to collect and use a wide range of personal information about their citizens. This poses "a wide range of privacy concerns" (Anderson, 2003, p.1).

This research examines and evaluates privacy and data protection issues in in e-government implementation in a developing country, such as Ghana. Since the literature on e-government and privacy and data protection are broad, the review will focus on:

- the steps towards a successful implementation of e-government in Ghana;
- the similarities and differences between e-government implementation in industrialised countries and in less industrialised countries with low ICT penetration;
- the stages of e-government model;
- the main obstacles (i.e. Government commitment, trust, corruption, digital divide, organisational, technological infrastructure, human resources/IT experts, public education etc.) that impede the successful implementation of e-government;
- the extent to which privacy and data protection is crucial to successful implementation of e-government;
- the role of stakeholders in the implementation of e-government, privacy and data protection;
- how e-government is implemented in countries without a history of data protection legislation;
- breaches of privacy and data protection.

The review of literature shows that even though there have been many studies in e-government as well as privacy and data protection. However, studies which have been done on these two areas in one research and which focus on a developing country like Ghana are rare. This chapter thus reviews the above points and link them to the research topic.

2.2 E-government

Chaffey (2009, p.189) defines e-government as "the use of internet technologies to provide government services to citizens". Also, through e-government, governments are able to use ICT to provide better, cost-effective, convenient and efficient services, which allow greater public access to information, and make government more accountable to citizens (Wescott, 2003).

According to Heeks (2001), the implementation of e-government enables governments to efficiently and effectively produce:

- the same outputs at lower total cost;

- more outputs at the same total cost; and
- same outputs at the same total cost in less time.

This can be interpreted as a cost saving for the government which is a benefit of e-government implementation.

2.3 Concepts of e-government

The concept behind e-government is to (if possible) move away from the manual way of providing services thus making transactions between governments and citizens, businesses and government organisations more paperless. However, with Ghana's low Internet penetration (CIA-The World Factbook, 2013; Bowen, 2010), low literacy rate (CIA-The World Factbook, 2013) and lack of basic e-skills (Frempong, 2011; James, 2011), the government attempt to offer paperless services or withdraw manual provision of services may face problems in terms of citizens' access.

The classification of e-government is based on electronic services that governments provide to stakeholders, that is, the citizens of the country (G2C), the business community (G2B) and the government departments, agencies and organisations (G2G) (Lee et al., 2005).

The first of these Government to Citizen (G2C) "facilitates for dissemination of information and use of online services at local and national levels" (Chaffey, 2006, p.14); for instance citizens can apply for or renew their driving licence or passport online. In Government to Business (G2B), government provides its services to the business community electronically. There is also Government to Government (G2G) where inter-governmental services or interactions between government departments take place electronically through email and other online facilities (Reddick, 2004; Lee et al, 2005).

According to the World Bank (2011), e-Government usually describes relationships across 3 modalities:

1. *Government to Citizen:* deals with the relationship between government and citizens. G2C allows citizens to access government information and services instantly, conveniently, from everywhere, by use of multiple channels.
2. *Government to Business*: consists of e-interactions between government and the private sector. The opportunity to conduct online transactions with government reduces red tape and simplifies regulatory processes, therefore helping businesses to become more competitive.

3. *Government to Government:* Governments depend on other levels of government within the state to effectively deliver services and allocate responsibilities. In promoting citizen-centric service, a single access point to government is the ultimate goal, for which cooperation among different governmental departments and agencies is necessary. G2G facilitates the sharing of databases, resources and capabilities, enhancing the efficiency and effectiveness of processes.

In G2C, apart from being able to apply for services online, citizens have "the ability to participate in society online" (Mossberger, 2008, p.1). For example, citizens are able to communicate with their elected representatives online; and they can also find needed information about government policies and available services on the local and national websites. To facilitate this, Fairweather and Rogerson (2006) suggest that "there is a need for morally defensible government to make available human (as well as automated) guidance about where to find relevant information". This suggestion, if adhered to, will support citizens in their online information searching. Web access and computer kiosks are products of G2C initiatives and facilitate online access to information.

G2B initiatives include transactions and services government provide online to the business community. The services may be tax and legal regulations (Chaffey, 2007, p.12), tax payment, businesses registration, obtaining and renewal of licences, and other information provided online.

G2G can best be explained by the following statement at the United States (US) government website:

> *The goal of the Government to Government (G2G) portfolio is to forge new partnerships among levels of government. These partnerships will facilitate collaboration between levels of government, and empower State and Local governments to deliver citizen services more effectively (The White House, 2013).*

G2G facilitates internal communications among government departments and agencies; "this includes information collection and dissemination and email and workflow systems for improving efficiency within government departments" (Chaffey, 2006, p.14).

According to UNESCO (2005) the implementation of e-government entails the active participation and involvement of "stakeholders in the entire process". A stakeholder is "any individual or group who can affect or is affected by the actions, decisions, policies, practices, or goals of the organization" (Freeman, 1984, p. 25). Pardo et al. (2000) point out the importance of identifying stakeholders and incorporating their requirements in e-government implementation. Some of the stakeholders (see figure 2.1) identified are:

- Political leaders
- Government departments/agencies
- Citizens
- Legislative bodies
- Private sector
- International organisations and non-governmental organisations (NGOs).

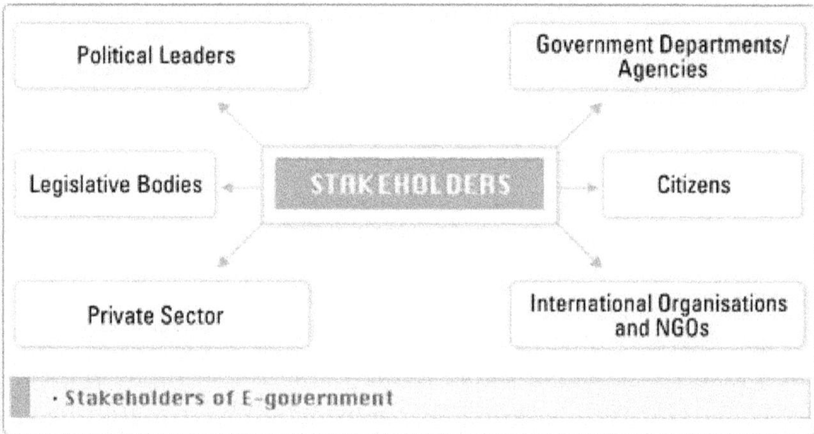

Figure 2.1: Stakeholders of e-government

Source – UNESCO (2005)

There are other identifiable stakeholders (Rowley, 2011) but the above are mentioned here for the purposes of the research phenomena. For instance, Donaldson and Preston (1995) explanation of stakeholders as individuals who are identified through the actual or potential harms and benefits that they experience or anticipate as a result of an organization's actions or inactions justifies citizens as e-government stakeholders. The justification is strengthened by Layne and Lee (2001) pointing out that "citizens' concern on privacy of their life and confidentiality of the personal data they are providing as part of obtaining government services" is a critical obstacle in realising e-government. In other words, the personal data citizens provide in exchange for e-government services carries potential risks to them. The potential for online identity theft and fraud raises privacy concerns, as already mentioned in Chapter 1.

Information and Communication Technology (ICT) has changed the way personal data are collected, processed, stored and even communicated. UNESCO (2005) has identified "Electronic Service Delivery" (which is the use of ICT to offer service) as one of the characteristics of e-government (see figure 2.2).

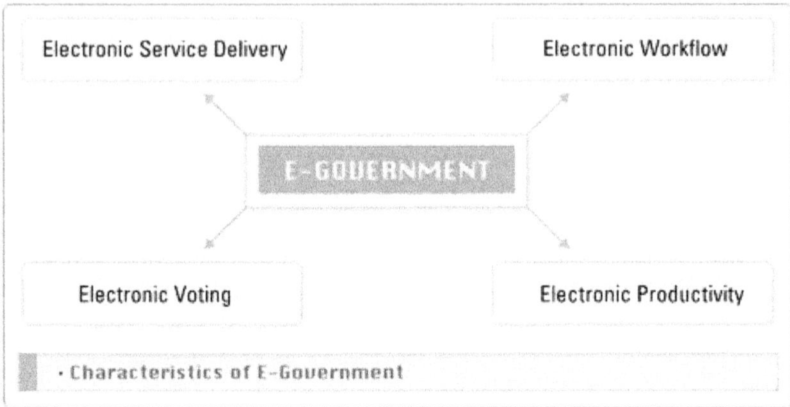

Figure 2.2: Characteristics of E-government

Source - UNESCO (2005)

This leads to conclusion that ICT is the key element in the implementation of e-government. The achievement of e-government is through the medium of ICT. As can be seen from table 2.1 all the definitions of e-government in the various perspectives involve or mention ICT.

Perspective	E-government Definition	Authors
Using technology for political reasons	The use of Information and Communication Technologies (ICTs), and particularly the Internet, as tools to achieve better government	OECD (2004)
Reforming public sector	The use of ICTs to improve the efficiency, effectiveness, transparency and accountability of government	World Bank Group (2004)
Change Management	The use of ICT in public administrations combined with organisational change and new skills in order to improve public services, democratic processes and strengthen support to the public policies.	European Information Society (2004:20)
E-government dimensions	E-government should be divided into four distinct areas of activity, namely e-democracy, e-service provision, e-management and e-governance.	Berri (2004)
Technology	Utilizing the Internet and the World-Wide Web for delivering government information and services to citizens.	United Nations (2003)
Relationships with partners	A government's use of technology, such as the Internet, to aid the delivery of information and services to citizens, employees, business partners, other agencies and other government entities	Layne and Lee (2001)
Political	E-government offers an opportunity for governments to re-organise themselves, get closer to the citizen and co-operate with a variety of societies.	Dunleavy (2002) (Caldow, 1999).

Table 2.1: Examples of e-government broad and narrow definitions

Source - Al-Shehry (2010)

2.3.1 The impact of ICT on Ghana's e-government implementation

It is important to note that even though ICT is a key component of e-government implementation, Ghana's access to ICT as shown on figure 2.3 is inadequate. This suggests a likely major challenge to the country's e-government implementation, if the ICT infrastructure is not developed to the required standard. In a survey conducted by AudienceScapes, Bowen (2010) reports that, only 4% of the total population had access to the Internet. The Ghana Minister of Communications in a speech to First Ghana Internet Governance Forum held in March 11, 2011, stated that "the Internet access in Ghana is still low and hovering around 18% covering about 4 million people, most of whom use the mobile Internet" (IGF, 2011). Ghana places 93 among world ranking of Internet users (CIA World Factbook, 2013). The aforementioned suggest that the country lacks the necessary infrastructures in terms of information, communication and technologies to enable it successfully implement e-government project.

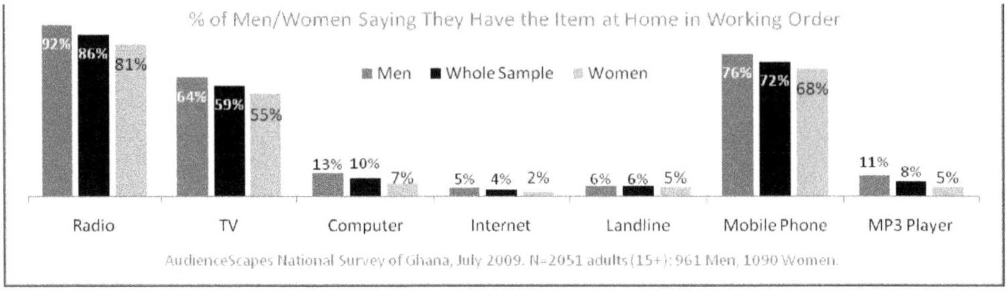

Figure 2.3: Access to Information and Communication Technologies

Source – Bowen (2010)

As can be seen from figure 2.3, there is wide gap between those who have access to Internet (4%) and mobile phone users (72%). According to International Telecommunication Union (2011) "the low Internet user penetration remains low because of a lack of fixed Internet structures". The Union suggests that there is "enormous potential to expand the use of the Internet via mobile networks and phones, particularly as competition [between service providers] increases and prices decline". This is a very important suggestion to be taken in the e-government implementation process. Also since the number of people with access to TV and radio is quite high the government can use these media to reach out to them and even through that educate them about privacy and e-government.

2.4 The four-stage e-government model

A number of e-Government stage models have been suggested by individual researchers (Lee, 2010). Regan (2008, p.129) points out that "when considering privacy in the context of electronic government, the clearest way to identify the privacy issues is to use Layne and Lee's four stage model [see figure 2.4]: 1) cataloguing; 2) transaction; 3) vertical integration: and 4) horizontal".

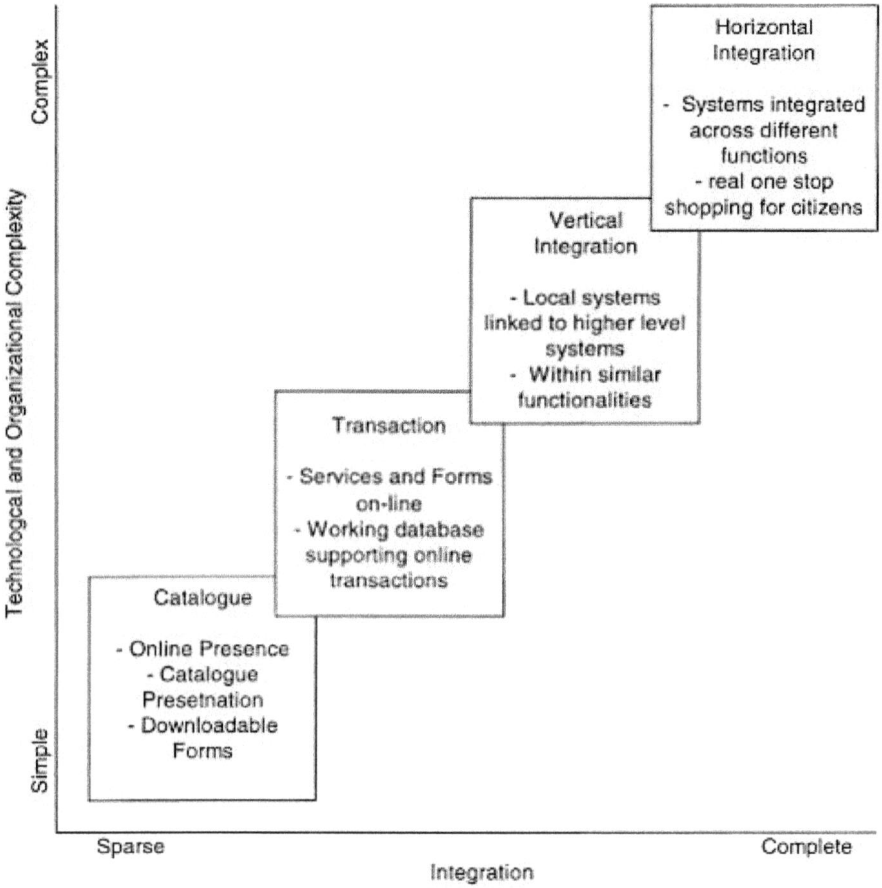

Figure 2.4: Dimensions and stages of e-government development

Source - Layne and Lee (2001, p.124)

Layne and Lee's four stage model is a sequential evolution of e-services which starts with online presence stage and progressed gradually to the stage of sharing information among government departments and agencies (Zakaria, 2013). Regan (2008) makes us aware that different information privacy issues take place in every stage of the model.

2.4.1 Cataloguing

This is the stage where there is online presence of the government. Information dissemination is the most basic form of e-government implementation at this stage, where the government simply make information available to the citizens on its website ((Lee, 2010); Hiller and Belanger,

2001, p.15). Even though at this stage there is no transaction and citizens do not have to submit their personal details, however, Regan (2008) points out two privacy issues occur at this stage. That is, "tracking of individual users and compromising the privacy of data subjects". Layne and Lee (2001) explain "it is possible for the government to track on-line activities like frequently accessed products, the length of time spent on each page, and the length of time spent searching". Regan (2008, p.129) adds that the information collected "reveals not only what pages the user viewed but also how the user arrived at the website and where the user went on departure". Considering Snowden revelation about the tracking of US citizens by the government (The Guardian, 2013), this should be a privacy concern to online users.

These may have been done for national security purposes, but as Saxby (2014) points out "citizens should not be subjected to intrusive monitoring and data collection until a reasonable suspicion of illegal activity exists". In view of this, a former privacy commissioner of Canada, Radwanski, advises governments to "guard against the tendency of governments to create new databases of privacy-invasive information on justified, exceptional grounds of enhancing security, and then seek to use that information for a whole range of other law enforcement or governmental purposes, simply because it's there and available" (The New York Times, 2003). As reported in the UN (2012) survey report "usage of e-services is often associated with security and privacy assurances provided to users". Governments therefore need to post privacy policy on their websites to assure citizens the protection of their online personal data privacy.

Similarly, in the light of Snowden's revelation (The Guardian, 2013) "citizens need to be assured that e-government services are offered to provide benefits rather than monitoring the society" (Akkaya et al., 2012).

2.4.2 Transaction

This stage involves services and financial transaction on the web (Lee, 2010). At this stage government put services and forms online and "establishes or maintains a direct relationship with citizens in order to deliver a service" (Hiller and Belanger, 2001 p.14; p.124; Regan, 2008, p.131). This is an electronic transaction where, for example, individuals can go online and apply or renew their driving licences or passports. As part of obtaining the services at this stage citizens provide personal data which according to Layne and Lee (2001) is a critical obstacle in realizing e-government due to the citizens' concern on privacy.

2.4.3 Vertical integration

In this vertical integration stage, government services are integrated, where local systems are linked to higher level systems, within similar functionalities. Regan (2008, p.134) explains that at this stage of e-government implementation when a citizen conducts a transaction with one level of government any changes with other levels of government will be directly communicated and transacted. For instance, citizens can register and vote online and the information is captured on file locally and at the national level (Hiller and Belanger, 2001 p.16; Layne and Lee, 2001). The integration is beneficial to both e-government providers and users, in terms of, accuracy and timeliness of the information that government agencies use to make decisions about individuals. However, it raises privacy issues vis-à-vis whether the receiving agencies need that information; whether the data subject is aware the transfer is taking place; and also whether the "receiving agencies retains, uses, and communicates the information under similar privacy protections as the original agency" (Regan, 2008, p.134). Also, if "material [is] monitored by the government for unauthorized purposes, the danger to political expression and association" (Fried, 1968) can lead to mistrust in both government and e-government, which can then negatively affect citizens' usage of online services.

2.4.4 Horizontal integration

This is the last stage where systems are integrated across different functions and there is real one stop shopping for citizens. At this stage a single portal is established and citizens or businesses can access the services online no matter which government departments or agencies offer them (Hiller and Belanger, 2001 p.15-16; Layne and Lee, 2001; Regan, 2008, p.135). Hiller and Belanger (2001) point out that, at this stage, "where government services are all accessible through one portal, the government should ensure that all privacy and security practices are consistently displayed no matter what direction an individual is taken on the site when requesting information. It is also important to realize that as government agencies move through the stages of e-government, the level of data collection and constituent privacy concerns increase".

Lee et al (2005) point out that e-government progress does not necessarily follow a linear path as shown in figure 2.4. It is possible for government implementing e-government to skip over certain stages or offer services from different stages simultaneously in a single initiative. The current state of e-government status in Ghana can be classified as stage one, which is catalogue. This means, there is an online presence on the Worldwide Web (WWW) where the government provides information on the Internet and individuals and organisations can access them (Government of Ghana, 2013). Stage 2 of the model (that is the transaction stage), where citizens and businesses can file tax returns, apply for or renew driving licences, etc online are non-existent.

2.5 E-government in developed and developing countries

Rahman (2009) identifies "lack of access to the Internet and other technologies, low literacy levels, and often lack of interest or willingness to use the new technologies," as the main differences between developed countries and less developed countries[9] when it comes to implementation of e-government.

Whereas previous studies (Alshehri et al., 2012; Ambali, 2009; Ndou, 2004) have found *Internet and other technologies; low computer literacy levels; and lack of qualified IT and expert personnel* to be among the main challenges of e-government implementation in developing countries, in developed countries the challenge is the less *"willingness to use the new technologies* [e-government services]" (Ambali, 2009) due to *privacy concerns* (AlGhamdi et al., 2012, Belanger and Hiller, 2006). In the developed countries, for example the US, citizens may be sceptical and mistrust e-government implementation, believing that the implementation may result in invasion of citizen privacy by government (Belanger and Hiller, 2006).

The quest for governments in developed countries to improve the services they offer to their citizens has led to the implementation of e-government being a major issue in governments' programmes. Beynon-Davies (2004) points out that "the political environment of Western [developed] countries has been much subject to the influence of ICT in the areas of electronic government (e-government) and electronic democracy (e-democracy) in recent times". Developing countries in order not to be left behind and also in an effort to bridge the digital divide, are adopting ICT and e-government policies.

The implementation of e-government in developed countries has been possible due to the fact that the infrastructure in terms of internet and other technologies are already in place. Moreover some citizens show an interest and are more than willing to use online services. The same cannot be said about developing countries in that infrastructures are inadequate; and access to the Internet is limited (Sang et al., 2009). Also low level of Internet access in the case of Ghana (see figure 2.3) implies that only a few will be

[9] Less developed country refers to any country whose per capita income is low by world standards. The meaning is much the same as developing country (see footnote in section 1.1). (Source: *Deardorff's Glossary of International Economics*)

able to use electronic services. Table 2.2 presents the major differences between developed and developing countries.

	Developed Countries	**Developing Countries**
History and Culture	• Government and economy developed early, immediately after independence • Economy growing at a constant rate, productivity increasing, high standard of living • Relatively long history of democracy and more transparent government policy and rule	• Government usually not specifically defined; economy not increasing in productivity • Economy not growing or increasing productivity; low standard of living • Relatively short history of democracy and less transparent government policy and rule
Technical Staff	• Has a current staff, needs to increase technical abilities and hire younger professionals • Has outsourcing abilities and financial resources to outsource; current staff would be able to define requirements for development	• Does not have a staff, or has very limited in-house Staff • Does not have local outsourcing abilities and rarely has the financial ability to outsource; current staff may be unable to define specific requirements
Infrastructure	• Good current infrastructure • High Internet access for employees and citizens	• Bad current infrastructure • Low Internet access for employees and citizens
Citizens	• High Internet access and computer literacy; still has digital divide and privacy issues • Relatively more experienced in democratic system and more actively participate in governmental policy-making process	• Low Internet access and citizens are reluctant to trust online services; few citizens know how to operate computers • Relatively less experienced in democratic system and less active participation in governmental policy-making process
Government Officers	• Decent computer literacy and dedication of resources; many do not place e-government at a high priority	• Low computer literacy and dedication of resources; many do not place e-government at a high priority due to lack of knowledge on the issue

Table 2.2: Major differences between developed and developing countries

Source - Chen te al. (2006)

In outlining the differences between developed and developing countries, as presented in table 2.2, Chen et al (2006) point out that "citizens [*in developing countries*] are reluctant to trust online services". Carter and Belanger (2005) in a study find that trustworthiness is a significant factor in citizens' intention to use an e-government service. This suggests that people in developing countries [Ghana included] may possibly be less willing to use e-government services. This poses a challenge to e-government implementation in developing countries, in the sense that, "the success of online public services [and for that matter e-government services], however, depends largely on how well the citizens make use of them (Kumar, Mukerji, Butt and Persaud, 2007)."

Having discussed e-government implementation in developed and developing countries, the next sections takes a look at Ghana's e-government implementation project, with a focus on the challenges the country faces. Sang et al.'s (2009) identified e-government implementation challenges in least developed countries[10] are used for the discussion.

2.6 E-government implementation in Ghana

Knowing how important e-government is to the economic growth and the democratic governance in the country, the Government of Ghana has already taken steps to provide services to the citizens electronically. The government has a website in place to disseminate information to the citizenry. This website is accessible to a minority of the citizens who are privileged to have access to the internet. As shown in table 1.4, out of a population of 25,199,609 only 14.1% are internet users. This low figure of internet users means when e-government is successfully implemented most people would not be able to use it or benefit from it.

Currently, many government departments are operating manual processes. The Ghana e-government implementing agency, NITA (2013), has identified some areas that it hopes to computerise their operations soon, for example e-tax payment and online application for passports and driving licences.

It is anticipated that after the successful completion of these e-projects the citizens will have a preference to access government services online instead of going to the departments or agencies' offices. However this anticipation faces some challenges in terms of access to the new technology and the skills required to use it.

2.7 Challenges of e-government implementation in Ghana

Ghana, as a developing country in Sub-Sahara Africa, faces challenges in its e-government project. Its ICT4AD policy (Republic of Ghana, 2003) identifies the following challenges: limited human resources capacity characterised by low professional; technical and managerial manpower base; as well as poor performance of the economy and those related to the low job creation capacity of the economy. Even though not mentioned in the poli-

[10] Least developed country is a country designated by the UN as least developed based on criteria of low per capita GDP, weak human resources (life expectancy, calorie intake, etc.), and a low level of economic diversification (share of manufacturing and other measures). (Source: *Deardorff's Glossary of International Economics*). It must be pointed out that, least developed countries are also classified as developing countries, therefore the e-government challenges identified by Sang et al (2009) can be used to discuss Ghana's e-government project.

cy, Internet access is also a challenge to e-government implementation due to its low penetration (14.1% - see table 1.4). Likewise corruption among government officials which was previously mentioned in sections 1.2 and 1.6. These and other challenges identified by Sang et al (2009) are used to discuss the e-government implementation issues in Ghana.

Sang et al (2009) have identified the following as the challenges facing e-government in least developed countries. These challenges are applicable to many developing countries, for instance Ghana, where e-government is being implemented. The six categories as shown in figure 2.5 are summarised as follows (Sang et al, 2009):

- infrastructure development - deals with the development of basic telecommunication and ICT infrastructure;
- law and ICT policy - concerned with the laws, rules, regulations, and policies, which must be implemented or changed in order to facilitate the development of both the new infrastructure and information services;
- management - includes strategic issues, human resource management, budget support and allocation, coordination and collaboration between agency leaders, and monitoring and evaluation of the projects;
- equity issues - associated with differential access of traditionally disadvantaged groups;
- the digital divide - is about the gap between those who have access to and use of ICT versus those who do not; and
- privacy and security - dealing with the protection of the personal information the government collects about individuals as well as the protection of e-Government sites from attack and misuse.

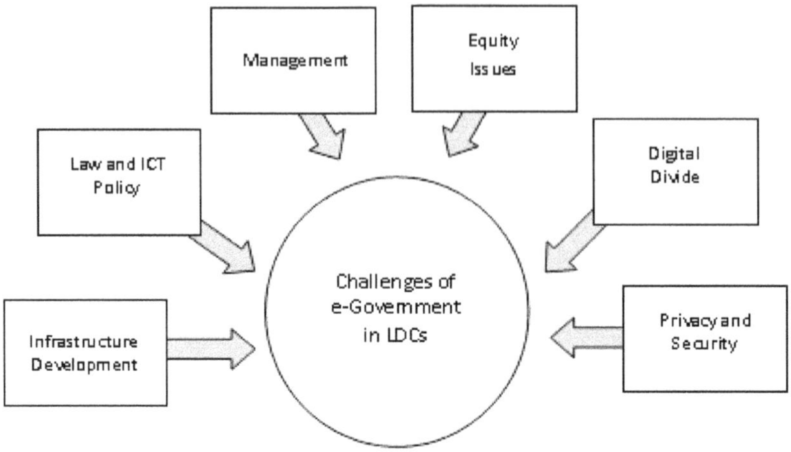

Figure 2.5: Challenges of E-government in LDCs

Source - Sang, Lee and Lee (2009)

Using figure 2.5 and the other challenges highlighted at the beginning of this section the next sub-sections 2.7.1-2.7.8 discuss some of the possible challenges of the implementation in Ghana. They are discussed in no particular order of significance.

2.7.1 Trust and corruption

Vinod (2008, p.121) defines corruption as abuse of a position of trust for dishonest gain, such as taking a bribe. Richey (2010) points out that "stories of political corruption are constantly in the media". For example, a UK newspaper, The Guardian (2009), reported that two ministers of state were forced to resign after a British construction firm, Mabey and Johnson, acknowledged having paid a total of US$ 761,725 in bribes to the Ghanaian government officials during the 1980s and 1990s. In another instance, Aning and Edu-Afful (2013) report that the Ghana Commission on Human Rights and Administrative Justice (CHRAJ)[11] conducted investigations into allegations of corruption and illegal acquisition of assets against four ministers of state and some senior government officials. The Commission made adverse findings against three of the officials but the government at that time issued a White Paper challenging the Commission's findings. All the recommendations by the commission to the Attorney General to prosecute the corrupt ministers were not carried out. Two issues, both bordering

[11] CHRAJ is a human rights commission in Ghana charge to investigate, among other issues, complaints of violations of fundamental rights and freedoms, injustice, corruption, abuse of power and unfair treatment of any person by a public officer in the exercise of his official duties (CHRAJ, 2012).

on trust can be deduced here: the adverse findings against the ministers and the Ghanaian government failing to prosecute them are recipe for the citizens to mistrust the government.

The World Bank (2014b) Enterprise Survey reports that 35.2% of firms operating in Ghana are expected to give gifts to secure government contract. This is not encouraging to IT companies, especially foreign based ones, which may want to establish businesses in the country. It can be a possible discouragement to these potential private IT companies which may want to forge public-private partnership with the government for successful implementation of e-government.

The Ghanaian people seem to be aware of this widespread social and economic canker. Ghana Integrity Initiative (2005) in a survey reports that 92.5% at least, agreed that corruption is prevalent in Ghana and 90.1% consider corruption as a serious problem. Richey (2010) in a research survey reveals that "governmental corruption has large corrosive effects on civil society." One of these effects is that citizens tend to trust less when they perceive that corruption in the country is high (Uslaner, 2004). High corruption, as Mauro (1997, p.5) reveals, leads to ineffective government, and in the survey conducted by Richey (2010), the findings showed that increased corruption lowers the trust people have in government. Mistrust as already found in the literature (section 2.5) poses a challenge to e-government implementation. Carter and Belanger (2005) in a study find that trustworthiness is a significant factor in citizens' intention to use an e-government service.

This notwithstanding, Bowen (2010) survey report indicates Ghanaians have high trust in institutions. The trusting of institutions is evident in the losing party in the 2012 Ghana presidential election contesting the election results in the Supreme Court. Instead of calling on its supporters to go on demonstration or riot, a phenomenon which is gaining normalcy in many African countries, the losing party chose to contest the election results in the court (Pryce and Oidtmann, 2013).

Even though it has been pointed out that corruption influences mistrust in government which may in tend be a challenge to e-government implementation, researchers (Garcia-Murillo, 2013; Bertot et al (2010); Basu, 2004) have found that e-government implementation can itself reduce corruption. It "offers a partial solution to the multifaceted problem of corruption. It reduces discretion, thereby curbing some opportunities for arbitrary action. It increases chances of exposure by maintaining detailed data on transactions, making it possible to track and link the corrupt with their wrongful acts. By making rules simpler and more transparent, e-government emboldens citizens and businesses to question unreasonable procedures and their arbitrary application." Global Corruption Report (2003, p. 30).

2.7.2 Law and ICT policy

Jaeger and Thompson (2003 point out that in implementing e-government, a government must consider elements of policy, including regulatory issues, economic issues, and the rights of users. As previously mentioned in section 1.4, the Ghana ICT for Accelerated Development (ICT4AD) policy has been in place since 2003 and it highlights strategies for the implementation of e-government as well as privacy and data protection. In line with this ICT policy the Ghana DPA 2012 was eventually passed in 2012.

Before the Ghana DPA 2012, Parliament had passed the following laws to deal with issues relating to Ghana ICT industry:

- the National Communications Authority Act (NCA) 769 of 2008;
- the National Information Technology Agency (NITA) Act 771 of 2008;
- the Electronic Transactions Act (ETA) 772 of 2008; and
- the Electronic Communications Act (ECA) 775 of 2008.

However, Frempong (2012) points out that these laws are yet to be fully implemented. The NCA Act 769 for instance, is "to regulate communications by wire, cable, radio, television, satellite and similar means of technology for the orderly development and operation of efficient communications services in Ghana" (Frempong, 2007; NCA, 2014). NITA Act 771 also established NITA, the agency charged with the e-government implementation. The agency also maintains registers for approval given for equipment under ETA Act 772 (NITA, 2014). The ETA Act 772 makes provision for the establishment of an Electronic Communications Tribunal to arbitrate in industry-related disputes (Frempong, 2012).

The privacy and data protection legislation and its impact on e-government is discussed in section 2.9.

2.7.3 Management

Some Ghanaians have expressed their concerns about the challenges facing the e-government implementation. For instance, a prominent Ghanaian academic and lawyer, Professor Takyiwaa Manuh, presenting a paper on *ICT for Government,* is reported as saying that, in the government-to-government sector the challenge of the e-government implementaion is identified as ability and commitment of government and its workers (Ghana News Agency, 2006).

Lack of qualified IT staff and expert personnel and government workers' inability to use the new technology could be a challenge to the e-government implementation. This was evident in the Ghana 2012 election (Pryce and Oidtmann, 2013). Among some of the issues which came up during the elections is the failure of the *new technology,* that is the Biometric Verifying Machine (introduced for the first time to check election fraud), to function properly (BBC, 2012). Inability of the election officials to operate the new technology, as reported by the media (BBC, 2012) was a factor. According to the report, the election officials struggled with the setting up of the machines; and more so they did not know how to use them. A supposedly one-day election therefore took two days and the results were therefore disputed by the losing political party (Pryce and Oidtmann, 2013). This instance brings out two issues namely – inability to use *new technology* and *lack of qualified IT staff and expert personnel.* These are crucial to successful implementation of e-government (Alshehri et al., 2012; Ambali, 2009; Ndou, 2004).

Government has sought assistance from some developed countries and Italy for instances, has been assisting in the in the e-government implementation project with financial aid and infrastructure (GNA, 2008).

2.7.4 Awareness and e-skills

"Before citizens are able to appreciate the relative advantages of e-government services, they must first be aware of this electronic option" (Carter and Weerakkody, 2008). Not only that, they must also be aware of the privacy risks involve in submitting their personal information in exchange for the electronic services.

Bowen (2010) in her survey report points out that:

> *"Although a lack of telecommunications infrastructure and cost factors clearly impede internet access for many in Ghana, another major challenge appears to be lack of knowledge about the web itself. A third of respondents say they do not know what the internet is; half say they do not know how to use it".*

If a third of the people do not know what the Internet is, then the e-government implementation faces a possible challenge, since it is the main enabler of the electronic services.

The survey report finding above suggests *lack of awareness* and *lack of e-skills* among the Ghanaian population. The lack of e-skills permeates the whole society, including end-users and even the service provider staff (that is government workers tasked with the handling of the e-services). The government has already envisaged the challenge the aforementioned pose to the e-Ghana project. It has therefore through the Ghana Education Services (GES) has introduced the teaching of ICT into the educational curriculum (Agyei and Voogt, 2011); and has also initiated free laptops to students (Jamil et al., 2014). This initiative seeks to expand the use of computer technology to the poorer and more rural areas (Buchele and Owusu-Aning, 2007). It is aimed at creating awareness of the computer/Internet technology and also bridging the digital divide in the country, which is discussed below in the next section.

2.7.5 Digital divide

Professor Manuh notes that the implementation of e-government in Ghana is being hampered by obstacles such as access and knowledge gap in the government-to-citizen sector (Ghana News Agency, 2006). This is confirmed by Bowen's (2010) survey report where he states that a third of Ghanaians do not know what the internet is; half say they do not know how to use it. The aforementioned is an indication of a digital divide. The gap in "Internet [access and] usage, naturally, have a significant impact on e-government usage" (Jaeger and Thompson 2004).

Efforts have been made by the government to bridge the digital divide by providing computers and internet access to the people in the rural areas through the Community Information Centre (CIC) project (Awotwi, 2010). However, these Centres are managed by untrained staff with limited knowledge of computers and Internet (IICD, 2012). According to a manager at one of the Centres, they have a limited number of computers with very slow Internet connectivity (IICD, 2012). She adds that, these have always caused long queues to be formed at the centre. Those who did not have patience to wait always left without having access.

In spite of the challenges the CIC project face, the UN e-government (2012; 2014) survey reports indicate Ghana has made progress, a positive change, in its quest of bridging the digital divide – see table 2.3.

Possibly the high subscription rate of mobile phones in the country can be encouraged and supported by the Ghana Government to make up for the digital divide. Ghana mobile phone subscriptions currently stand at 26.5 million (Ghanaweb, 2013). Comparing this figure with the country's current population, 25,199,609 million (CIA World Factbook, 2013), shows that mobile phone subscription is more than the population. This anomaly can be attributed to the fact that some individuals subscribe to more than one mobile phone as already explained in section 1.3. The high mobile subscription is significant in the e-government implementation.

In fact, Bowen's (2010) survey report highlights the usage of mobile phones by stating that:

> *Nearly as many respondents report getting news and information from SMS services as from newspapers, suggesting that at least in terms of national averages, mobile phones are already as important a source of information as some traditional media sources.*

The report adds that "less than 10 percent of mobile phone users say they have accessed or currently access the internet via their mobile"). This suggests that even though mobile phones are widespread they are mostly used for making and receiving calls rather than accessing the Internet.

The Ghana Government can take advantage of this finding in its e-government implementation by raising awareness and encouraging people to use mobile phones to access the e-government services. The high subscription rate of mobile phones can therefore make up for the low Internet penetration.

2.7.6 Equity issues

As previously mentioned in Chapter 1, Internet connectivity is very low in the country, however, the differential access between the rural and urban communities needs to be discussed. Bowen (2010) highlights significant variations in Internet access between rural and urban communities. Figure 2.3 shows how access to ICTs differs in a general sense in rural and urban settings, which is the ratio 1 to 7 (1% to 7%). These figures suggest Internet access seems to be more of a barrier for many rural dwellers than the urbanites. "This limits the utility of digital government and denies the advantages of e-government" (West, 2005) to the rural dwellers.

Williams et al (2012) in a study title *Enhancing rural connectivity through an extended internet cafés business models* point out that the rural areas in Ghana lack of Internet connectivity due to commercial unviability of such investment. Bowen (2010) adds that an obstacle to accessing ICT in rural areas is lack of adequate and reliable electricity. According to the International Energy Agency (2011), the electrification rate in the rural areas is about 14%. "A looming energy supply crisis in sub-Saharan Africa (SSA) [Ghana included] raises concerns about a long-lasting energy shortage" (Suberu et al., 2013). This suggest that even as connectivity improves in rural areas, there are still more obstacles to accessing ICT there.

Lack of resources therefore prevents rural communities from accessing the internet. It must be pointed out that the implementation of e-government is not for a privileged few who are experienced with Internet technology (Booz Allen Hamilton, 2002) or have access to it but for the use by all citizens (Jaeger and Thompson, 2004). In order to address this equity issue the government must therefore develop the rural infrastructure or encourage its development by others, such as by mandating universal service obligations of (mobile) phone companies.

The next section addresses the inadequate ICT infrastructure in the country which is a possible major challenge to the e-government implementation.

2.7.7 Infrastructure development

As previously stated in 2.1.2, the government has taken measures to improve the ICT infrastructure. This is reflected in Ghana moving 22 places up in the global ranking in the e-government development index (EGDI)[12] as in table 2.3.

EGDI 2014	EGDI 2012	2014 Rank	2012 Rank	Change in Rank
0.3735	0.3159	123	145	↑ 22

Table 2.3: Ghana's EGDI for the years 2012 and 2014

Source: UN (2012, 2014)

The 2014 UN e-government *Survey* reports that Ghana has made progress in its e-government implementation. As the table 2.3 shows, its EGDI increased from 0.3159 in 2012 to 0.3735 in 2014. While this may be an achievement, it is inadequate for successful implementation of e-government.

The Ghana Minister of Communications is reported to have said that the "ministry has commenced the implementation of the E-government infrastructure project to provide a national network for networking Ministries, Department, Municipal and District Assemblies as well as other public sector organisations" (Ghana Government, 2010). The Minister's statement suggests that, government recognises the limited ICT infrastructure as a challenge to the G2G sector and it is therefore addressing it.

Fairweather and Rogerson (2006, p.179) point out that "there are benefits to be gained from the provision of e-government facilities to citizens" notably cost savings to the government and convenience to the citizens. These benefits, however, will not be achieved without a cost: the loss of privacy of the Ghanaian citizens (Hiller and Belanger, 2001 p.17).

[12] The EGDI is a composite measure of three important dimensions of e-government, namely: provision of online services, telecommunication connectivity and human capacity. It aims to give a performance rating of national governments relative to one another (UN, 2014).

2.7.8 Privacy and security

The significance of privacy and security in e-government implementation cannot be under-rated. Previous researchers (Millard, 2008b; Norris, 2007) argue that issues such as privacy and security remain as barriers for e-government. Spinello (1995) points out that privacy has been one of the most explosive issues to emerge in this information communication and technology age. Smith and Jamieson (2006) define security as ways of protecting data and records that are kept to record, administrate and monitor e-government agencies' actions and policies.

The UN e-government survey report (2014) emphasises that "privacy and data security issues greatly influence the user uptake of e-government". It therefore behoves on governments to see these issues as challenges to e-government implementation and address them accordingly.

Some organisations in Ghana recognises this challenge in their electronic transaction services and are addressing it. Especially, Bank of Ghana (BoG) has taken extra measures to secure and protect the privacy of their customers. Ghana News Agency (2009) reports that BoG secured for itself ISO/IEC 27001:2005 Certification. The "ISO 27001 certification demonstrated that the BoG had addressed, implemented and controlled the security of the Bank's information, and that BoG's management information and systems were secure to ensure the integrity of data sent out as well as data received, significantly limiting security and privacy breaches" (Ghana News Agency, 2009).

The challenge privacy poses to e-government implementation is further discussed in section 2.11. In the next section, the concept of privacy, with a focus on the type of privacy this research aligns itself with, is discussed.

2.8 The concept of privacy

McQuoid-Mason (1978) highlights different societies' perspective of privacy as follows:

> *[E]ven modern societies have differing concepts of privacy. For instance, while Germans demand closed office doors, fenced yards, separate rooms and strict person to person distancing, the Americans are content with open office doors, unfenced properties and informal rules of personal and social distance. The English on the other hand are accustomed to shared offices and bedrooms, and use 'reserve' rather than doors and walls to preserve their privacy. The French and the Arabs have been described as 'sensually involved' with individual members of their society in a manner which would be offensive to Germans, Englishmen and Americans. It has been suggested that because the Japanese and the Arabs enjoy crowding*

> *together they have no word for 'privacy' [...] but one cannot say that the concept of privacy does not exist [...] only that it is very different from the Western conception.*

The above quotation shows that privacy is recognised in every culture and jurisdiction; however the limits to the exercise of the right to privacy may depend on the social group (Dagbanja, 2014). With Ghana being a collectivist society (Hofstede, 2014), Dagbanja (2014) explains that Ghanaians, in their perception of privacy, would want matters that intimately concern them that they do not want others to have anything to do with to be accorded the needed distance.

Ghanaians' understanding of privacy makes it "seems to be related to secrecy, to limiting the knowledge of others about oneself" (Fried, 1968). It must however be pointed out that people are keen to limit or prevent only negative things about them from the knowledge of others - things that they are worried would bring shame to the family. Fried (1968) however, disagrees with Ghanaians notion of privacy and says that "privacy is not simply an absence of information about us in the minds of others; rather it is the *control* we have over information about ourselves". What Fried wants to put across as the meaning of privacy is just the western conception – having control over one's personal information.

This is not significantly different from Westin's (1967) definition of privacy which states that privacy is the ability of an individual to control the terms under which personal information is acquired and used.

Personal information is information identifiable to a person (Culnan and Armstrong, 1999). The significance of personal information in the context of this research is, it provides value to organizations (government departments and agencies) and their customers (citizens) however its collection (as already mentioned) raises privacy concerns (Culnan and Armstrong, 1999; Bloom et al. 1994). Concerns arise over how the citizens' personal details are collected, processed, stored and even the possibility of disclosure to a third party without their consent. Personal privacy is therefore concern over the loss of privacy and the need for protection against unwarranted communication and use of personal information (Smith et al., 1996).

Privacy is also a human right (see section 1.4) and therefore anything untoward personal information is an interference in an individual right to privacy. However, Dagbanja (2014) argues that "given the group-focused rather than individual-focused nature of Ghanaian society, it is not likely that what will justify interference with the right to privacy in individual-oriented societies will in all cases apply to the Ghanaian context." This brings to the fore the influence of the national culture of privacy which is discussed in Chapter 3.

2.9 Privacy and data protection

Privacy and data protection are two different issues, but are interrelated. They are different in the sense that according to Westin (1967, p.7) and Cate (1997), privacy is "the claim of individuals, groups or institutions to determine for themselves when, how, and to what extent information about them is communicated to others". Data protection on the other hand refers "to the law relating to the use of personally identifiable data" (Hook, 1989). In other words it is the "regulation of the way organizations collect, store, manage and disclose personal information" (Bennett, 2000).

Researchers and writers on privacy issues agree that privacy is difficult to define and that there is no one definition for the term (Clarke, 1999; Tavani, 2004). However some authorities on privacy have come out with various definitions and descriptions. Clarke (1999) defines privacy as "the interest that individuals have in sustaining a 'personal space', free from interference by other people and organisations". Ratson et al (2000) describe privacy "as the desire for individual control over oneself and how that information is used". Chaffey et al. (2003) also refer to privacy as "a moral right of individuals to avoid intrusion into their personal affairs by third parties". These are just a few of the many definitions for privacy.

McRobb and Stahl (2007, p.232) ask whether privacy refers to a "situation, a right, a claim, a form of control, or a value". In the Ghanaian perspective it is a right (The Constitution of Republic of Ghana, 1992). This right of privacy however does not protect online personal data of Ghanaians in this ICT age. Thus the Ghana Data Protection Act 2012 enacted thus seeks to give meaning to Article 18(2) of the 1992 Ghana constitution (BIZTECH AFRICA, 2011). As discussed in the next section with a specific example (Ghana News Agency, 2011c), until the passing of Ghana 2012 DPA, any data privacy violation dispute brought before any court of the country was subject to the interpretation of the presiding judge. Ghana DPA therefore brings article 18(2) to life in the field of computerised data. The way in which ICT has changed how personal data are collected, processed and stored has made privacy to be understood and defined in developed countries (for instance US and the EU member states) as "access to and control of personal information" (Grodzinsky and Tavani, 2005). In the EU countries, it involves access to and control of personal information (European Union, 1995). McRobb and Stahl (2007) add that privacy is about "individual's control over his or her personal information".

In essence the definition of privacy depends on whether one is talking, among other things, about: personal privacy, communication privacy or information privacy. While there is no one agreed definition for privacy

(Clarke, 1999; Tavani, 2004), this research in the context of the research phenomena aligns itself to Westin's definition of information privacy (1967, p.7): *"claim of individuals, groups, or institutions to determine for themselves when, how, and to what extent information about them is communicated to others"*. This definition is in line with the discussion of privacy in this section and in section 2.8 above.

Lange and Lampe (2008) quote the United States the Supreme Court as describing privacy as "including the right of the individual to be free in his private affairs from government surveillance and intrusion and the right of an individual not to have his private affairs made public by the government". Privacy to Ghanaians is "protecting individuals from any overreaching control of others" (Sheehan, 2002). This definition is used in the context of individuals' private affairs which is devoid of online personal information. There is therefore a difference between Ghanaians conception of privacy and that of the western developed countries, especially UK. In spite of this difference, when the time came for the government to implement privacy and data protection legislation it adopted that of the UK and for that matter the EU data protection principles.

Data protection is defined as "essentially that area of the law that governs what may, and what may not, be done with personal information" (Privacy and Data Protection Limited, 2002). Macaulay and Watts (2002) explain that "Data Protection is about looking after people's privacy by making them aware of how information about them is obtained, how it is used and so that it is processed in way that is fair to them". It seeks to legally protect the privacy rights of individuals. In other words it is the law that safeguards an individual's personal information or data from being misused.

Cate (1997) points out that, "privacy and data protection overlap, with each having a wider scope". This research thus recognises the close interrelationship between these two issues and as such deals with privacy and data protection together, while still recognising the possible dissimilarity between them. The Ghanaian Minister of Communications, Haruna Iddrisu, on August 24, 2010, upon opening a National Stakeholders Consultation on the Ghana Data Protection Bill 2010 explains that "Data protection is enacted in order to protect us, our privacy and our data. Data protection is a specific right on its own, and protects the sacred precincts of personal life," (Ghana News Agency, 2010). Thus one can say, data protection protects the privacy of individuals.

A review of countries which already have privacy and data protection legislation shows that although they may have different number of privacy principles they all almost specify the same thing. Whereas UK Data Protection Act (DPA) 1998 has eight principles, Hong Kong Personal Data (Privacy) Ordinance Principles has six and Canada's privacy legislation also has ten principles. Some countries seem to have their legislation more strict than others. In particularly, data protection laws in the EU are regarded as stringent (Informationweek Government, 2011).

The EU directive which required all member states to implement national privacy legislation (European Union, 1995) prompted United Kingdom to create the Data Protection Act 1998. The Act had at its core eight principles (The National Archives, 2011) stating that:

> *Personal data shall be processed fairly and lawfully and, in particular, shall not be processed unless —*
>
> *[...]*
>
> *2. Personal data shall be obtained only for one or more specified and lawful purposes, and shall not be further processed in any manner incompatible with that purpose or those purposes.*
>
> *3. Personal data shall be adequate, relevant and not excessive in relation to the purpose or purposes for which they are processed.*
>
> *4. Personal data shall be accurate and, where necessary, kept up to date.*
>
> *5. Personal data processed for any purpose or purposes shall not be kept for longer than is necessary for that purpose or those purposes.*
>
> *6. Personal data shall be processed in accordance with the rights of data subjects under this Act.*
>
> *7. Appropriate technical and organisational measures shall be taken against unauthorised or unlawful processing of personal data and against accidental loss or destruction of, or damage to, personal data.*
>
> *8. Personal data shall not be transferred to a country or territory outside the European Economic Area unless that country or territory ensures an adequate level of protection for the rights and freedoms of data subjects in relation to the processing of personal data.*

The Hong Kong Data Protection Principles (Office of the Privacy Commissioner for Personal Data, 2001) also states that:

> *Principle 1- Purpose and manner of collection. This provides for the lawful and fair collection of personal data and sets out the*

> *information a data user must give to a data subject when collecting personal data from that subject.*
>
> *Principle 2 - Accuracy and duration of retention. This provides that personal data should be accurate, up-to-date and kept no longer than necessary.*
>
> *Principle 3- Use of personal data. This provides that unless the data subject gives consent otherwise personal data should be used for the purposes for which they were collected or a directly related purpose.*
>
> *Principle 4- Security of personal data. This requires appropriate security measures to be applied to personal data (including data in a form in which access to or processing of the data is not practicable).*
>
> *Principle 5- Information to be generally available. This provides for openness by data users about the kinds of personal data they hold and the main purposes for which personal data are used.*
>
> *Principle 6- Access to personal data. This provides for data subjects to have rights of access to and correction of their personal data.*

According to Hiller and Bélanger (2001) before the Safe Harbor was implemented, the US Privacy Act had been passed in 1974 and amended in 1988. This Act requires that

> *"any agency that maintains a system of records that collects information about an individual that is identifiable by name, number, or other identifier must:*
>
> 1. *Give notice in the Federal Register when new systems of records are created.*
> 2. *Make systems of records accessible.*
> 3. *Inform the individual when information is being collected and about its purpose, and disclose the possible consequences of nonparticipation.*
> 4. *Obtain permission from the individual to share the information.*
> 5. *Give individuals the right to review records and disclosures of records and to submit corrections.*
> 6. *Ensure the accuracy (obtain information directly from the individual when possible) and security of information.'*

The US Safe Harbor principles are categorised under the following: Notice; Choice; Onward Transfer (Transfers to Third Parties); Access; Security; Data integrity; and Enforcement.

Comparing the principles of the UK DPA 1998 and the US Safe Harbor Agreement we can see that they entail almost the same principles. This is not a surprise since the Safe Harbor was put together to bridge the different privacy approaches and provide a streamlined means for US organisations to comply with the data sharing requirements of the 1995 EU Directive on Data Protection (Safe Harbor Review).

This literature review shows that countries which have enacted PDP legislations stipulate what Macaulay and Watts (2002) put in a mnemonic form as FARSTARS which stands for ***Fair, Adequate, Rights, Specific, Transfer, Accuracy, Retention*** and ***Security***.

Considering FARSTARS, ***transfer*** (of data) seems to stand out as the most significant difference between some of the countries which already have data protection legislation in place. For instance, whereas organisations in EU countries can only transfer data to another country which has "adequate' privacy legislation in place, the same thing cannot be said about some other countries, for example, the US.

2.10 Privacy and data protection in Ghana

Privacy and data protection has been a matter of concern to many online users. In a recent survey conducted by European Commission (2011) the results show that three out of four Europeans are concerned about how companies use their information. In view of this, many societies throughout the world are designing or implementing national schemes for privacy and data protection (Howley et al, 2002).

Ghana, as a developing country, enacted the Data Protection Act in 2012. The enactment was necessary because its 1992 constitution makes provision for the fundamental human rights and freedoms of the individuals (The Constitution of the Republic of Ghana, 1992).

Article 18(2) of the 1992 Republic of Ghana constitution states that:

> *'No one shall be subjected to arbitrary interference with his privacy, family, home or correspondence, nor to attacks upon his honor and reputation. Everyone has the right to the protection of the law against such interference or attacks.'*

Although, not specifically mentioned, privacy and data protection of persons (irrespective of colour, gender, religion, creed, race and place of origin) living in Ghana could be taken to be among the fundamental human rights and freedoms under the constitution. The constitution makes provision for privacy of home, property, correspondence or communication (The Constitution of the Republic of Ghana, 1992).

The foundation of what originally represented the Ghana's privacy and data protection regulation was the 1992 Constitution, which stipulates a right to confidentiality of personal life (The Constitution of the Republic of Ghana, 1992). The constitution is however silent on citizens' privacy of online personal data and protection. Until the passing of Ghana 2012 DPA, any privacy violation dispute, for example, the Ghana Football Association (GFA) versus Economic and Organized Crime Office (EOCO) (Ghana News Agency, 2011c)[13], brought before any court of the country was subject to the interpretation of the presiding judge.

The fact that the United Nations published in December 1990 Resolution 45/95 (Guidelines for the Regulation of Computerized Personal Data Files), gives credence to belief that the issue of privacy and data protection is very important. This resolution among other things urges member countries to "develop regulations that require fairness, accuracy and transparency of data files" (Reilly, 2004, p.629). Until Ghana passed the Data Protection Act 2012, the government has in some ways ensured that data or information it collects is secured. For example, the Government started the construction of a primary and secondary national data centres in 2010 to store national information (GraphicOnline, 2013). The centre houses a call centre which would fight cyber security.

Even though the Data Protection Act has been passed, it lacks enforcement, which raises some concern. For example, the Ghana government can show the presence of some form of e-government through its website (Government of Ghana, 2013) there is ignorance and neglect of privacy issues. Another issue is, the Ghana Consumer Advocacy Centre (CAC), as already mentioned in section 1.2, has as at May 2014 drawn the government attention to the fact "people used the SIM card registration as an opportunity to retrieve consumers' personal information to engage in criminal activities, which leads most of the consumers into trouble" (GraphicOnline, 2014). However, there is no evidence to show that this has been acted upon. Even though the enforcing body, the Ghana Data Protection Commission, has already been inaugurated (GNA, 2012), and more than 2 years since Ghana DPA 2012 was enacted the law is yet to be enforced.

The national banks which offer online transactions to their customers have not posted any online privacy policies on their website (Ghana Commercial Bank Limited, 2011; Bank of Ghana, 2011). However there are presence of privacy policies on the foreign banks with their headquarters

[13] This story is discussed in section 2.11

in countries which have enacted privacy laws (Barclays-Ghana, 2013; Standard Chartered-Ghana, 2013).

Danielsson (2007, p.1361) explains that "the privacy policy of an organisation documents how personal data should be used by the organisation, including who has access to which data and under what circumstances, and for how long personal data is retained before being deleted, or made anonymous and aggregated for further use as statistics". The reason for these lacks of privacy policies could be attributed to the non-enforcement of the DPA.

Now that the Ghana DPA 2012 has been passed, when it comes into force it will be obligatory for private and public organisations to host a privacy policy. The Data Protection Commission must enforce it since the policy explains to users how their data are collected, processed and stored.

The Ghana Minister of Communications (Ghanaweb, 2010) directed all mobile phones operators to start collecting information aimed at identifying existing and subscribers. This directive was issued without considering any data protection implications. In other words the directive was issued without consideration as to how the personal data collected would be processed, stored and secured. One may argue that since there was no data protection law in place at that time, the government enforced the directive without any data protection implications. However, since the constitution makes provision for privacy as a human right, subscribers' personal details could not have been collected arbitrarily without letting them know first and foremost how their data would be collected, processed and stored. This was a violation of individuals' privacy, but there was no protest. The public seemed to have accepted this instance as normal.

In UK not only do mobile phones companies collect data about their customers, they also retain data about who subscribers call, when they make the call and where they are when they make the call (BBC NEWS, 2007). For example, in a court case in which a gang is alleged to have stolen £105,000 in a robbery at Fareham's Nationwide Building Society, Jurors were shown mobile phone records which showed the defendants were in the vicinity of the area before and after the robbery (BBC, 2013). Since the disclosure was for prosecution of offenders (which is deem as an exemption in the Data Protection Act) the aforementioned may not be considered as a breach of the UK DPA 1998.

The difference between mobile phone companies in UK and Ghana collecting their subscribers data is, in UK the data collected is protected under the Data Protection Act 1998 while in Ghana there was no privacy legislation at the time to safeguard the data.

Perhaps the reason why there was no privacy legislation in Ghana until 2012 was that, there is low privacy risk. This could result from the fact that "the level of computer literacy and awareness in the country is very low" (Docstoc, 2013). The awareness is not there, thus the public is not very much concerned about data collected on them, the purpose or use. It is interesting to note that people are more than willing and happy to keep their names and contact details in the public telephone directory.

People in Ghana do not really bother themselves with privacy issues until it happens that someone or an organisation has intruded into their personal life or private matters. It is interesting to note that most publically aired violations of privacy cases are about the media publishing private stories about individuals. For instance the Ghana News Agency (2011a) reports that the "media were disregarding the rights and privacy of children" when they published "the name of the 14-year-old girl who was alleged to have murdered her father". In the absence of Data Protection law at the time the incident happened there have been other legislations like Juvenile Justice Act which spells the "protection and privacy of children" thus publishing of the girl's name by the media "constituted a violation" of her privacy (Ghana News Agency, 2011a).

It is probable that the reason why it took Ghana a while to enact any privacy legislation is that, privacy has not been an important issue and also the awareness and consciousness, as mentioned earlier, is not there. With just 59,086 Internet hosts and 1.297 million Internet access (CIA-World Factbook, 2013) it could be deduced that the country has not advanced in ICT so much so that privacy would be an important issue for government to enact legislation on. Another possible reason could also be that the Government is not concern because the processing and storing of peoples personal data is more of manual than computerised, so the threat of someone hacking into an organisation's system from a remote site is non-existent or minimal. It is anticipated that when the Ghana 2012 Data Protection Act is enforced it will make provision for how personal data can be accessed, collected, processed and stored.

Most organisations in Ghana, especially the state owned banks, do not have privacy policies (Bank of Ghana, 2011; Ghana Commercial Bank, 2011). It has been more than 2 years since the DPA was passed yet the law is not being enforced to make these organisations (government departments included) comply with or compel them to come out with any privacy policy. No individuals, or advocacy/pressure groups, civil societies have raised any concerns about it. According to Sarnaik (2001), "a civil society is a public space between the state, the market and the ordinary household, in which people can debate and tackle action". He adds that, it "could include any voluntary collective activity in which people combine to achieve change on a particular issue". Considering how privacy issues, as mentioned above, are overlooked in the country suggest low value of privacy concerns of the people. However, depending on the circumstances, some individuals, may to some extent, show concern about their examination results, bank accounts balance, salary and medical records being made public. For instance, due to the stigma and shame that come to the family, if a person has HIV AIDS he/she would want it to be kept private and confidential; likewise if student fails his/her exams. In a situation like this individuals may have privacy concerns because of the embarrassment and negative impact on the family.

The above discussion suggests the low of value concern organisations (data controllers) and citizens (data subjects) in Ghana seem to attach to information privacy. Yet the country is reported to be "ranked among the world's top 10 countries in cybercrime" (Warner, 2011; Ghana News Agency, 2011; Ghanaweb, 2009) with its associated identity theft cases as mentioned in section 1.2. Guermazi and Satola (2005, p.42) write that:

> *'An FBI investigation of global credit card internet fraud revealed that over $5 million of online shopping fraud was detected to have generated from Ghana. The report shows that even if credit card usage is not very common in Ghana, the offenders managed to hack into credit cards account in Ghana to conduct online transactions.'*
>
> *'Ghana is yet to update its legal environment to respond to such fraudulent activities. The lack of laws protecting against cyber fraud simply means that perpetrators of such crimes can still get away. The implications for the lack of reform can be very costly for Ghana. First as a result of the FBI report, Internet shopping was banned for Ghana, credit card holders in Ghana can no longer use their cards to buy online. The implications for the banks can also be onerous as the combination of lack of an adequate regime for compliance with security procedure and for deterrence of cyber fraud threatens to scare away potential business with wider economic implications for the country.'*

This may have prompted the Ghana Government to pass the DPA in 2012. This study finds out that the Ghanaian population attitude towards privacy differs from that of the Western world. It differs more especially in individual's privacy concerns over online personal data. While the Ghanaian society has low privacy concern over their online personal information, previous studies (Belanger and Hillier, 2006; Carter and McBride, 2010) have shown that privacy concern is high among the people developed countries. The Ghanaian society seems to put their trust in the government; with a notion that it is the government responsibility to protect the personal information it collects from them.

With Ghana named as the one of the locations mostly notably for online romance scams (Internet Crime Complaint Center, 2011) and also reported as among top ten countries in cyber fraud (Internet Crime Complaint Center, 2010), the Data Protection Act 2012 was probably enacted to let the International community see the country is taking measures to curb the menace. In other words it seems the law was passed to allay the fears foreign investors and visitors may have over their personal information and hence increase their trust in the country.

The enactment may have other implications as well. That is, to satisfy the eighth principle EU DP directive and hence boost trade with EU countries as mentioned in section 2.9. It could also be taken as compliant with UN, OECD and the ECOWAS directives.

Considering the account the bad publicity Ghana has in terms cyber fraud, specifically, *the Sakawa menace* (Warner, 2011), the passing of privacy and data protection legislation is timely.

2.11 Breaches of privacy and data protection

As mentioned earlier, Ghana is already involved with the processing of people's personal data. There is even a trans-border flow of data transferred from the US. The Ghana office of the United States firm, Affiliated Computer Systems - Business Process Solutions (ACS-BPS) provides remote data entry of medical records for insurance company Aetna (Turner et al, 2004). ACS sells data processing services to insurance companies in the US.

Some organisations have breached EU data protection laws by transferring customer data to outsourcing companies in India. Actually, the European Data Protection Directive states that: "the transfer to a third country of personal data which are undergoing processing or are intended for processing after transfer may take place if ...the third country in question ensures adequate level of protection". According to Privacy and Data Protection Journal issue of 2004, India did not "have adequate data protection laws" yet some companies in the EU member states were outsourcing in the country.

Brooks (2004) wrote about a customer of Lloyds TSB who objected to the fact that his personal data is transferred to India for processing. According to Brooks, the customer claims that the bank outsourcing its operations to India is a breach of the UK DPA 1998 and also EU data export laws.

Interestingly, the bank has rejected the claims by maintaining that "it has complied with the Act by putting in place appropriate measures to protect customer data".

Perhaps it is the EU Directive that prohibits trans-border flows of personal data which has prompted India to be working on its privacy legislation for approval. Most EU countries and the US have been outsourcing in India which is a boost to the Indian economy. On April 11, 2011 a new privacy and data protection law was passed by the Indian Government (Dalmia, 2011).

Privacy laws enacted by the EU member states, US, Canada, Australia and other developed countries seek to safeguard personal data, yet "reports of privacy abuses abound". In the UK there are reported incidents of government departments and agencies losing sensitive personal data of their citizens. For instance, a medical practice lost patients' details including names, addresses and NHS numbers (BBC, 2011); Sturcke (2008) also reports that "computer discs holding personal information on 25 million people and 7.2 million families had gone missing"; and a Royal Navy officer's laptop which contained the personal details of 600,000 people who had applied to join the UK armed forces got stolen. The US has also had reported cases of privacy breaches. The Identity Theft Resource Center 2009 Data Breach Statistics report showed that 222,477,043 records were exposed from 498 private data breaches.

The US Department of State (2011) reports that even though Ghana 1992 constitution prohibits "*arbitrary Interference with privacy, family, home, or correspondence...*the government sometimes infringed on privacy rights. The report adds that "although the law requires judicial search warrants, police seldom obtained them in practice".

It is evident that "even when privacy legislation is enacted, it does not guarantee good privacy practice, even on the part of government agencies" Appel (2006). It therefore suggests that the passing of Ghana's DPA 2012, commendable effort by the government, will not totally eliminate or prevent possible privacy violations in the country. It may at best reduce occurrences when enforced.

Ghana News Agency (2011c) reports that on December 8, 2010, the Economic and Organised Crime Organisation (EOCO), a government law enforcement agency, in executing an order of the court, proceeded to the offices of the Ghana Football Association (GFA) (which is also a government agency) and took away some computers and documents. The EOCO also took away mobile phones of some of the GFA's personnel as well. The GFA filed an application in the Human Rights Court against EOCO for breaching their rights and privacy. The trial judge in a ruling said the EOCO had exceeded its statutory mandate and by so doing violated the privacy of GFA.

2.12 E-government and privacy

Moon and Welch (2005, p.258) have identified high levels of concern about security and privacy as one of the factors that slows the implementation of e-government initiatives. Arnesen and Danielsson (2007, p.1358) identify some examples of threats to privacy in the implementation of e-government as follows:

- *Data collection capabilities increase as new technology for continuous and automatic data collection is introduced. Examples of such technologies include digital video surveillance, biometric identification and radio frequency identification (RFID).*
- *Data processing capabilities are rapidly increasing. The very existence of large amounts of stored personal data, together with the availability of sophisticated tools for analysis, increases the probability for misuse of data.*
- *There is a trend towards integration of formerly separated governmental services, including physical offices. Providing a single point of contact is more user friendly, but it may also provide an attacker with a single point of attack.*
- *Outsourcing of services (e.g., customer relationship management) is increasingly popular both among companies and governmental organizations. Those who deliver such services to many customers have a unique opportunity to gather personal information from many different sources. If services are outsourced across country borders, and perhaps in several layers, responsibilities soon become unclear.*
- *Even if the organization responsible for stored personal information does not have malicious intents, one cannot expect all its employees to be equally trustworthy. Disloyal employees are a severe threat when increasing amounts of information are stored.*
- *Tax records and other public records made available on the Internet enable efficient searches and aggregation of information about individuals. Identity thefts and fraud are common uses of information gathered in this way.*

These threats are of global concern to on-line users. The speed at which governments are enacting or amending privacy legislation attest to this fact.

An aim of countries developing or enacting privacy and data protection laws is to safeguard the privacy and personal data of their citizens. One can also say that it is to promote economic growth, security and to meet international standards. For instance, without the passing of Safe Harbor Agreement in the US, it would not have been possible to legally transfer airline passenger data from EU member countries to the US authorities; and also it would not have been possible for organisations in the same EU member states to legally transfer personal data of individuals to the US for whatever purpose. This is due to the initial requirement that, organisations in EU countries can only transfer data to another country which has 'adequate' systems for the protection of personal data in place.

2.13 Summary

E-government involves governments using ICT as a means to deliver services and information to citizens. ICT is the "enabled route to achieving good" (Heeks 2001) e-government implementation. There are benefits to be gained from the provision of e-government facilities to citizens, notably cost savings to the government and convenience to the citizens. "These benefits, however, do not come without cost: lost of privacy" (Privacy Working Group, 1995).

Comparing the privacy principles adopted by various countries shows that, even though stated differently, the meaning is the same. These principles set out guidelines as to how personal data of individuals are collected, processed and secured. The only main difference is the transfer of data across international borders. While principle eight of the EU Directive specify that personal data must not be "transferred to any other country without adequate protection in situ", the 1994 US Privacy Act does not mention it. It is for this reason that Safe Harbor was introduced – "to deal with international transfers of personal data" from the EU to US.

This literature review showed that even though some public and private organisations offer online services to Ghanaian citizens no privacy policy and statements have been posted on their websites. Currently the new privacy law to regulate data collection of individuals in Ghana is not being enforced. This may account for the lack of privacy policies on the organisations websites.

The literature search revealed previous studies' (Cullen, 2009; Bellman et al., 2004; Milberg et al., 2000; Milberg et al. 1995) findings which suggest that a country's cultural dimensions may influence citizens' concerns about information privacy and even their adoption of e-government. Ghana was identified as a collectivist society, which suggests the people have low privacy (Hofstede et al., 2010).

The literature review identified digital divide, equity issues, management, law and ICT policy, inadequate ICT infrastructure, and privacy and security as possible hindrance to the successful implementation of e-government.

2.14 Conclusion

Even though this literature review finds that Ghanaians have low privacy concerns, which is in contrast to developed countries; Ghana's new Data Protection Act 2012 and the privacy policies of some organisations/ institutions within the country are all based upon western conceptions of privacy, especially the EU.

Now that the Ghana Data Protection Act 2012 has been passed by parliament every organisation, including government departments and agencies should be made to embrace data protection positively. Staff should undergo training to know their obligations towards protection of customers' personal information and also the consequences and implications of data privacy breach. A report on the government website reveals that the only time a workshop was organised only a few government officials attended (Government of Ghana, 2012); suggesting how little insignificance the public attached privacy and data protection issues.

The Ghana Government has made an effort to bridge the digital divide however, due to inadequate computers, slow Internet connectivity and non-availability of staff with the requisite level of knowledge and skills, the level of achievement has not been as desired.

The CIC project, for instance, may have achieved some little success where "today people living in poorer neighborhoods may be able to surf the web from...community centers...but this is not the same as having automatic access via high-speed connections at home and at the office" (Norris, 2001, p. 92).

E-government is the use of ICT by Governments to offer electronic services to their citizens. ICT is a major factor in the implementation of e-government with a range of associated privacy and data protection issues. E-government cannot be implemented without the provision for PDP. As identified by Howley et al (2002, 2004) IS staff are playing an important role to the provision of PDP. Thus it can be concluded that apart from Government officials and the civil servants, IS staff have also have a contribution towards e-government processes. These contributions of IS staff are very important since in this ICT age, any e-government implementation without PDP consideration can be very risky and costly.

Due to low literacy rate and inadequate technology infrastructure the question of whether the implementation of e-government will be a success is still very much an open one.

The current Internet penetration rate of 14.1% suggests that more than half of the citizenship will not have access to e-government services if government does not take steps to bridge the digital divide. This indicates that what the citizens need most is Internet accessibility and the skills to use the new technology and not privacy and data protection legislation.

Even though Internet penetration is still low it has made progress since the year 2005. According to the World Bank and ITU Internet usage has increased 9% since then. The increase in Internet activity has also come with increase in cyber fraud called "Sakawa" (Warner, 2011) in local parlance. This poses a privacy risks to the e-government users. Privacy and data protection must therefore be in place to safe guard the online personal information of users.

E-government is a key factor for governments in providing better, efficient and effective services to their citizens. Likewise privacy and data protection is crucial to the implementation of e-government. Despite the potential benefits of e-government individuals are wary of its use, due to the privacy risks to their personal information.

Carter and McBride (2010) point out that "when conducting transactions over the Internet it is necessary for [government departments and] agencies to collect data from citizens, therefore collection is integral to the success of e-services". In a situation where citizens submit false personal data due to mistrust in government and for that matter fear of violation of their personal data by government workers is a hindrance to the successful implementation of e-government. Therefore, privacy regulation cannot be an afterthought in the implementation of e-government; it should be incorporated from the initial design and throughout implementation of any e-government project.

There is no empirical evidence to show a similar study has been conducted in developing countries, especially, in Sub-Sahara Africa, such as Ghana. Previous studies which sought to investigate privacy and data protection issues in e-government implementation were undertaken with the survey or fieldwork conducted in developed countries. For instance, Belanger and Hiller (2006) study is the one that comes close to the research phenomena being understudied. They sought to find a framework for understanding the implications of privacy in the electronic federal government. However, the study was undertaken in the US. Similarly, Beldad et al (2011), in a study, also investigated the factors influencing Dutch Internet users' perceptions of the risks in disclosing personal data for e-government services. This was an Internet-based survey which was implemented in The Netherlands, a developed country. This study therefore seeks to contribute to knowledge by investigating privacy and data protection issues that arises when e-government is introduced in a developing country like Ghana.

The next chapter discusses the theoretical framework of the research. It lays out the theoretical framework that examines the impact of national culture on privacy concerns of citizens in the implementation of e-government.

3

Theoretical Framework

3.1 Introduction

Chapter 2 set the scene for the study regarding the crucial role of privacy and data protection in e-government implementation in a developing country like Ghana. Employing Hofstede's dimensions of national cultural model this chapter lays out the theoretical framework that examines the impact of national culture on privacy concerns of citizens in the implementation of e-government.

Research questions, as already highlighted in section 1.7, guiding the study are as follows:

- *To what extent is privacy and data protection crucial to e-government?*
- *What current issues or challenges, regarding Ghana's e-government implementation, do stakeholders consider particularly significant issues?*

The research questions sought to explore the role of privacy and data protection in e-government implementation. They also aimed at identifying factors which affect e-government implementation and empirically investigate the relationship between them.

This chapter discusses the theoretical framework of the research. There are many theories that IS researchers have employed to investigate individuals adoption and use of new technology like e-government. The most common ones include:

- Davis' (1989) technology acceptance model (TAM);
- Rogers' (2003) diffusion of innovation theory (DOI);
- Venkatesch et al.'s (2003) unified theory of acceptance and use of technology (UTAUT); and
- Hofstede's (1980) dimensions national culture model.

The theory that is used is Hofstede's dimensions of national culture

(Hofstede et al., 2010, p.31). Kagitçibasi (1997, p. 11) points out that, "Hofstede's [theoretical] framework is still the most comprehensive comparative study in terms of both the range of countries and the number of respondents involved".

3.2 Hofstede's national culture model

The Hofstede's cultural dimensional model (Hofsetde et al., 2010, p.31) was developed by Geert Hofstede. He worked on the problem of employees' values orientations in the 1970s. He undertook a large scale research in the IBM multinational corporation and its subsidiaries in 40 countries (he later increased the number to 50 countries). His research involved analysis of 117,000 reports which comprised a wide range of professions. He sought to see the differences in the system of national values. He analysed the value orientations of IBM employees who had similar problems in different countries and nevertheless gave different answers to the same questions. From the statistical analysis of the answers, he formulated a four-factor[14] dimensional model of national cultural differences namely: *power distance* (from small to large), *individualism versus collectivism, masculinity versus femininity* and *uncertainty avoidance* (from weak to strong). He defined dimension as "an aspect of a culture that can be measured relative to other cultures" (Hofsetde et al., 2010, p.31)[15].

Previous studies (Cullen, 2009; Milberg et al., 2000; Bellman et al., 2004) have shown that the four dimensions of culture, aforementioned, affect relationships within an organisation (and for that matter country), and may influence citizens' concerns about information privacy. In the same vein, Zhao (2011) and Kovačić (2005) employing these dimensions in separate studies found that worldwide e-government readiness and its components are related to culture.

Among the Hofstede dimensions of national culture, uncertainty avoidance index has been identified as the most influential dimension affecting the adoption of IS (Sundqvist et al. (2005); de Luque and Javidan, 2004; Straub, Keil and Brenner, 1997). Similarly, previous studies (Cullen, 2009; Bellman et al., 2004; Milberg et al., 2000) have identified *individualism versus collectivism* as the most influential national culture dimension affecting information privacy.

[14] Hofstede's model of cultural differences is now made up of six dimensions (Hofstede et al., 2010, p.31) – the other two dimensions, *long-term orientation* and *indulgence versus restraint,* are briefly explained in section 3.6 below.

[15] The information in this paragraph was extracted from Hofstede et al. (2010).

3.3 Criticism and limitation of Hofstede's national culture model

Hofstede's work has attracted criticisms from some researchers notably, Ailon (2008), Baskerville (2003) and McSweeney (2002a). For instance, Ailon's (2008) study of Hofstede's work reveals several inconsistencies in both theory and methodology and therefore cautions researchers against an uncritical reading of Hofstede's cultural dimensions. Baskerville (2003) also identifies problems such as: "(i) the assumption of equating nation with culture (ii) the difficulties of, and limitations on, a quantification of culture represented by cultural dimensions and matrices; and (iii) the status of the observer outside the culture".

Among these critiques, McSweeney (2002a) is the most cited critique (from Google Scholar search). McSweeney (2002a) main argument is that results extracted from a company level, *irrespective of how multinational the research participants are*[16], cannot be generalised to a nation. He supports his argument with the fact that: IBM Company, as a micro-location, is not typical of a nation; and that its employees are not representatives of a country. He also points out that, the main dimensions of culture cannot be identified by a questionnaire. McSweeney (2002a) had a problem with the sampling to which he said "was flawed, being sparse and unevenly distributed".

To make a case for how valid and reliable his national culture model is, Hofstede (2009; 2003; 2002) has painstakingly responded to the critics mentioned above. To McSweeney (2002) criticism, in particular, Hofstede (2002) responds that, what was measured in his study were differences between national cultures; and that the IBM set of data consisted of unusually well matched samples for an unusually large number of countries. He added that "the country scores obtained correlated highly with all kinds of other data, including results obtained from representative samples of entire national populations" (Hofstede, 2002).

Ailon (2009), Baskerville-Morley (2005) and McSweeney (2002b), still not satisfied with aforementioned responses, have counter-responded to insist that Hofstede's national culture model is relied "on fundamentally flawed assumptions and the evidence of the predictive capacity of those depictions is contrived (confirming not validating)" (McSweeney, 2003).

The many criticisms of Hofstede's work from these researchers and the responses from Hofstede himself may probably be due to the fact that "culture is so complex and dynamic; problems of reliability and validity make it difficult to measure" (Davidson, 2009).

[16] The emphasis is mine.

The next section highlights attempts made by this study to avoid the criticisms raised about Hofstede's work and the rationale for employing the model.

3.4 Rationale for employing Hofstede's national culture model

In spite of these criticisms, researchers (see tables 3.2 and 3.3 below) in the field of IS continue to employ Hofstede's national culture model in their studies. Jones and Alony (2007) study into the arena of information systems proving IS scholars additional insight into Hofstede work concluded that it "is the most widely cited in existence...[and] remains the most valuable piece of work on culture for both scholars and practitioners".

This study's attempt to avoid the criticisms raised about Hofsteds's work is presented in table 3.1. It, in particular, addresses the issue of methodology, in terms of data collection appropriateness.

Limitations of Hofstede's study	**Evaluation based on this research**
Data collection appropriateness	Hofstede's study was criticised for using surveys. Considering the concern of using surveys as the data collection method, this study used one-to-one in-depth interviews and focus group interviews as a mechanism to collect data. The researcher believed this study will benefit by using interviews, as understanding the culture in depth can be aided by asking more leading questions as appropriate. For example, the researcher sought to explore why in spite of the potential benefits e-government in terms of convenience and cost, some Ghanaians would still want to use traditional government services; and whether the reasons presented by participants have any cultural connotations.
One company approach	To avoid this limitation, the study involved collecting data from multiple organisations, for example Government's ministries, departments and agencies as well as universities, Internet Service Providers and the general public.

Data too old	As presented in chapter 5 new data was collected for the study.
Cultural heterogeneity	Hofstede assumes national culture to be homogeneous. To avoid assumption of cultural homogeneity, this study collected data from smaller groups (comprising the stakeholders – e-government providers and users) such as academic community, politicians, civil servants, students.

Table 3.1: Review study based on Hofstede's limitations

Adapted from Sutharshan (2013)

Hofstede's dimension of national cultural model has a bearing to this study. As presented in table 3.2 below, previous studies have employed this model to show that the national culture affects relationships within an organisation (and for that matter country), and may influence citizens' concerns about information privacy.

Study title	**Source**
Culture, identity and information privacy in the age of digital government	Cullen (2009)
International differences in information privacy concerns: A global survey of consumers	Bellman et al. (2004)
Does national culture influence consumers' evaluation of travel services? A test of Hofstede's model of cross-cultural differences.	Crotts and Erdmann (2000)
Information privacy: Corporate management and national regulation	Milberg et al. (2000)
Values, personal information privacy, and regulatory approaches	Milberg et al. (1995)
A field experiment comparing information-privacy values, beliefs, and attitudes across several types of organizations	Stone et al. (1983)

Table 3.2: Examples of researchers that employed Hostede's model in their study of information privacy

Table 3.3, also highlights previous studies that have examined the influence of national culture in e-government adoption. Kovačić (2005), for instance, conducted an analysis of the impact national culture has on e-Government readiness and its components for 95 countries by using Hofstede's dimensions of national cultures. Employing the dimensions, Zhao (2011) also examined empirically whether national culture has an impact on e-government development in 84 countries around the world.

Study title	Source
The surprisingly low effect of national culture on e-government adoption: a cross-cultural comparison	Akkaya et al. (2012)
Impact of national culture on e-government development: a global study	Zhao (2011)
The impact of national culture on e-government implementation: a comparison case study	Ali et al. (2009)
E-government adoption: A cultural comparison	Carter and Weerakkody (2008)
The impact of national culture on worldwide egovernment readiness	Kovacic (2005)

Table 3.3: Examples of researchers that employed Hofstede's model in their study of e-government adoption

As seen in tables 3.2 and 3.3, previous researchers have used Hofstede's dimensions of national culture model to investigate the two phenomena understudy (that is, privacy and data protection and e-government implementation) separately. Unlike the previous studies mentioned above in this section, the use of the model in this study focuses on the combination of these two important areas at the same time. The model is used in this study, as the theoretical framework, to discuss the impact of culture on privacy and data protection (for example privacy concerns) in e-government implementation in developing countries in Sub-Saharan Africa, with particular focus on Ghana.

The sections in this chapter explain what culture is and also discuss Hofstede's dimensions of national cultures. The influence of national culture on privacy and data protection and e-government implementation is also discussed.

3.5 What is culture?

A literature search for the meaning of culture resulted in a variety of meanings. The study therefore limits itself to the definitions which are in the context of the phenomena understudied. Hofstede et al. (2010, p.516) define culture as *"the collective programming of the mind distinguishing the members of one group or category of people from others"*. McCort and Malhotra (1993, p.97) cites Taylor (1871) as defining culture "the complex whole which includes knowledge, belief, art, morals, custom and any other capabilities and habit acquired by man as a member of society". This definition relates very well to Ghanaian culture. *Belief for instance, plays an important role in the choices and decisions people take.*[17]

Culture is what makes people from one country different from the other. The differences may due to their "knowledge, belief, art, morals, custom and any other capabilities and habit acquired by man as a member of society" McCort and Malhotra (1993, p.97). Chen (2001, p.56) highlights the importance of culture by stating that "...to understand a person's communication behavior or to communicate effectively with a person from a different culture, it is first necessary to understand the person's culture". Akkaya et al. (2012) point out that national culture shapes the values, norms and behaviours of individuals. They therefore recommend that "governments should offer services considering the cultural characteristics of their nations" It is probably for these reasons why e-government researchers, for instance, Zhao (2011) and Kovačić (2005), employed Hofstede national culture model to examine the e-government readiness of countries and the impact it has on countries' e-government development. Similarly, in Bellman et al. (2004) study, as mentioned in section 3.2 above, they found out those differences in internet privacy concerns are due to the different cultural values that countries have.

As shown in table 3.4, the dimensions of national culture, as identified by Hofstede, correspond to significant issues in social life, which are: identity, hierarchy, gender and truth respectively (Hofstede et al., 2010).

Power distance	Hierarchy	Hierarchy has to do with the extent and nature of inequality between people and groups, and whether or not this is seen as natural or not. The **'power distance'** in different countries varies according to prosperity - generally in more wealthy, there is a **smaller** power distance between individuals, this becomes **larger** is less wealthy countries.
Individualism versus collectivism	Identity	Identity has to do with the relationship between the individual and the group. **Collectivism** is an adaptation to poverty and limited resources and **individualism** as an adaptation to wealth and plenty. As societies become wealthier, they move towards individualism, but remain collective as they deal with the challenge of scarcity.

[17] Researcher personal view

Masculinity versus femininity	Gender	Unequal role distributions between men and women are consistent with tougher societies because there is more emphasis on achievement and fighting and less on caring and compromise. Where there is more equal role distribution, a more 'feminised' society results. Unequal role distribution equates to **masculine**, equal distributions would equate to **feminine** societies.
Uncertainty avoidance	Truth	Anxiety and the search for (the) truth are closely related. Cultures which are concerned with Truth with a capital 'T' are usually unfriendly to outsiders. What is different is dangerous. This is referred to by Hofstede as **'Uncertainty Avoidance'** in contrast to **Uncertainty Tolerance**.

Table 3.4: The basic issues of society (that societies respond to, to produce 'culture')

Adapted from Davidson (2009)

The four dimensions, as preesented in the above table, are discussed in detail in the next section vis-a-vis their influence in information privacy and e-government implementation.

Kumaraguru and Cranor (2006) in a study state that culture affects a population's attitude toward privacy. Similarly, drawing on cross-cultural research in IS adoption and diffusion, Akkaya et al. (2012) posit that "differences among adoption behaviors of nations may be attributed to cultural differences". They add that "national culture shapes the core values and beliefs of individuals, which in turn influence attitudes and behaviors". It is in the light of this that, Hofstede's national culture of dimensions model is being employed in this study to investigate the influence of culture in e-government implementation in Ghana.

The next section discusses Hofstede's cultural dimensional model with particular focus on Ghana.

3.6 Discussion of Hofstede's national culture model

National cultural dimensions, as presented in table 3.5 below, affect relationships within an organisation (Hofstede et al., 2010, p.31), and for that matter a country. The table is an adapted version of Hofstede national cultural dimensional model and it is used here to discuss how attitudes towards privacy and e-government adoption in a society (in particular Ghanaian society) are influenced by its cultural orientation.

	Dimension	What it means	Score - Ghana
PDI	Power distance (from small to large)	It is the extent to which the less powerful members of institutions and organisations within a country expect and accept that power is distributed unequally.	80 - Large power distance society
IDV	Individualism versus collectivism	It is the degree of interdependence a society maintains among its members.	15 - collectivist society
MAS	Masculinity versus femininity[18]	It is what motivates people, wanting to be the best (masculine) or liking what you do (feminine).	40 – low masculine society
UAI	Uncertainty avoidance (from weak to strong)	The extent to which the members of a culture feel threatened by ambiguous or unknown situations and have created beliefs and institutions that try to avoid these is reflected in the UAI score.	65 – Strong uncertainty avoidance society

Table 3.5: Cultural dimensions of Ghana

Source: Hofstede et al. (2010, p.31) and Hofstede (2014)

Ghana's dimensional scores as indicated in table 3.5 and figure 3.1 depict the country as a large power distance, collectivist and strong uncertainty avoidance society. Its score of 40 in the masculinity dimension expects Ghanaians to have low value for privacy concerns.

[18] Hofstede et al. (2010, p.156) caution readers not to be confused about femininity with feminism. They explain that feminism is an ideology that wants to change the role of women in society. In the context of this study, femininity is used for countries that scored from 0-49 in the masculinity dimension.

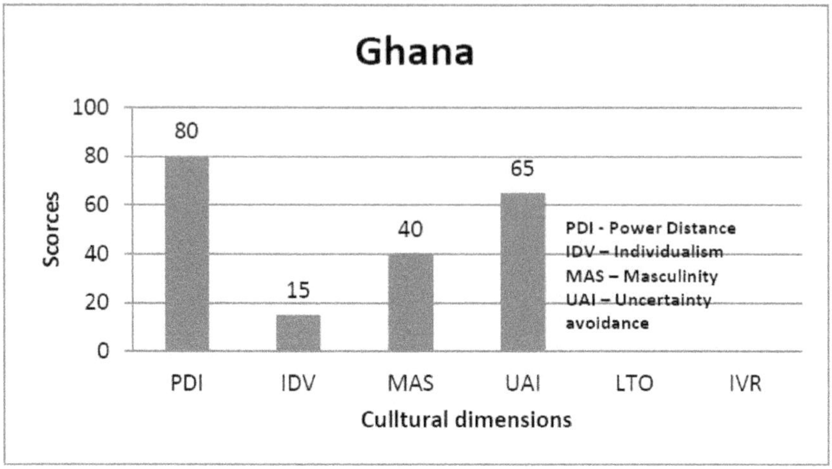

Figure 3.1: National cultural dimensions of Ghana

Adapted from Hofstede (2014)

As already mentioned in section 3.2 and shown in figure 3.1, Hofstede's model of cultural differences is made up of six dimensions (Hofstede et al., 2010, p.31). The two additional dimensions are *long-term orientation (LTO)*[19] and *indulgence versus restraint (LVR)*[20].

For the purpose of this study, only *power distance* (from small to large), *individualism versus collectivism, masculinity versus femininity* and *uncertainty avoidance* (from weak to strong) are discussed. The two latest additional dimensions would not be discussed since there are no available scores on them for Ghana.

3.7 Power distance

Hofstede et al. (2010) explain that power distance is "the extent to which the less powerful members of institutions and organisations within a country expect and accept that power is distributed unequally". It is the

[19] This dimension is the extent to which a society shows a pragmatic future-oriented perspective rather than a conventional historical short-term point of view. Societies with a short-term orientation generally have a strong concern with establishing the absolute truth. They are normative in their thinking. They exhibit great respect for traditions, a relatively small propensity to save for the future, and a focus on achieving quick results (Hofstede et al., 2010).

[20] Indulgence stands for a society that allows relatively free gratification of basic and natural human drives related to enjoying life and having fun. Restraint stands for a society that suppresses gratification of needs and regulates it by means of strict social norms (Hofstede et al., 2010).

conviction of very many people from large power distance societies that "whoever holds the power is right and good" (as highlighted in table 3.6 below) and, by extension, could be trusted with their personal details. It also suggests that citizens from such society are more likely to comply with directives from the government.

Power distance	
Small power distance	*Large power distance*
The use of power should be legitimate and follow criteria of good and evil.	Might prevail over right: whoever holds the power is right and good.
Subordinates expect to be consulted.	Subordinates expect to be told what to do.
Less powerful people and more powerful people should be interdependent.	Less powerful people should be dependent.
Inequalities among people should be minimized.	Inequalities among people are expected and desired.
Scandals end political careers of those involved.	Scandals involving power holders are usually covered up.

Table 3.6: Extracts of the key differences between small- and large-power distance societies

Source: Hofstede et al. (2010, p.72, p.76, p.83)

As shown in figure 3.1, Ghana scores 80 in this dimension, this makes it a large power distance society, which suggests Ghanaians are expected to have high levels of privacy concerns.

3.8 Individualism

Hofstede et al. (2010) explain that individualism is "the degree of interdependence a society maintains among its members". Its opposite, collectivism[21], represents a preference for a tightly-knit framework in society in which individuals can expect their relatives or members of a particular in-group to look after them in exchange for unquestioning loyalty. This means that in collectivist society, intrusion is acceptable and it is not viewed as breach of individuals' privacy.

According to Hofstede et al. (2010) "the right to privacy is a central theme in many individualist societies that does not find the same sympa-

[21] A collectivist society is a society or country that has a dimensional score of 0-49 (Hofstede et al., 2010).

thy in collectivist societies, where it is seen as normal and right that one's in-group can at any time invade one's private life." In the latter, "private life is invaded by group(s)" (see table 3.7 below) which does not raise any privacy concerns among the people. The implication of this is that, people from this society are more likely to accept the intrusion by groups (government and organisations) into their personal life without much of a concern for their personal privacy. They provide personal information to these groups without much of a thought of the risks involved. For instance, a low dimensional index score of 15 by Ghana (see figure 3.1) portrays the country as a collectivist society. It suggests, Ghanaians are more likely to accept intrusion by government and its agencies into their private life (Hofstede et al, 2010, p.130).

This was evident in the mobile phone SIM card registration in 2010 (Ghanaweb, 2010; Malakata, 2010) which was discussed in Chapter 2. It gives credence to the reason why the directive by government to all mobile phone companies in the country to register all their subscribers was successfully carried out. As mentioned in Chapter 2, even though the directive raises privacy concerns the people complied without resistance. There is an implication for this in the context of the e-government implementation. It implies that Ghanaians are more likely to access e-government services without having too much concern about their privacy.

As highlighted in table 3.7, in a collectivist society like Ghana, "people are born into extended families" which make them "interdependent" Hofstede et al. (2010). It means that things that people do privately, for example committing adultery, lead to shame to oneself and the extended family. "Whether shame is felt depends on whether infringement has become known by others. This becoming known is more of a source of shame than the infringement" (Hofstede et al., 2010, p.110). It suggests that people in Ghana are more likely to protect private matter than online personal information privacy.

Individualism	
Collectivist	***Individualist***
Private life is invaded by group(s).	Everyone has a right to privacy.
People are born into extended families or other in-groups that continue protecting them in exchange for loyalty.	Everyone grows up to look after him- or herself and his or her immediate (nuclear) family only.
Interdependent self.	Independent self.

Consumption patterns show dependence on others.	Consumption patterns show self-supporting lifestyles.
Relationship prevails over task.	Task prevails over relationship.
The Internet and email is less attractive and infrequently used.	The Internet and email hold strong appeal and are frequently used to link individuals.

Table 3.7: Extracts of the key differences between individualist versus collectivist society

Source: Hofstede et al. (2010, p.155, p.165, p.180)

The findings of other empirical studies (Bellman et al., 2004, Milberg et al., 1995, 2000) show that the level of individualism-collectivism influences the privacy concerns of personal information submitted online.

3.9 Masculinity

It is what motivates people, wanting to be the best (masculine) or liking what you do (Hofstede et al., 2010). Societies with high masculinity (MAS) scores tend to place greater emphasis on achievement and material success, and possibly on the economic benefits of using private information, over caring relationships and quality of life (Bellman et al., 2004). Its opposite, femininity, stands for a preference for cooperation, modesty, caring for the weak and quality of life. Society at large is more consensus-oriented. Ghana's score of 40 on this dimension is relatively low. This means that the dominant values in the Ghanaian society are caring for others and quality of life.

Masculinity	
Feminine	***Masculine***
Relationships and quality of life are important.	Challenge, earnings, recognition, and advancement are important.
The Internet is used for rapport building	The Internet is used for fact gathering.
Permissive society	Corrective society
Welfare society, help for the needy	Performance society ideal; support for the strong

Table 3.8: Extracts of the key differences between masculinity versus femininity

Source: Hofstede et al. (2010, p.113, p.117, p.124, p.130)

As highlighted in table 3.8, individuals in the feminine society cherish "relationships and quality of life". They are tolerant of each other; and *tend to have little privacy concerns.*

3.10 Uncertainty avoidance

Hofstede et al (2010) explain that the extent to which the members of a culture feel threatened by ambiguous or unknown situations and have created beliefs and institutions that try to avoid these is reflected in the UAI score. Ghana's score of 65 makes it a strong uncertainty avoidance society. According to Bellman et al. (2004), societies with a strong uncertainty avoidance index tend to reduce uncertainty by embracing clear written rules and regulations, and may be more likely to introduce higher levels of government regulation of privacy.

Uncertainty avoidance	
Weak uncertainty avoidance	***Strong uncertainty avoidance***
Comfortable in ambiguous situations and with unfamiliar risks.	Acceptance of familiar risks; fear of ambiguous situations and of unfamiliar risks.
What is different is curious.	What is different is dangerous.
Belief in generalist and common sense	Belief in experts and technical solutions
Citizen protest is acceptable	Citizen protest should be repressed
Citizens trust politicians, civil servants, and the legal system.	Citizens are negative toward politicians, civil servants, and the legal system.
There is fast acceptance of new features such as mobile phones, email and the Internet.	There is hesitancy toward new products and technologies.

Table 3.9: Extracts of the key differences between weak and strong uncertainty avoidance

Source: Hofstede et al. (2010, p.203, p.208, p.217, p.223)

Table 3.9 portrays individuals from strong uncertainty avoidance society to see what is different as dangerous. Unlike weak uncertainty avoidance society, "there is hesitancy toward new products and technologies" (Hofstede et al., 2010). In other words, the willingness to use e-government services by individuals from low uncertainty avoidance is more likely than individuals from high uncertainty avoidance. These suggest that, Ghana's high score in uncertainty avoidance index dimension can negatively affect people acceptance and usage of e-government services.

Having discussed the Hofstede's dimensions of national culture model, with particular focus on Ghana, the next section explores how the dimensional scores affect privacy and data protection and e-government implementation in Ghanaian society.

3.11 Influence of culture on PDP and e-government in Ghana

As already discussed in section 3.3, cultural values are a set of strongly held beliefs that guide the attitudes and behaviour of people in a society (Bellman et al., 2004). Previous studies have been carried out to find out how national culture influences privacy and data protection and individuals adoption and use of electronic services. Kumaraguru and Cranor (2006) for instance found out that culture affects a population's attitude toward privacy. Similarly, Crotts and Erdmann (2000, p.410) also found out that "national cultural differences are one of many forces influencing consumer [citizen] decision making" in their adoption of a service. In view of this, Hofstede's dimensions of national culture as explained above are used to discuss their influence on privacy and data protection and e-government implementation in Ghana.

3.11.1 Culture in privacy and data protection

As was mentioned in section 3.6, in a collectivist society like Ghana, things that people do privately (and are deemed as taboo or against the norms of the society) lead to shame. "Whether shame is felt depends on whether infringement has become known by others. This becoming known is more of a source of shame than the infringement" (Hofstede et al., 2010, p.110). This means Ghanaians are more wont to be concerned about their personal life or private matter than their online personal information privacy.

Stone et al. (1983) define personal information privacy, as "the ability of the individual to personally control information about oneself". What this definition means to an individual in a collectivist society, like Ghana, is the ability to control his or her private matter from becoming public, especially, personal matter that might bring shame to the family.

In other words, individuals are more likely to safeguard personal private matters (especially if they are negative or things that the society disapprove of and will bring shame to the family) than personal online data. In such situations, individuals' privacy concerns are more about preventing or protecting private matter that might cause damage to ones reputation from the public domain. However, in the Ghanaian society, "private life is invaded by group(s)" (see table 3.7). Hofstede et al. (2010) explain that, this does not raise any privacy concerns among the people and it is accepted by the people as normal.

The implication of this to Ghana as a collectivist society is that people are more likely to accept the intrusion by groups (government and organisations) into their personal life without much of a concern for their personal privacy. They provide personal information to these groups without much of a thought of the privacy risks involved. This suggests the Ghanaian people have low privacy concerns.

As mentioned in Chapter 2 and section 3.6, the mobile phone SIM card registration in 2010 is an example of organisations or government institutions intruding on peoples' privacy, yet there seem not to be any protest, and it is deem acceptable. Even though the registration raises privacy concerns but due to the collectivist nature of the people it was faithfully complied with. As pointed out by Totterdale (2012) people from a collectivist society tend to have more trust which suggests "perhaps less concern over the use of personal information and general privacy concerns".

Makulilo (2012) points out that "collectivism denies an individual a space to advance [a] claim for privacy". He found out in a study that although "collectivist culture is an important factor in explaining the limited state of privacy in Africa [Ghana included], it is not a catch-all phenomenon". He adds that "instead, technological, economic, political and social processes have significantly affected privacy consciousness and consequently the systems of privacy and data protection in the [African] continent".

According to Makulilo (2013), "commentators in the field of data privacy are in agreement that the adoption of data protection legislation outside of Europe is largely a result of the influence of the European regime of data protection." Particularly, "the Directive dealing with data transfers to countries outside of the EU have an absolute impact on the data protection policies of every nation that trades with an EU member" (Hobby, 2005). A review of Ghana DPA 2012 supports the aforementioned. The Act incorporates the principles of UK Data Protection Act 1998 (which in itself resulted from EU Directive 95/46/EC). Just like the UK Information Commissioner Office, the Act makes provision for a supervisory authority to enforce the law. There is one major difference though. Whereas, Ghana's DPA 2012 is silent on the international transfer of personal data, the EU Directive is binding for all member countries to ensure "adequate" protection for transfer of personal data outside the EU.

Due to its influence in the other jurisdictions the EU Directive 95/46/EC has been identified as the "most influential instrument of all international codes of data protection policies in the world" (Kuner, 2011). Makulilo (2013) attributes the influence to be "mainly from the Directive's spillover effect". It seems what might have caused the Directive to have so much influence globally is the Article 25 of the EU Directive, which among other things enjoins member countries to ensure an "adequate" level of protection of personal data transfer to countries outside the EU. This implies countries that want to boost trade relationship with the EU, must comply with the Directive, at least with respect to data from the EU.

This means countries outside the EU, Ghana included, are enacting privacy and data protection laws, not just to protect the personal details of their citizens but for economic reasons. However, "no country likes to feel the downward pressure of being dictated to concerning issues that may have significance in terms of a nation's ability to regulate its own affairs, ergo national sovereignty, simply because of economic leverage" Hobby (2005).

The aforementioned suggest Ghana, for instance, with its low concern for privacy due to its cultural collectivist nature would not have bothered to enact the DPA 2012 at the time it did. It would have taken some time since citizens privacy concerns were not an issue. Bellman et al (2004) and Milberg et al (1995) found out that countries implement privacy and data protection legislations when there is growing concerns among the citizens for their personal data privacy. This study is therefore of the view that, considering the country's collectivism nature with its connotation of low value for privacy, Ghana's main reason for implementing privacy and data protection legislation is economic.

3.11.2 Culture in e-government implementation

The discussion in the above section suggests Ghanaians have low concern for information privacy and that its national culture dimensions, specifically collectivism, may be an influential factor. This section discusses whether the dimensions also affect the country's e-government implementation.

As already mentioned in section 3.2, previous researchers have explored the possible influence of national culture in e-government implementation. Akkaya et al. (2012), for example point out that "cultural differences among the nations may be one of the main causes for the different usage and adoption patterns of e-government." National culture explains why individuals in a particular society may prefer face-to-face interaction with public officials/civil servants, when applying for government services, even though online services (as already found out in Chapter 2) may be convenient and cost saving.

Ghana as a collectivist society, as mentioned in section 3.6, is characterised by long-lasting, strong relationship between people. "Face-to-face dependence relationship" (Crozier, 1964, p.222) is a significant trait in this society and people look up to others in assisting them to get task done. As highlighted in table 3.7, in a collectivist society, "relationship prevails over task" where "only natural persons are worthy of trust" (Hofstede et al., 2010) but not computers or the Internet. Also, "consumption patterns show dependence on others" (Hofstede et al., 2010), that is, the use of government services is done with face-to-face with assistance from public officials.

Studies have been carried out to find out how national culture influence services. Crotts and Erdmann (2000, p.410) for instance, found out that "national cultural differences are one of many forces influencing consumer [citizen] decision making" in accepting to use a service. In another study, Warkentin et al. (2002) state "culture is likely to contribute to the adoption or resistance to e-Government".

As found out from section 3.8, Ghana's uncertainty avoidance score of 65 which is high (Hofstede, 2014), can negatively affect peoples' acceptance and usage of e-government services.

As indicated in table 3.9 strong uncertainty avoidance cultures have the tendency to view new, unfamiliar things being introduced into their community as threatening and "dangerous" and try to avoid them. *There is hesitancy toward new products and technologies* (Hofstede et al., 2010), for instance e-government services.

3.12 Conclusion

The applications of the Hofstede's dimensions of national culture have been used to investigate the link between culture and privacy and data protection in e-government implementation in Ghana. The investigation revealed that national culture significantly affects peoples' value of privacy. It was found out from the discussion in this chapter that, Ghana is a collectivist society, which suggests Ghanaians have low value for privacy and this may, to an extent, possibly influence their privacy concerns for their online personal data when accessing e-services. It can be deduced that privacy concerns and absence or presence of data protection law may not be a hindrance to most people accessing e-government.

The long delay of Ghana's Data Protection Bill to until 2012 when it was finally passed into law could be attributed to the collectivism nature of the society where as mentioned in section 3.6 the *people are more likely to accept the intrusion by groups (government and organisations) into their personal life without much of a concern for their personal privacy* thus privacy and data protection legislation is not so much of a priority. Likewise, the femininity nature of the society which (which as discussed in section 3.6) places little or no emphasis on privacy concerns of the people. Privacy and data protection legislation and its enforcement may not be a priority to the government.

The discussion as presented in this chapter has show that there is a link between a country's culture and privacy. It has been found out that people from collectivist society, for example Ghanaians, have low privacy concerns for their online personal data. It has also shown that a country's national culture influences its adoption and use of electronic services, for example e-government services. For instance, people in a highly individualistic country like the UK, are more likely to adopt e-government services than the people from Ghana. This assertion is supported by Ling and Bauer (2000) study which found out that the cultural differences between different countries may influence its adoption and use of e-services.

Using Hofstede's model of national dimension as the theoretical framework for the investigation of this study's topic – the role of privacy and data protection in the implementation of e-government in Ghana, it is concluded that Ghana is significantly characterized as a strong power index (personal relationships), collectivism (power of the group), low masculinity and strong uncertainty avoidance society. These characteristics have the tendency to negatively influence the people's adoption of e-services and for that matter, e-government. However, its collectivism nature also depicts it as a country with low privacy concerns, which suggests, privacy and data protection may not necessarily be an issue in its e-government implementation. In the same vein, Ghana score of 65 in the uncertainty avoidance dimension, which is relatively high, suggests the people may be less willing to use the e-government services when it implemented. This is due to the fact that, high uncertainty avoidance cultures have the tendency to view new, unfamiliar things being introduced into their community as threatening and try to avoid them.

Drawing from above, it is concluded that Ghanaians may not adopt or use the e-government services, not because of their concern for their online information privacy, but probably, for the reason that, they may find the new technology unfamiliar and threatening.

Overall, the theoretical framework revealed how influential national culture can have on citizens concern for information privacy and also their adoption and use of e-government. Akkaya et al. (2012) therefore recommend that "Governments worldwide should design and deliver their e-government services after a very careful examination of their national cultures". Also drawing from the findings of Bellman et al. (2004) and Milberg et al. (2000, 1995) studies which revealed that countries implement privacy and data protection legislations when there is growing concerns among the citizens for their personal data privacy, it suggests that Ghana, for instance, with its low concern for privacy due to its cultural collectivism nature would not have been bothered to implement the DPA 2012 at the time it did. It would have taken sometime for it to be implemented since citizens concerns for their privacy were not an issue.

Having explored the theoretical framework of the study, the next chapter gives details of the methodology employed in carrying out the research. The, philosophy, strategy, methods and design used in answering the research questions are presented.

4

Research Methodology

4.1 Introduction

In this chapter the research philosophy, strategy, method and design used to address the research questions stated in Chapter 1 are presented, discussed and evaluated. The philosophical assumptions underlying approaches to information systems (IS) research; qualitative research methods and data collection techniques are discussed. All these are explained in detail taking into consideration the research questions, aims and objectives. The data analysis approach, discussed in detail in Chapter 7, is also introduced later in this chapter.

4.2 Philosophical assumptions

Myers (2009, p.34-35) explains that every piece of research has underlying assumptions. Such underlying assumptions make it possible to determine which methods are regarded as suitable for the whole research process. These assumptions are philosophical in nature. All research whether quantitative or qualitative is based on these philosophical assumptions.

Sobh and Perry (2006) explain that "a core issue for researchers is not related to choice of methodologies but related to acknowledgement of the research paradigms". A paradigm is defined as "a basic set of beliefs that guides action" (Guba 1990).

Information systems research has strategies "with different underlying philosophical paradigms" (Oates, 2006, p.282). According to Oates (2006, p.282), a paradigm is a "set of shared assumptions or ways of thinking about some aspect of the world". It is also the "basic belief system or world view that guides the investigator" (Guba & Lincoln, 1994, p.105) in a piece of research.

The importance of a coherent philosophy in research cannot be overemphasised. Easterby-Smith et al. (2012, p.17) point out that it helps researchers to choose research methods that they will use to decide on their overall research strategy. They add that knowledge of research philosophy will enable and assist researchers to evaluate different research methods and avoid inappropriate use and unnecessary work by identifying the limitations of particular approaches at an early stage of their study.

Myers (1997) identifies three philosophical paradigms in information systems research as:

i. Positivist

ii. Interpretive

iii. Critical research

These paradigms "have different views about the nature of our world (ontology) and the ways we can acquire knowledge about it (epistemology)" (Oates, 2006, p.291). Sobh and Perry (2006) state that, ontology is "reality", and epistemology is the relationship between that reality and the researcher, and methodology is the technique used by the researcher to discover that reality.

4.2.1 Positivism

This paradigm comes from natural science and uses scientific methods in social sciences research. In the words of Orlikowski and Baroudi (1991) in social science research positivism is "evidence of formal propositions, quantifiable measures of variables, hypotheses tested, and the drawing of inferences about a phenomenon from the sample to a stated population". It is a model that "treats social facts as existing independently of the activities of both participants and researchers" (Silverman, 2013, p.103). Positivist research is about the social world which, which it is claimed, exists independent of human action and beliefs and can be discovered and described using measurable variables (Orlikowski and Baroudi, 1991).

Lincoln and Guba (1985) claim that, researchers who make use of the positivist paradigm rely on the following five points:

i. The phenomenon under study is tangible and there is a unique description for each of its aspects.

ii. The researcher and the participant are distinct and independent entities for the purpose of explaining the phenomenon under study.

iii. The aspects of the phenomenon being studied are considered to be precise and have a fixed meaning, which therefore allows for generalisation like, for example, law.

iv. The "Truth" is obtained by using methods based on theory and deductive analysis with the goal of testing and confirming the hypothesis.

v. Inquiry is value-free (i.e. the enquiry is not influenced by the inquirer).

Orlikowski and Baroudi (1991) support the last point by adding that (in positivist research) the variables are independent of the researcher and human action and experience. In relationship to the research topic, this point is also underpinned by Heeks and Bailur (2007, p.249) when he states that:

> Positivist e-government studies would hold an empiricist epistemology (set of assumptions about how one should gather data about the world) that would seek to observe key e-government variables and to experiment in order to build knowledge about underlying relations and laws. They would assume that *data and data gathering are independent of the observer and of his/her interests and qualities*[22].

It can be concluded from the aforementioned that, in using positivism as a philosophical paradigm in e-government study the variables/data should be free from the researcher's influence. It is not adopted for this study, for a reason that the "approach [positivism] views knowledge as something external to the Individual, not based on the meaning an individual assigns it...It does not depend on the perception of any one individual" (Creswell and Miller, 1997). As mentioned in Chapter 1, this study investigates the privacy and data protection issues which arise when e-government is implemented in a developing country like Ghana. The appropriate way to carry out a study of this nature is to collect the views and shared experiences of individuals, analyse and interpret them. Positivism is therefore rejected as a research philosophy.

4.2.2 Interpretivism

According to Oates (2006, p.292), "interpretive research in IS and computing is concerned with understanding the social context of an information system: the social processes by which it is developed and construed by people and which it influences, and it is influenced by, its social setting". She adds that unlike positivism, "interpretive studies do not prove or disprove a hypothesis" but rather attempt to give explanation to how social settings are related and interdependent.

In this philosophical paradigm, "individuals seek understanding of the world in which they live and work" Creswell (2013, p.24). The paradigm assumes that "people create and associate their own subjective and intersubjective meanings as they interact with the world around them" Orlikowski and Baroudi (1991).

---

[22] My emphasis

Walsham (1995) explains that "interpretive methods of research start from the position that our knowledge of reality, including the domain of human action, is a social construction by human actors and that this applies equally to researchers. There is no objective reality which can be discovered by researchers and replicated by others, in contrast to the assumptions of positivist science". Researchers who adopt interpretive paradigm in their study "thus attempt to understand phenomena through accessing the meanings participants assign to them" Orlikowski and Baroudi (1991). It is therefore considered for adoption by this study, which seeks to investigate the role of privacy and data protection in e-government implementation in Ghana by interpreting stakeholders perception of the phenomena.

4.2.3 Critical research

Critical research is one of the three philosophical paradigms in information systems research. According to Myers (1997), the main task of critical research is seen as being one of social critique, whereby the restrictive and alienating conditions of the status quo are brought to light. Critical research focuses on the oppositions, conflicts and contradictions in contemporary society, and seeks to be emancipatory i.e. it tries to eliminate the "sources of alienation and domination" (Oates, 2006, p.296). Researchers whose study is based on this philosophical paradigm make the assumption that social reality is historically constituted and that it is produced and reproduced by people (Myers and Avison, 2002).

4.2.4 Comparison of the three identified IS philosophical paradigms

Table 4.1 presents the comparison of the three IS paradigms discussed above.

	Positivist	Interpretivist	Critical Research
Ontological Assumptions	• "Naive Realism" in which an understandable reality is assumed to exist, driven by immutable natural laws. True nature of reality can only be obtained by testing theories about actual objects, processes or structures in the real world.	• Relativist; the social world is produced and reinforced by humans through their action and interaction	• Historical realist; social reality is historically constituted; human beings, organizations, and societies are not confined to existing in a particular state
Epistemological Assumptions	• Verification of hypothesis through rigorous empirical testing • Search for universal laws or principles • Tight coupling among explanation, prediction and control	• Understanding of the social world from the participants' perspective, through interpretation of their meanings and actions • Researchers' prior assumptions, beliefs, values, and interests always intervene to shape their investigations	• Knowledge is grounded in social and historical practices • Knowledge is generated and justified by a critical evaluation of social systems in the context of researchers' theoretical framework adopted to conduct research

Relationship between Theory and Practice	• It is possible to discover universal laws that govern the external world	• Generative mechanisms identified for phenomena in the social sciences should be viewed as 'tendencies', which are valuable in explanations of past data but not wholly predictive for future situations	• Generalizations point to regularities of process rather than cross-sectional differences • Generalization in critical research focuses on the "totality" of relationships • There can be no theory independent collection and interpretation of evidence to conclusively prove or disprove a theory
Role of the Researcher	• Objective, impartial observer, passive, value-neutral	• Interactive; the researcher interacts with the human subjects of the enquiry, changing the perceptions of both parties	• Transformative; initiating change in social relations and practices, helping to eliminate the bases of alienation and domination

Table 4.1: Comparison of IS research paradigms

Source – Khazanchi and Munkvold (2003)

Implicit in the table 4.1 is the role of the researcher. In interpretivist paradigm researchers interact with the participants and attempt to understand the phenomena from their (participants') views. Whereas in positivist paradigm researchers remain passive and neutral. In critical research rather than simply describing current knowledge and beliefs, as an interpretive researcher might do, the idea is to challenge those prevailing beliefs, values, and assumptions that might be taken for granted by subjects themselves (Myers, 2009, p.42).

4.2.5 Chosen research paradigm

Interpretive approach was judged appropriate to answer the research questions outlined in Chapter 1. This is due to the fact that it answers ontological question that is reality which is a social construct and is fabricated by human beings in relation to each other (Lincoln and Guba, 1994; Oates, 2006).

As already elaborated in Chapter 1, the study seeks to investigate the role of privacy and data protection in the implementation of e-government in Ghana. Emphasis of the study is on how individuals perceive privacy and data protection, in particular privacy concerns, in their use of e-government services. Other related issues which arise when e-government is introduced in developing countries like Ghana are also explored.

To answer the research questions, views, experiences and direct knowledge are needed from individuals (stakeholders). Knowledge is contributed based on the findings from the analysis, interpretation and meaning the researcher gives to individuals' personal perspectives on the phenomena. As justified in section 4.9 below, the empirical data could be appropriately gathered by using in-depth interviews and focus groups. The research questions are answered by also exploring *current knowledge and beliefs* of the phenomena held by participants in those phenomena which are line with interpretive research.

4.3 Research method

In all research, the researcher has the choice to choose either quantitative or qualitative methodology or a combination of the two methodologies. Borch and Arthur (1995) suggest that using both quantitative and qualitative methodologies together in a piece of research may sometimes be appropriate.

The research methodology and methods chosen for this study are influenced by the research topic, aim and objectives. Halaweh et al. (2008) explain the difference between methodology and method. According to them, methodology refers to the entire research process, from the identification of one or more research questions and the selection of a research method through to the formulation of the findings and results, in which the entire process is based on philosophical assumptions (ontology and epistemology), whilst method is a procedure or technique used to collect and/or analyse data.

Potter (1996, p.50) also makes a clear distinction between methodologies and methods by explaining that methodologies are "perspective on research [which] set out a vision for what research is and how it should be conducted" and methods are "tools-techniques of data gathering, techniques of analysis and techniques of writing".

Silverman (2013, p.122) summarises the aforementioned by stating that "methodology shapes which methods are used and how each method is used". In other words research methodology influences the research methods that are employed to conduct a study.

Research method is essential to every piece of research. It influences researchers' data collection. Myers (1997) explains a research method as "a strategy of inquiry which moves from the underlying philosophical assumptions to research design and data collection". Jankowicz (1991, p.158) adds that it is the systematic and orderly way by which data is collected so that information can be obtained from those data. This makes research method instrumental in every piece of research. It influences how data is collected from the field and also how it is analysed.

Research methods are categorised into two main groups of methods namely: quantitative and qualitative. The choice of either of these two groups of methods influences the way in which a researcher collects data. Choosing a specific research method (quantitative or qualitative or combination of both) imply different skills, assumptions and research practices.

4.4 Quantitative research methods

According to Myers (2013, p.7), quantitative research methods were originally developed in the natural sciences to study natural phenomena. A quantitative approach in a piece of research involves collecting and analysing numerical data and applying statistical tests (Collis and Hussey, 2003). The emphasis, when doing quantitative research, is most of the time on analysing a large number of cases using carefully constructed instruments that have been evaluated for their reliability and validity (Patton, 1990).

Quantitative research is more about numbers, that is, data that can be quantified. In other words, it is about "collecting data about things that can be counted" (Moore, 2000, p.120). Survey is an example of a quantitative research data collection technique. It is a detailed and formal examination of a subject (Remenyi, 2013a, p.216). Researchers often employ quantitative research methods to answer research questions which have underpinnings of positivist philosophy and emphasis is on quantitative data (Recker, 2013, p.66).

4.5 Qualitative research methods

The use of qualitative methods as means of data collection enables researchers to gather a detailed description of situations, events and people. It allows the use of direct quotations from people about their experiences, attitudes, beliefs, and thoughts. It also allows the researcher to study selected issues with an in-depth detail (Patton, 1990; Collis and Hussey, 2003). Pope and Mays (2006) point out that qualitative research is more of an interpretative and subjective exercise, to which the researcher is intimately involved in the process.

Qualitative research methods were developed in the social sciences to enable researchers to study social and cultural phenomena (Myers, 2009, p.8). Ethnography, case study research, action research and grounded theory are examples of qualitative research methods (Recker, 2013, p.88; Creswell, 2013, p.10; Myers, 2009, p.8). These are categorised as research strategies and discussed in section 4.9. Qualitative data sources of evidence from using these approaches include direct observation and participant observation (fieldwork), interviews and questionnaires, documents and texts, archival records and physical artifacts, and the researcher's impressions and reactions (Myers, 2009, p.119; Yin, 2009, p.102).

4.6 Differences between qualitative and quantitative research methods

The differences between the two identified research methods are presented in Table 4.2.

Quantitative	Qualitative
Numbers used as data	Words - written and spoken language-(and images) used as data
Seeks to identify relationships between variables, to explain or predict - with the aim of generalising the findings to a wider population	Seeks to understand and interpret more local meanings, recognises data as gathered in a context; sometimes produces knowledge that contributes to more general understandings
Generates 'shallow' but broad data - not a lot of complex detail obtained from each participant, but lots of participants take part (to generate the necessary statistical power)	Generates 'narrow' but rich, 'thick descriptions' – detailed and complex accounts from each participant; not many take part

Seeks consensus, norms, or general patterns; often aims to reduce diversity of responses to an average response	Tends to seek patterns, but accommodates and explores difference and divergence within data
Tends to be theory-testing, and deductive	Tends to be theory generating, and inductive (working up from the data)
Values detachment and impartiality (objectively)	Values personal involvement and partially (subjectively, reflexivity)
Has a fixed method (harder to change focus once data collection has begun)	Method is less fixed (can accommodate a shift in focus in the same study)
Can be completed quickly	Tends to take longer to complete because it is interpretive and there is no formula

Table 4.2: Some broad differences between qualitative and quantitative paradigms

Source – Braun and Clarke (2013, p.4)

It can be concluded from the table that qualitative research methods collect data that answers the "why", "what", or "how" questions; whereas quantitative research generates numerical data that are better suited to answer "how many" or "how much" questions.

Sechrest and Sidani (1995, p. 78) point out that, both qualitative and quantitative methodologies "describe their data, construct explanatory arguments from their data, and speculate about why the outcomes they observed happened as they did". The differences between data collected using the two research methods are highlighted in table 4.3 below.

Quantitative data	Qualitative data
• Based on meanings derived from numbers • Collection results in numerical and statistical data • Analysis conducted through the use of diagrams and statistics	• Based on meanings expressed through words • Collection results in non-standardised data requiring classification into categories • Analysis conducted through the use of conceptualisation

Table 4.3: Distinctions between quantitative and qualitative data

Sources – Saunders et al. (2009, p.482)

Saunders et al (2009, p.482) point out that *meaning* does not always depend on *numbers*. However Dey (2005, p.28) asserts that, "numbers depends on meaning". He explains that, numbers are analysed through statistics; and meanings through conceptualisation.

Patton (1990, p.464) explains that "it is likely that quantitative methods and qualitative methods will eventually answer questions that do not easily come together to provide a single, well-integrated picture of the situation". In other words combining the methods in research adds insights and understanding that might be missed when only quantitative or qualitative method is used (Recker, 2013, p.105). The combination of the two research approaches is called mixed methods (Braun and Clarke, 2013, p.333).

4.7 Mixed methods

Johnson et al. (2007) define mixed methods research as a type of "research in which a researcher or team of researchers combines elements of qualitative and quantitative research approaches (e.g., use of qualitative and quantitative viewpoints, data collection, analysis, inference techniques) for the broad purposes of breadth and depth of understanding and corroboration".

As a method, *mixed method* focuses on "collecting, analyzing, and mixing both quantitative and qualitative data in a single study or series of studies. Its central premise is that the use of quantitative and qualitative approaches, in combination, provides a better understanding of research problems than either approach alone" Creswell and Plano Clark (2007, p.3).

The above definition goes beyond mixed methods being seen or understood as a "methodology that spanned viewpoints to inferences and that included the combination of qualitative and quantitative research" Creswell and Plano Clark (2010, p.4).

Employing mixed methods in a piece of research "can benefit from both quantitative and qualitative method strengths" (Recker, 2013, p.105), where a researcher:

- collects and analyses persuasively and rigorously both qualitative and quantitative data (based on research questions);
- mixes (or integrates or links) the two forms of data concurrently by combining them (or merging them), sequentially by having one on the other, or embedding one within the other;
- gives priority to one or to both forms of data (in terms of what the research emphasizes);

- uses these procedures in a single study or in multiple phases of a program of study;
- frames these procedures within philosophical worldviews and theoretical lenses; and
- combines procedures into specific research designs that direct the plan for conducting the study (Creswell and Plano Clark (2010, p.5).

Johnson and Onwuegbuzie (2004) highlight the strengths and weaknesses of mixed methods as presented in table 4.4.

Strengths
• Words, pictures, and narrative can be used to add meaning to numbers.
• Numbers can be used to add precision to words, pictures, and narrative.
• Can provide quantitative and qualitative research strengths.
• Researcher can generate and test a grounded theory.
• Can answer a broader and more complete range of research questions because the researcher is not confined to a single method or approach.
• The specific mixed research designs discussed [...]have specific strengths and weaknesses that should be considered (e.g., in a two-stage sequential design, the Stage 1 results can be used to develop and inform the purpose and design of the Stage 2 component).
• A researcher can use the strengths of an additional method to overcome the weaknesses in another method by using both in a research study.
• Can provide stronger evidence for a conclusion through convergence and corroboration of findings.
• Can add insights and understanding that might be missed when only a single method is used.
• Can be used to increase the generalizability of the results.
• Qualitative and quantitative research used together produce more complete knowledge necessary to inform theory and practice.

Weaknesses
• Can be difficult for a single researcher to carry out both qualitative and quantitative research, especially if two or more approaches are expected to be used concurrently; it may require a research team.
• Researcher has to learn about multiple methods and approaches and understand how to mix them appropriately.
• Methodological purists contend that one should always work within either a qualitative or a quantitative paradigm.
• More expensive.
• More time consuming.
• Some of the details of mixed research remain to be worked out fully by research methodologists (e.g., problems of paradigm mixing, how to qualitatively analyze quantitative data, how to interpret conflicting results).

Table 4.4: Strengths and weaknesses of mixed research

Source - Johnson and Onwuegbuzie (2004)

Even though mixed methods would have been appropriate research for this study due to its characteristics of making up for the limitations of qualitative methods (for example, a possible chance of bias). It was however not considered due to some of the weaknesses as presented in table 4.4. For instance, combining the methods in a piece of research involve a lot more than singly using quantitative or qualitative methods. Therefore, due to time pressure and resource (funding) limit, it would have been expensive and time consuming to adopt the mixed methods.

4.8 Rationale for choosing qualitative research methods

Considering the research questions the use of qualitative method for this research was influenced by the differences between the two research methods as highlighted in tables 4.2 and 4.3. For instance, as shown in table 4.3, data analysis in quantitative research is *based on meanings derived from numbers.* However this study is investigating phenomena which are sparse in a developing country like Ghana. Quantitative research "with its focus on measurement, has the tendency to isolate specific aspects of phenomena" (Recker, 2013, p.13). This study, as stated in Chapter 1, seeks to investigate the role of privacy and data protection in e-government implementation in Ghana. This requires analysing and interpreting stakeholders' perceptions on privacy risks, in particular peoples' privacy concerns, in e-government adoption. "Why people make decisions and act the way they do is often highly contextual, qualitative research methods are designed to explore this very context, in order to offer explanations for why the phenomena occurred the way they do" (Recker, 2013, p.88). This places emphasis on in-depth interviews with stakeholders to solicit qualitative data. It is therefore appropriate to employ qualitative research methods.

4.9 Research strategies

A research strategy is a general plan of action that gives directions in a research and which intend to enable the researcher to conduct it in a systematic manner (Altinay and Paraskevas, 2008, p.76). The strategies considered before choosing the most appropriate method for the research design and data collection are:

- Ethnography
- Grounded theory
- Case study
- Action research

The strategies are individually discussed in the next sections. The rational for choosing the appropriate method to answer the research questions is also discussed.

4.9.1 Ethnography

According to Myer (1997), ethnography is a research method that comes from the discipline of social and cultural anthropology. In this type of research method ethnographers are expected to spend a considerable amount of time in the field and absorb themselves in the lives of the people they study (Lewis, 1985, p.380). Through this they are able to place the phenomena studied in their social and cultural context (Myer, 1997).

This strategy was not used due to the fact "a good ethnography requires prolonged stay at the research site" (Wolcott, 2008). Staying at the research site to observe and interact with the research sites would have been impossible due to time and financial constraints.

4.9.2 Grounded theory

Myer (2009, p.106) states that, "grounded theory is a qualitative research method that seeks to develop theory that is grounded in data systematically and analysed". It is different from the other qualitative research methods in the sense of "its specific approach to theory development". In the words of the founders of grounded theory, Glaser and Strauss (1967, p.65):

> *In Grounded Theory Study, neither one kind of data on a category nor technique for data collection is necessarily appropriate. Different kinds of data give the analyst different views or vantage points from which to understand a category and to develop its properties.*

The idea about grounded theory research, which is mostly inductive, is to become grounded in the data and to allow understanding to emerge from close study of the text (Bernard, 2012, p.524).

Recker (2013, p.102) highlights the following as the characteristics of grounded theory:

- The main purpose of the grounded theory method is theory building, not testing.
- Prior domain knowledge should not lead to pre-conceived hypotheses or conjectures about the research that the research then seeks to falsify or verify.
- The research process involves the constant endeavour to jointly collect and compare data, and to constantly contrast new data to any emerging concepts and constructs of the theory being built.
- All kinds of data are applicable, and are selected by the researcher through theoretical sampling.

Adapting the Straussian version of the grounded theory as a data analysis technique, all the above points, with the exception of the second one, were employed in the data analysis phase of this study (see Chapters 7 and 8). The second point was ignored on the basis that it seems to suggest that researchers should not have any *preconceived theoretical ideas* before embarking on their research. This was impossible in the case of this study, since research proposal was written and submitted for approval before the research was started. The proposal made use of available theoretical ideas found in the literature. Grounded theory as research methodology was not used due to the fact that review of literature of the phenomena was undertaken before data analysis. Likewise fieldwork data was collected and transcribed before thorough data analysis.

The Straussian version of grounded theory "is a style of doing qualitative analysis that includes a number of distinct features…and the use of a coding paradigm to ensure conceptual development and density" (Strauss, 1987). It was borrowed for the data analysis of the fieldwork data for the reasons:

- it allows researchers to become immersed in the data at a detailed level;

- It encourages systematic, detailed analysis of the data and provides a method for doing so;
- It gives researchers ample evidence to back up their claims; and
- It encourages a constant interplay between data collection and analysis (Myer, 2009, p.111).

4.9.3 Case study

Yin (2009, p.13) defines case study in two parts:

1. The case study is an empirical inquiry that
    - *Investigates a contemporary phenomenon in depth and within its real-life context, especially when*
    - *The boundaries between phenomenon and context are not clearly evident.*
2. The case study inquiry
    - *Copes with the technically distinctive situation in which there will be many more variables of interest than data points, and as one result*
    - *Relies on multiple sources of evidence, with data needing to converge in a triangulating fashion, and as another result*
    - *Benefits from the prior development of theoretical propositions to guide data collection.*

Myers (2009, p.75) explains that part 1 of Yin's definition "specifies the scope of the study" and the part 2 "the data collection and the data collection analysis".

Case study research is a "strategy for doing research which involves an empirical investigation of a particular contemporary phenomenon within its real life context using multiple source of evidence". According to Yin (2009, p.4) the choice of case study largely depends on the research questions. He explains that the more research questions seek to "explain some present circumstances the more that the case study method will be relevant". He adds that case study is also relevant if the research questions "require an extensive and in-depth description of some social phenomenon".

Table 4.5 highlights some of the key characteristics of case studies. The choice of case study as a strategy for this study was informed by these characteristics.

1. Phenomenon is examined in a natural setting.
2. Data are collected by multiple means.
3. One or few entities (person, group, or organization) are examined.
4. The complexity of the unit is studied intensively.
5. Case studies are more suitable for the exploration, classification and hypothesis development stages of the knowledge building process; the investigator should have a receptive attitude towards exploration.
6. No experimental controls or manipulation are involved.
7. The investigator may not specify the set of independent and dependent variables in advance.
8. The results derived depend heavily on the integrative powers of the investigator.
9. Changes in site selection and data collection methods could take place as the investigator develops new hypotheses.
10. Case research is useful in the study of "why" and "how" questions because these deal with operational links to be traced over time rather than with frequency or incidence.
11. The focus is on contemporary events.

Table 4.5: Key Characteristics of Case Studies

Source - Benbasat et al., 1987

The research problem asked the "why" and "how" questions which solicited an in-depth responses from the stakeholders and other research participants during data gathering.

Furthermore, Otley and Berry (1994) point out that, case study also allows a researcher to generate new knowledge when the existing knowledge is inadequate and incomplete. This assertion therefore supports the use of case study as an appropriate strategy to answer the research questions, since studies into the role of privacy and data protection in e-government implementation in developing countries, and for that matter sub-Saharan African countries such as Ghana are rare.

Yin (2009, p.14) points out that, in adopting the case study strategy in research there is the tendency for the researcher to have "biased views to influence the direction of the findings and conclusions". The strategy reliance of getting access to a case site is also a challenge (Recker, 2013, p.95).

To limit or avoid any bias as mentioned above, documentation was adopted as a secondary source of evidence. For example, the Ghanaian citizens' comments on media reports of the passing of the 2012 Data Protection Act were accessed and compared with the views of the study participants on the phenomena. In the same vein the challenge of getting access to stakeholders was not a problem. The stakeholders seemed interested in the study and its findings and thus gave their full cooperation and participation.

4.9.4 Action research

Oates (2006, p.301) points that action research like case study can be in any of the three paradigms discussed in section 4.2 above, however it tends to be more in the interpretive paradigm than the other two. It "aims to contribute both to the practical concerns of people in an immediate problematic situation and to the goals of social science by joint collaboration within a mutually acceptable ethical framework" (Rapoport, 1970, p.499). It is more concerned with collaboration and change involving researchers and research participants (Myers, 2009, p.56-57).

What makes Action research so distinctive from the other research methods discussed above is the "collaboration with practitioners and the deliberate intervention of the researcher… [Researchers using case study, grounded theory and ethnography] try not to interfere with their subject matter" (Myers, 2009, p.57). For instance, in action research, if observation is adopted as source of evidence, the researcher not only observes, "but also find a role within the group observed from which to participate in some manner" (Recker, 2013, p.101). Therefore participation of researchers is essential in action research.

Even though action research is exemplary in terms of its unique contribution to practice and research – that is, solving current practical problems while also expanding scientific knowledge - (Myers, 2009, p.62), it was not useful to be adopted for data collection due to the fact that the researcher was not in a position to bring about change..

4.10 Data collection techniques

This section presents the source of evidence most commonly used in doing case study research (Yin, 2009, p.101) namely: *documentation, archival records, interviews, direct observations, participant-observation and physical artefacts.* Table 4.6 shows their comparative strengths and weaknesses.

Source of Evidence	**Strengths**	**Weaknesses**
Documentation	• Stable-can be reviewed repeatedly • Unobtrusive-not created as a result of the case study • Exact-contains exact names, references, and details of an event • Broad coverage-long span of time, many events, and many settings	• Retrievability - can be difficult to find • Biased selectivity, if collection is incomplete • Reporting bias-reflects (unknown) bias of author • Access-may be deliberately withheld
Archival Records	• *[Same as those for documentation]* • Precise and usually quantitative	• *[Same as those for documentation]* • Accessibility due to privacy reasons
Interviews	• Targeted-focuses directly on case study topics • Insightful-provides perceived causal inferences and explanations	• Biased due to poorly articulated questions • Response bias • Inaccuracies due to poor recall • Reflexivity-interviewee gives what interviewer wants to hear
Direct Observations	• Reality-covers events in real time • Contextual-covers context of "case"	• Time consuming • Selectivity-broad coverage difficult without a team of observers • Reflexivity-event may proceed differently because it being observed • Cost-hours needed by human observers

Participant-Observation	• *[Same as those for direct observations]* • Insightful into inter-personal behavior and motives	• *[Same as those for direct observations]* • Bias due to participant-observer's manipulation of events
Physical artefacts	• Insightful into cultural features • Insightful into technical operations	• Selectivity • Availability

Table 4.6: Six sources as evidences - strengths and weaknesses

Source – Yin (2009, p.102)

According to Yin (2009, p.101), no single source presented in the table has a complete advantage over all the others. However, the choice of any of these techniques for data gathering is explored in relation to the aims and objectives of the research as outlined in Chapter 1. Out of the six data resources evidences presented in table 4.6, this study employed interviews (including focus groups) and documentation as data collection instruments.

4.10.1 Direct and participant observation

In *direct observation* the researcher acts as a passive and neutral bystander that is not involved in the phenomenon being studied; while as in *participant observation* the researcher is an active participant and influences the phenomenon (Recker, 2013, p.91).

According to Ritchie (2003, p.35) observation offers a researcher the opportunity to record and analyse behaviour and interactions as they occur. This makes it possible for events, actions and experiences to be observed through the eyes of the researcher. It is particularly useful where a study is "concerned with investigating a 'process' involving players, where an understanding of non-verbal communications are likely to be important or where the behavioural consequences of events form a focal point of study".

This technique could have been adopted for this study to observe and hear discussions among the key stakeholders implementing the e-Ghana project. However, as previously mentioned, due to time pressure and financial constraints, it was not possible.

4.10.2 Documentation

According to Yin (2009, p.101), documentation is relevant to case study topic. He however cautions that it is not "always accurate and may not be lacking in bias"; its important use is to "corroborate and augment evidence from other source". Creswell (2013, p.160) suggests analysing public documents in qualitative research.

It must be noted that, documents collection (documentation) was not initially chosen as a data collection method in the research design, however during the fieldwork, some participants made available documents to complement their responses. For example, Participant P13, a Member of Parliament, made available a draft copy of the Data Protection Bill, to support his claim that, the Bill was before Parliament, waiting to be passed into law. People's comments on media reports of the passing of the 2012 Data Protection Act in Ghana were accessed and compared with the views of the study participants on the phenomena.

The use of documentation to complement the interview data is called triangulation of data. It helps researchers to "gain a more nuanced picture of the situation, and increase reliability and validity of their findings" (Recker, 2013, p.91).

4.10.3 Interviews

Interviewing as a data collection technique is the systematic collection of data through asking questions, then carefully listening to and recording or noting the responses concerning the research question (Altinay and Paraskevas, 2008, p.107). It is the most prominent form of data collection techniques; and it can be either face-to-face or one-to-many, as in focus groups (Recker, 2013, p.90). It provides the platform which allows a researcher to gain an in-depth knowledge from the responses. It has an advantage of the researcher having full grip of the interview and controlling the flow of the responses. It also gives participants the chance to respond to questions in their own way. However this has a disadvantage of producing data which at times is not easy to analyse due to the fact that it may be too diverse. A solution to this problem is to structure the interview questions in such way they solicit responses from participants that are focused on the research question. To achieve this, Yin (2009, p.92) recommends first piloting the interview questions and then refining them.

Altinay and Paraskevas (2008, p.107) highlights the following difficulties associated with interviews:

- It may be difficult to secure the interview in the first place
- Access to people may be denied for a number of reasons
- Organising, preparing for and conducting an interview can often be very time consuming.

The researcher considered all these difficulties and eliminated them before embarking on the field work. For example, direct assistance was sought from the then Deputy Speaker of Parliament to interview the members of the Select Committee of Communication and this was granted. A date was arranged and the interviews took place on the premises of the Parliament House in Accra, Ghana.

4.10.4 Focus group

Focus group is a data collection technique where fieldwork data is simultaneously collected from multiple participants (Braun and Clarke, 2013, p.108). It provides direct evidence about similarities and differences in participants' opinions and experiences (Morgan, 1998). It is based on facilitating an organised discussion with a group of individuals selected because they were believed to be representative of some class (Altinay and Paraskevas, 2008, p.117, Myers, 2009, p.125). This technique is ideal because it is possible to group participants at one place for interviewing or discussion. The discussion is used to bring out insights and understandings in ways in which simple questionnaire items may not be able to tap. At times people get caught up in the spirit of group discussion and may reveal more than they would normally do in the more formal one-to-one interview setting. Interaction is the key to successful focus group. Due to its unique characteristic of participants' responses giving cue to others to further express their views on phenomena when it is used in a piece of research, it would have been appropriate to use it as the sole data collection technique. However, there is the difficulty of grouping some participants at one place at the same time. For instance, in this study fieldwork, it would been difficult to put the selected Members of Parliament and Directors of government departments and agencies together for focus group interviewing, due to their busy daily schedule.

One limitation to this technique is there is a possibility that one or two participants could dominate the proceedings and others may not have the chance to contribute at all. Remenyi (2013a, p.74) cautions researchers to watch out for this. The fore knowledge of this limitation was useful in curtailing a particular instance[23] during the main fieldwork, as was reported in section 6.4.2. Also to prevent the occurrence of such situation in subsequent focus groups, where one person dominates the discussion, the inter-

[23] During one of the fieldwork focus groups interviews one of the participants tried to dominate the discussions. With no reference to anybody in particular, the moderator politely stopped proceedings and reiterated the ground rules, stressing on the need to allow other participants to also share their opinions. Also, as recommended by Braun and Clarke (2013, p.128), the quieter participants were encouraged to express their views.

viewer familiarised himself with participants' names and called them to solicit for their views. This was particularly useful in getting participants who were reluctant to contribute to share some views on issues under discussion.

4.11 Rationale for choice of data collection technique

Considering the fact that this research took place in Ghana and the researcher was based in the United Kingdom it would have been cheaper in terms of cost to use questionnaire rather than face-to-face interviewing as a data collection technique. Moreover as compared to face-to-face interviewing, questionnaire would have given a wide coverage; and also save the researcher time of travelling to Ghana. Questionnaires in general are easier to administer than arranging interviews. It however does not allow the researcher to understand or explore answers (Gillham, 2008). It is for this reason that the researcher used interview as a data collection method rather than questionnaire. The interview as a qualitative research data collection technique collects data which "are usually in a text form, and offer a richer, more in-depth representation of people's experiences, attitudes and beliefs" (Altinay and Paraskevas, 2008, p.75).

In spite of its limitation of anticipated voluminous pages of transcripts which takes great deal of time to analyse, interviews and focus group were the main data collection and fact finding methods. The choice was influenced by the nature of the research questions. That is, the ability to have a face-to-face personal interaction with participants enables researchers to probe further and seek clarification where there is ambiguity in the responses provided by participants.

The choice of interview was made for the reason by using this technique there is a possibility to check the clarity of answers given by research participants and ask further probing questions, which give in-depth knowledge about the phenomena being investigated. Also as compared to focus group, interview is relatively easy to arrange. However (as explained in Chapter 5), it was found out that that apart from interviewing it was useful to also consider focus group as a data collection technique where the stakeholders met and shared ideas (or discussed issues) on the role of privacy and data protection on the implementation of e-government in Ghana.

As stated in Chapter 1, this study sought to evaluate the role of privacy and data protection in the implementation of e-government in Ghana. Stakeholders and other research participants in-depth views were sought to answer the research questions. Qualitative approach was used to collect data. This was in-line with qualitative research definition by Hussey and Hussey (1997, p.20) which states that "a subjective approach which includes examining and reflecting on perceptions in order to gain understanding of social and human activities".

The next section discusses how CADQAS can be employed to analyse qualitative data collected in the field.

4.12 The use of CADQAS in data analysis

In qualitative research, the researcher is more often than not faced with large volume of data. Previous researchers (Hoover and Koerber, 2011; Bringer et al., 2006; Weitzman, 2000) therefore recommend the use of Computer Assisted Qualitative Software (CAQDAS) in data analysis in order to save time.

Hoover and Koerber (2011) cite Blakeslee and Fleischer (2007) and Hughes and Hayhoe (2007) in pointing out the important role CAQDAS plays in "storing, managing, and analysing qualitative data". They identify the following CAQDAS, with their distinguishing features, as some of the well-known examples:

- Nvivo – Interface similar to Microsoft Outlook; advanced querying functions; and powerful source data and coding organization;
- ATLAS.ti – Advanced multimedia support; native PDF support (looks like the original) and Google earth is embedded in it;
- MAXQDA – Interface is clean and intuitive; good use of colour for separating project elements; and integrates qualitative analysis well with quantitative analysis features;
- NUD*IST – predecessor to Nvivo version 8.

It must be stated that the use of any of these software does not entirely do the data analysis which results in research findings. They only facilitate the data analysis process. They have a unique feature of "increasing efficiency of data analysis, facilitating multiplicity in research methodologies, and enabling transparency of the process as a whole" (Hoover and Koerber, 2011). Welsh (2002) explains that CAQDAS keep track of data and ongoing analysis; and they support transparency and accuracy requirements of the analysis process.

The use of one over the other CAQDAS is at times a matter of choice. It also depends on the kind of data a researcher is dealing with. For instance, MAXQDA may be a better choice if a researcher employs mixed method in a piece of research and is overwhelmed with both qualitative and quantitative data. Cost, that is the price of the software, may also influence a researcher decision to use any of the above software.

For this study, cost did actually influence the choice of Nvivo as a data analysis tool, since the research institution, De Montfort University (DMU), has a site licence for the software, so it was free for the researcher to use. Its "advanced querying functions; and powerful source data and coding organization" (Hoover and Koerber, 2011) were also influential in it being selected as data analysis tool of choice. In other words, Nvivo was chosen as a data analysis due to its ability to deal with large volume of data (Walsh, 2003) and thereby reducing it to a manageable size (Rouse and Dick, 1994) which make it convenient for the researcher in terms of channelling the time saved to the interpretive, creative dimensions of their work (Hoover and Koerber, 2011).

Using the Nvivo software to analyse the pilot study data gave the researcher the much needed experience and confidence to use it again in the analyses of the fieldwork data which is discussed in Chapters 7 and 8.

4.13 Pilot study

Easterby-Smith (2008 te al., p.24) points out that "in a [PhD study] time is short and one may then need to launch directly into the main study ... [however] there is usually time to carry out a pilot investigation to test methodologies and to assess the feasibility of initial ideas, which might lead into a larger study or be completely jettisoned at a later stage." It helps researchers to refine their "data collection plans with respect to both the content of the data and the procedures to be followed" Yin (2013, p.92).

Taking a cue from the aforementioned, the interview questions (see Appendix G) were piloted on the staff of the Ghana High Commission in London before the main fieldwork was undertaken in Ghana. The results of the pilot study were used to revise and refine the research design.

The next section discusses the selection method which used to select the participants for both the pilot study and the main fieldwork.

4.14 Purposive sampling method

Purposive sampling is a non-probability sampling method. A non-probability sampling means sampling without using random selection methods. It is a sample selection method based on purpose and it is used when a researcher wants to access a particular subset of people in order to select information-rich cases for detailed study (Denzin & Lincoln, 2000; Patton, 2002). In this case study, stakeholders, for example, users of e-government services and also policy makers in e-government implementation were purposely selected.

The sample sizes may or may not specifically be determined before the commencement of the fieldwork. Sample sizes are dependent on the resources and time available as well as the research objectives. They are also determined on the basis of theoretical saturation, that is, the point in data collection when new data no longer brings additional insights to the research questions (Bryant and Charmaz (2010); Glasser and Strauss, 1967; Eisenhardt, 1989).

Purposive sampling is therefore most successful when data review and analysis are carried out in conjunction with data collection, as recommended by Glasser and Strauss (1967).

4.15 Summary

In this chapter the philosophy (interpretive) behind the research was outlined. Various means by which the data could be collected and analysed were also considered. It was found out that basically there are two approaches to research, that is, quantitative and qualitative. The researcher was faced with the choice between these two, however considering the research aims and objectives, a qualitative method was chosen to answer the research questions.

Recognising the importance of survey, one-to-one interview was chosen as the main data collection method. However, as stated in Chapter 5, after the pilot study focus group was adopted to compliment this technique to solicit participants' views on the study phenomena. The choices for the study's methodology were made with consideration to the research aims, objectives and questions as outlined in Chapter 1.

This led to the definite choice of a qualitative data analysis method which was used to answer the research questions. The whole idea about qualitative data analysis was to come up with some insight that might help the researcher and others to understand or explain the subject at hand (Myer, 2009). A detailed account of the qualitative data analysis method is presented in the next chapter.

The interview questions (see Appendix G) were piloted on the staff of the Ghana High Commission in London before the main fieldwork was undertaken in Ghana. The pilot study process is discussed in the next chapter.

5

Pilot Study

5.1 Introduction

This chapter discusses the pilot study that took place among Ghanaians at the High Commission in London, before the main fieldwork was undertaken in Ghana. It highlights the reasons for conducting the pilot study, the data collection and analysis techniques used, and finally the contribution of the pilot study to the overall research. The pilot study was a one-day experience which took place on Thursday, June 10 2010 in participants' individual offices. Face-to-face semi-structured interviews were conducted with participants.

As required by the research institution, De Montfort University, an application to gain ethical approval was submitted to the Human Research Ethics Committee and was approved (see Appendices H and I) before the pilot study was undertaken. This is explained further in section 6.5.

5.2 Pilot study significance

Alreck and Settle (1995) describe a pilot study as a brief preliminary survey, often using a small convenient sample. De Vaus (1993, p.54) advice to researchers is, "do not take the risk. Pilot test first." Pilot study is therefore "done in preparation for the major study" (Polit et al., 2001, p.467).

The significance of undertaking a pilot study in research of this nature is captured in the words of Byrne (2001):

> *Performing a pilot study is always a good idea regardless of which research method is used. A pilot study provides the researcher with experiential logistics from actual procedural implementation. The pilot study facilitates a more systematic approach to actual data collection and analysis. Although many graduate students view a pilot study as busy work or a time-wasting step, in the long run, it will expedite the actual implementation phase of a research study.*

The pilot study process was therefore undertaken to ensure that there were no unanticipated difficulties in the investigation. The aim of the pilot study was to test the interview questions; and to find out if they would solicit the kind of data needed to inform the research questions (Braun and Clarke, 2013, p.85). It also aimed to confirm and, if appropriate, further identify stakeholders to be interviewed in the main study.

5.3 Pilot study sample

After permission was granted from the Ghana High Commission, in London, to interview some of their staff, purposive sampling was used to select 10 members of staff for the pilot study. Purposive sampling aims to create rich, in-depth information (Liamputtong, 2005; Zmijewska and Lawrence, 2005). The rationale for adopting this sampling method in the pilot study was to choose a setting or individuals where "the processes [phenomena] being studied are most likely to occur" (Denzin and Lincoln, 1994, p.202). In this case, participants who are conversant with e-government project issues in Ghana; and are also e-government service users themselves and thus could share their views on privacy concerns. There was also an influential factor as to whether the participants were "accessible and convenient" (Braun and Clarke, 2013, p.57) for the study. The Ghana High Commission, as a sponsor[24] of the research, was willing to make its staff available for the piloting.

On the scheduled date, Thursday, 10 June 2010, seven of the already selected participants were unavailable on that day due to a department meeting. Due to time constraints, it was impossible reschedule another date, therefore interviews took place with the available three participants. The participation of these three interviewees, apart from the aforementioned (that is their knowledge and experience in the study phenomena), were also based on convenient accessibility. Therefore the sampling method is a combination of purposive sampling and convenience sampling, with the former taking precedence over the latter. Convenience sampling is where study participants are selected based on accessibility (Braun and Clarke, 2013, p.329). One limitation for using this method is that the perceptions of these participants from the High Commission may differ from other participants from the Ghanaian community in UK and more so in Ghana. This is evident in the differences in the findings with respect to the role of privacy and data protection in e-government implementation (see sections 5.6 and 8.6.1).

---

[24] There is a possibility of sponsor bias here; however this was just a pilot study. The important part was the ability to pilot the research, rather than the substantive results from the pilot.

Methods using a small sample size are useful for pilot studies before committing the research to a large scale. However, a sample size of 3 is too small and may possibly affect the data quality. The findings from the piloting data analysis cannot therefore be used to generalise the entire population. However, for the fact that the participants were selected using purposive sample, that is, they were people specifically interviewed because of their knowledge and experience in the research phenomena, their responses were useful in testing and confirming the main fieldwork data collection and analysis strategy.

5.4 Procedure

As already mentioned the pilot study was a one-day fieldwork experience. Considering the interview was the technique chosen for the data collection. The rationale for choosing this technique has already been discussed in Chapter 4. As it was found out, with this technique, it is possible for the interviewer to have a personal contact with the participants.

A period of 50 minutes was allocated to each individual interview and one and half hours to meet participants and solicit their feedback, comments and suggestions. This became possible because all the participants work in the same building.

The data collected were responses from 3 participants. These same participants were later in the day grouped together for discussions, comments and feedback on the earlier one-to-one interviews. This proved to be a very useful exercise as it turned out be more like a focus group.

As a novice researcher with no experience in interviewing, Easterby-Smith et al. (2008, p.146) and Myers and Newman (2007) guidelines (see section 6.4.1) were adopted for the entire interview process. They were helpful in developing interview skills for the subsequent fieldwork in Ghana. As highlighted in section 8.1, in some instances, when the participants were hesitant, careful prompts were used to encourage them to speak.

This skill, for example, was acquired from piloting the interview questions in conjunction with the aforementioned guidelines.

5.5 Pilot study data analysis

In line with the methodology employed for this research (see Chapter 4), data analysis approach was borrowed from the Straussian version of grounded theory. The analysis of the pilot study data followed the same procedure as highlighted in Chapters 7 and 8.

As Sampson (2004, p.399) points out it is "only when data is evaluated that any gaps in a research design begin to show up". Analysing the data from the pilot study gave valuable insights. It gave a picture of issues that could possibly influence the implementation of e-government in Ghana.

5.6 Findings and discussions

Initial findings showed that privacy and data protection play a crucial role in e-government implementation in Ghana. Issues such as low Internet penetration and inadequate ICT infrastructure; digital divide; lack of awareness and e-skills; and unskilled technical staff could possibly hamper the e-government implementation in Ghana. However, from the experience of the Ghanaian community in the UK, potential benefits of the online services – in terms of convenience and cost saving – are likely to influence many citizens adoption and use of e-government services in Ghana.

The finding shows that, among the Ghanaians interviewed online personal privacy and data protection have significant relationship with e-government implementation. This means that citizens would be less willing to access e-government services in the absence of privacy and data protection law. Legislation would therefore be needed to allay citizens' fears and also safeguard their online privacy before they would adopt e-government services[25].

All the participants were of the view that the Internet is not a safe place to submit one's personal information. It was revealed that, this assertion though, is not as a result of personal experience of privacy breach, but through media reports. Participant PS3, for instance revealed that:

> *"as a T-mobile customer, I was worried to read in the newspapers that, personal details of thousands of customers of the phone company had been stolen a couple of months ago".*

They are of the view that, from their knowledge of privacy violations in the western countries, privacy and data protection is crucial and it would influence their decision to access e-government services.

Even though the participants highlighted the importance of privacy and data protection in e-government implementation they also however emphasised on ICT infrastructure as highly necessary. According to Participant PS2:

> *"The online passport application service we offer here [in the UK] has been successful because users have access to the Internet 24/7" Participant PS2.*

This emphasised the crucial role of Internet accessibility in e-govern-

[25] It must be stated here again that these interviews and data analysis took place before the Privacy and Data Protection Act was passed in February 2012.

ment implementation. It suggests that the Ghanaian people are more likely to use e-government services if they have convenient access to the Internet.

5.7 The contribution of the pilot study to the research

Considering the relevance of views and ideas which were raised by the participants during the feedback and group discussion the study adopted focus groups as the second data collection technique to complement the already chosen one-to-one interview technique.

The pilot study was instrumental in identifying some of the stakeholders for the main data collection. For instance, the National Information Technology Agency (NITA), Ghana, was pointed out as the main government body in-charge of the e-government implementation. This information was already known through literature search, but what was significant was the participants provided contact information of some key personalities at the e-government implementing agency. This was very useful for the fieldwork, as it enabled these staff to be recruited for interviews.

Also crucial issues which did not come to the fore during the literature review and research design emerged. For instance, Participant PS1, revealed that:

> *"The Ghanaian community in UK uses the High Commission website a lot to apply for or renew their passports. This is a good thing for us* [the High Commission]. *It's taken the pressure off us; it has curtailed long queues we used to experience."* PS1

Participant PS2 added that:

> *"I think the Ghanaian community are happy with the online service since those living outside London don't have to travel all the way here to renew or apply for a new passport."*

Literature searching showed that this facility (online passport application) is unavailable in Ghana. This gives credence to Heeks (2002) argument that ICT implementation and use in developed countries (for example UK) are different than it is in developing countries such as Ghana.

It is evident from the participants' responses that, the Ghanaian community have adopted and are really using the online passport application and renewal service. As can be deduced from the responses, the online service has been beneficial (in terms of convenience) to both the High Commission and the Ghanaians resident in the UK. Chen et al. (2006) point out that implementation of e-government has been successful in the developed countries, for example UK, due to (among other things) high Internet access and computer literacy for users; good current infrastructure; and dedication of resources. These may possibly have influenced the Ghanaian community acceptance and usage of the online service.

The above revelation prompted the study to include in the interview guide a topic which sought to explore online services people obtain from the government portal in Ghana; and also how often they browse the government portal.

It was observed that the participants were reluctant to answer questions around corruption among government officials/workers. For instance the following questions: *what is your view about corruption among government officials/workers? How can e-government eliminate or reduce corruption among government officials/workers?* did not yield any responses from participants.

In the group discussion and feedback, the interviewer sought to find out from the participants why they were reluctant to answer corruption related questions. One participant jokingly said: *"no one washes his dirty linen in public"*. This response, even though light-heartedly said, suggested participants were uncomfortable answering corruption related questions. It indicates their admittance of corruption in the Ghanaian society, especially among government officials[26], but they were not going to talk about it. It also confirmed the collectivist national cultural dimension of the Ghanaian society where people do not discuss intimate "family" matters in public, especially if they are shameful. It was apparent this type of questions was not going to yield responses and they were therefore deleted from the interview guide.

It emerged through the piloting that the mixed questions encompassing the phenomena, *e-government* and *privacy and data protection,* initially seemed confusing to the participants. This was rectified by grouping the interview questions under each phenomenon as shown in Appendix G.

5.8 Conclusion

It was concluded from the pilot study data analysis finding that privacy and data protection is an influential factor for individuals to access the e-government services. It thus seemed to suggest that in Ghana, privacy and data protection plays a crucial role in the implementation of e-government. Previous research (DeBenedictis et al., 2002) confirms this finding. The findings from the pilot study supported the chosen research methods as reliable to collect fieldwork data to answer the research questions.

By using purposive sampling, researchers believe that some participants are more appropriate for the research compared to other individuals

[26] As discussed in section 2.7.1.

(Castillo, 2009). For example, since this study draws on the knowledge, expertise and experience of persons involved in electronic government implementation, Participant PS1 was identified as an important source of knowledge. As was revealed the Ghanaian community in UK are able to renew and apply for passports online; the participant's shared experience with the developments in this electronic services and online privacy was useful to the study.

Likewise, it must be stated that even though convenience sampling is the least rigorous and justifiable sampling method (Sandelowski, 1995) it became necessary to incorporate it to complement the purposive sampling due to the pilot study sample convenient accessibility. The Ghana High Commission, as a sponsor of the research, willingly made its staff available for the piloting.

Feedback from participants confirmed that the interview questions were appropriate and understandable and that the resulting data was capable of being analysed using the proposed data analysis strategy. The refined research interview questions (see Appendix G) which resulted from piloting were used to collect the fieldwork data. A detailed report of the fieldwork is presented in the next chapter.

6

Fieldwork Report

6.1 Introduction

Creswell (2013, p.95) explains fieldwork is gathering of information in the context or setting where the participants live. This section presents the report of the main fieldwork and a subsequent follow-up that took place in Ghana. It emerged in the follow-up fieldwork trip that the situation in Ghana has not changed since the commencement of the research. The research questions that this research seeks to address still exists and remain unanswered. This research commenced before the Ghana Data Protection Act 2012 was passed in February 2012. However, the passing of the legislation did not affect the findings of the research. This became known through the comparison of the first interview data and the follow-up interview data. It was possible to compare the responses of both interviews due to the fact that the similar questions were asked in both cases.

As was highlighted in Chapter 4, this study employs case study methodology to investigate the role of privacy and protection in e-government implementation in Ghana. This chapter describes the purposive sampling that was used to select the research participants whose combined responses would enable the research questions to be answered.

As stated in Chapter 1, the research aimed to solicit views from the participants on the role of privacy and data protection in e-government implementation. Qualitative data was collected through semi-structured interviews with stakeholders from government departments and agencies, parliament, universities, private and public organisation and the general public. Participants' responses were not influenced by their respective managers or heads of department[27]. The data solicited are account of the participants' personal perspective of the phenomena being under studied.

---

[27] To detect any influence of Managers in participants' responses, the interview data were compared with each other and also with other sstakeholders to check if they seem to out of line – nothing untoward was found.

Guided by set criteria, purposive sampling is used to select the interview participants. In total, 53 participants were interviewed. Each individual one-to-one interview lasted approximately one hour. The focus group (comprising six participants in a group) was also conducted within an average time of three hours. The one-to-one interviews and the focus groups followed the same schedule and structure as presented in appendix F and G.

Criteria for the selection of participants were based on their knowledge and/or prominence in e-government implementation. This was done to limit bias in the collection of interview data. This is in line with Eisenhardt and Graebner (2007) who assert that highly knowledgeable participants who view the focal phenomena from diverse perspectives limit biases in the interview data collection. Overall the participants were enthusiastic to share their views on the study phenomena.

The process of interviews and focus groups along with the research's ethical considerations are also highlighted. A discussion of the field notes and the data transcriptions are also presented and a summary concludes the chapter.

6.2 Fieldwork follow-up

While the initial fieldwork took place in November 2010, a follow-up was undertaken from October 11 to 25, 2012. The data collected from this follow-up trip added value to the data analysis. The responses were similar to those collected in the previous fieldwork trip. It also emerged that the practiced situation in Ghana has not changed since the commencement of the research. The follow-up fieldwork trip confirmed that the problem that this research seeks to address still exists. The e-government inplementation project is on-going (but still at cataloguing stage). There are still reports of identity theft, cyberfraud and corruption in the country as discussed in sections 1.2 and 2.7.1. The only significant change in the country was the passing of Data Protection Act in February 2012. However, this development did not have any effect on the study findings.

6.3 Selection of research participants

In selecting the research participants the "time and resources available, and the number of suitable people who [could] be identified and contacted for inclusion" (Descombe, 2007, p.334) were considered. A purposive sampling method was chosen to select the research participants. This sampling method is in conformity with interpretive paradigm research (Llewellyn et al., 1999) and researchers like Patton (2002) and (Denzin and Lincoln, 2000) recommend it for a study of this nature.

6.3.1 Research participants

The Ghana government, in its ICT4D policy (Republic of Ghana, 2003), identified the following as the key implementation agencies, players and stakeholders in its e-government implementation project:

- All Government Ministries and Public Sector Organisations
- The Public Enterprise Commission
- The Labour Union

Even though the ICT4D policy has been reviewed (Ghana News Agency, 2011) since the start of this research, the identified stakeholders in the e-government implementation project remain the same. Freeman (1984, p.25) defines a stakeholder as "any group or individual who can affect or is affected by the achievement of the organization's objective". The literature search identified other stakeholders (see table 6.1 below) that also play a key role in e-government implementation.

Stakeholders of E-government	Source
Political Leaders	UN (2008), Orange et al. (2007), UNESCO (2005)
Government (including its Ministries, Departments and Agencies)	Millard (2008a), Yildiz (2007), Heeks (2006), Orange et al. (2007), UNESCO (2005)
Legislative Bodies	UNESCO (2005)
Public Administrators	UN (2008), Orange et al. (2007)
Private Sector (especially Internet Service Providers)	UNESCO (2005)
International Organisations and NGOs	Heeks (2006), UNESCO (2005)
Informed citizens (academic)	Millard (2008a), Irani et al. (2007)
Project managers/design developers/IS staff/Programmers	Orange et al. (2007), UN (2008)
End Users (Citizens, Businesses, Employees, Students etc.)	Millard (2008a), UN (2008),Yildiz (2007), Heeks (2006), UNESCO (2005), Mintzberg (1996)

Table 6.1: Identified stakeholders of e-government

Source - Adapted from Rowley (2011) and UNESCO (2005)

The findings from the literature review established that e-government implementation is a multi-stakeholder coordination process (Wright, 2010). One of the aims of the research design was to involve at least one participant from each of these identified categories of stakeholders. As presented in tables 6.2 and 7.2, this aim was achieved.

As presented in table 6.1 the implementation of e-government involves the active participation and contribution of the following identified key players and stakeholders in the entire process:

- Government (including its Ministries, Departments and Agencies): Similar to political leaders and the legislative bodies, the government stands out as a key player in the e-government project. It is the policy making body and, through its Ministry of Communications and affiliated agencies, coordinates the whole e-government implementation process and activities. UNESCO (2005) advises "the government departments at all levels in country need to ensure a perfect backend integration of systems and processes to ensure a smooth and seamless transformation of the government to a digital state". The government itself stands to benefit from this transformation since the ministries, departments and agencies can collaborate and provide services to one another.
- Legislative Bodies: These are key players in the e-government implementation in the sense that the onus lies on them to formulate and pass well-crafted ICT laws and policies which are a pre-requisite for the success of the project (UNESCO, 2005).
- Public Administrators: The awareness amongst the government employees and their willingness to embrace change plays a crucial role in the whole e-government implementation process (UNESCO, 2005).
- Private Sector (especially Internet Service Providers): The important role of the private sector in the e-government implementation cannot be ruled out. Currently there are nine Internet Service Providers (ISPs) in Ghana, namely: KNet, Broadband4u, Africa online, Internet Ghana, Network Computer Systems, Zipnet, Busy Internet, Accelon and Ecoband Networks Ltd Being the main service providers in a country with a low Internet penetration of only 14.1% Internet users (CIA World Factbook, 2013), a healthy collaboration and partnership between the government and the industry/private sector (especially the service providers) "shall lead to an easy fulfilment of e-government goals as both the parties can draw benefit out of the ventures". A Director of the Ministry of Communication (2010) stated in the data collection interview that apart from tax-

es, the service providers pay one percent of their annual revenue into the e-government project fund. UNESCO (2005) adds that "the private sector can be an investor for e-government initiatives and can also add value to the e-government initiatives through deployment of advanced technology and global expertise. Apart from the commercial aspect, they would in turn benefit from the increased efficiency, transparency and accountability of the government."

- International Organisations and NGOs: These also play an important role by being facilitators and motivators for the projects. The World Bank, for instance, has been funding some aspects of the e-government project. Through an effective promotion of e-government initiatives, organisations like the United Nations can raise awareness amongst citizens and can also contribute by carrying out research in the area and exchanging best practices with countries that have already proved successful in some areas of e-government (UNESCO, 2005).
- Informed citizens (Academics): Due to the nature of their profession (teaching and research - especially those in computer science/ ICT departments), their contribution to e-government implementation cannot be ruled out. They teach and train many of the Project Managers, Design Developers, Information Systems (IS) Staff and Programmers in university. Also Government policy making is sometimes based on evidence from their studies/research (Ferlie et al., 2003).
- Project Managers/Design Developers/IS Staff/Programmers: Research findings have shown that these professionals (especially IS Staff) are already contributing to the provision of privacy and data protection (Howley et al., 2004). As the literature review (Chapter 2) indicated, e-government cannot be implemented without provision for privacy and data protection; these professionals' role in the process is important hence their being selected to participate in the research interview.
- End Users (citizens, businesses, employees, students etc.): They are the key beneficiaries of e-government process. The end users "play a crucial role as they are the ones to expect a fast and convenient delivery of online information and services from the government" UNESCO (2005).

Since this study focussed on e-government, privacy and data protection implementations it was essential that the policy makers and legislators views were solicited. The main reason for choosing these research participants was that they could enlighten the phenomena of privacy and data protection issues, and e-government implantation in Ghana. They were specifically recruited because of their knowledge or experience relating to the phenomena.

The research design aimed to involve at least one participant from each of these identified categories of stakeholders. This was realised, and out of the fifty-three research participants, several participants were selected from each of the stakeholder categories as shown in table 6.2. Among these were politicians/parliamentarians (from both sides of the political divide), civil servants and government officials tasked with the responsibility for implementing the e-government project. Educators, students and industry experts were also sourced from the universities, Internet Service Providers, mobile phones network companies and banks.

	Stakeholders of E-government	**Number of Participants**
Providers[28]	Political leaders/ legislative bodies	4
	Government (including its ministries, departments and agencies officials - Public administrators/civil servants	6
	Private sector (especially Internet Service Providers, International organisations and NGOs)	3
	Informed citizens (academic/researchers)	9
	Project managers/design developers/IS staff/Programmers	1
Users[29]	Citizens, businesses, employees, employers, unemployed, students etc.)	30
Total number of participants		53

Table 6.2: Research participants

As shown in table 6.2, the research participants are all stakeholders and are classified into two groups: providers and users. They were selected to

[28] Provider is used here in the context of any person or body which is linked to e-government implementation. For instances, Government as electronic services provider; Members of Parliament as policy makers or influencing government decisions on e-government; academics/researchers as consultants to the e-project; and NGOs and ISPs in public private partnership with government to provide e-government services citizens.

[29] Users denote citizens (potential users) who are likely to adopt and use e-government services.

solicit their views on the role of privacy and data protection in e-government implementation in Ghana. Their views on what they consider most significant issues on e-government implementation were also considered.

The criteria for choosing the participants from these stakeholders were one or more of the following: involvement in e-government implementation; knowledge and experience of e-government usage; knowledge of the Internet or have been using the Internet to access information or e-services; academics/lecturers involved with research or teaching of the e-phenomena; and university students studying ICT/Computing.

Based on one of the criteria that participants should have *knowledge of the Internet or have been using the Internet to access information or e-services,* Internet cafes were chosen to recruit volunteers from the general public[30] to participate in the research. It must however be pointed out that "the Internet café as a space did not fully contain the social phenomena under study but rather served as an entry point" (Burrell, 2012, p.32) to recruiting volunteers from the general public who were Internet users to participate in the study.

Using these criteria means e-government *potential* users (especially those who did not know what the Internet is or have never used the Internet) were excluded from the selected participants. Their participation would not have added any value to the research due to their lack of knowledge and experience in the phenomena being studied.

The participants selected, based on the selection criteria, resulted in a multiple perspective of fieldwork data. Their knowledge and experience put them in a better position to share their opinions on the role of privacy and data protection in e-government implementation.

6.4 Data Collection

Letters (see Appendix A) asking for permission to interview the identified stakeholders were sent to the ministries, departments, agencies and organisations. The invitation letters were sent out to heads[31] of department of the participants. The letters stated the aim and purpose of the research and highlighted the fact that the research was being sponsored by

[30] Many of the general public participants heard about the term *e-government* for the first time during the interviews. However, as found out from section 8.1.2, when it was explained to them they were able to give potential benefits of e-government.

[31] The fact that invitation letters were sent through heads of departments raise possible influence or bias. As a precautionary measure to eliminate or reduce biases, participants' responses were compared with each other to check if they seem to out of line.

the Government of Ghana. Research consent forms (see Appendix E) assuring participants of their confidentially were attached to the letters.

Permission to conduct the interviews was granted from almost all the relevant stakeholders in the various organisations; and a convenient date was arranged with each willing participant. Organisations which were not in the position to participate in the research interviews referred the interviewer to the appropriate ones. For example, literature search revealed that, the Ghana-India Kofi Annan Centre of Excellence in ICT (KACE) was involved in stimulating ICT growth in the country. However, they declined an invitation to be part of the study and signposted the researcher to The National Information Technology Agency (NITA), the e-government implementing agency of the Ministry of Communications. NITA had already agreed to be part of the study, however, KACE's kind gesture was very much appreciated. The participants from NITA gave an insightful account of the phenomena which was helpful to the data analysis.

Convenient dates were arranged with participants so interviews could be conducted. Using the purposive sampling method, whose main aim is to obtain rich, in-depth information (Liamputtong, 2005; Zmijewska and Lawrence, 2005), the Select Committee of Communications of Ghana Parliament was identified; and permission from the Deputy Speaker was granted to interview some of its members. The committee is appointed by the Ghana Parliament to ensure that government ICT policy and decision-making is based on good professional advice and evidence. It has the mandate to examine the activities of ministries, departments and agencies involved with ICT projects in the country, for example the e-government project implementation.

Membership of the committee is made up of parliamentarians from both sides of the political divide, the majority and minority. The members were selected to be part of this study due to their experience and legislative work in ICT. This direct access offered the opportunity to solicit responses which were considered privileged information (Denscombe, 2007, pp.175-180) and enabled an in-depth understanding of the Ghana e-government implementation process to be gained. The Members of Parliament who were interviewed were kind enough to make available a draft copy of the Data Protection Bill. As mentioned in Chapter 2, this Bill has now been passed into law.

The Deputy Speaker's role in the selection of participants for the interviews did not in any way affect the fieldwork data. Many of the participants are experienced professionals and public officials who are involved in the e-government implementation project. They willingly gave their expert opinion on the phenomena under discussion.

Permission was also granted to interview some top civil servants from the Ministry of Communications during work time. The Ministry of Communications has an oversight role in the e-government implementation project; thus the selected participants from the sector ministry shared information which highlighted the e-government implementation project.

The general public were recruited by contacting Internet café managers with a request to interview their customers. Three Internet cafes were contacted; one opted out and one agreed to the request. The manager of the third café declined with the excuse that he did not have any space available for the interviews to take place. However, he volunteered to participate in the research and the interview was conducted in his office.

As an incentive, an agreement was reached with the second Internet café manager to allow each volunteer one hour of free browsing and the total cost of the Internet usage was to be passed on to the researcher. The manger therefore put up a notice at the reception a week before the scheduled meetings. The notice read: "VOLUNTEERS WANTED TO TAKE PART IN A RESEARCH INTERVIEW – 1 HOUR FREE INTERNET BROWSING FOR EACH VOLUNTEER AFTER THE INTERVIEWS". Any volunteer who wanted further information was asked to contact the researcher or the manager who had already been briefed about the research.

Interested volunteers left their names and contact details with the café receptionist. They were later contacted on the phone and email to brief them about the research interview and to remind them about the interviews date and time. The manager was kind enough to arrange a room in the café premises for the interviews to be conducted. The total cost of the free Internet usage by the volunteers was paid for by the researcher after the interviews.

Considering the research aims and objectives which sought to evaluate the role of privacy and data protection in the implementation of e-government in Ghana, interviews and focus groups were chosen as techniques for the data collection. With these techniques, it was possible to have personal contact with the participants. It also made it possible to explain and clarify certain aspects of the interview questions to the participants who might have had difficulties understanding them.

The fieldwork produced a total of 53 responses comprising of 35 individual face-to-face interviews and 4 focus groups with 6 participants in each group (see table 7.2). Crucial issues that came up during the interviews and focus groups, with the associated possible effect of data saturation, resulted in the 53 participants' responses collected. Data saturation is the point at which "no additional data are being found whereby the [investigator] can develop properties of the category" Glaser and Strauss (1967).

6.4.1 Fieldwork Interviews

As described in Chapter 4, Research methodology, interview is a useful research instrument for obtaining the story behind a participant's experiences. Researchers use it to pursue in-depth information around the study topic. The interview process for this study was informed by the guidelines outlined by Myers and Newman (2007) (see figure 6.1).

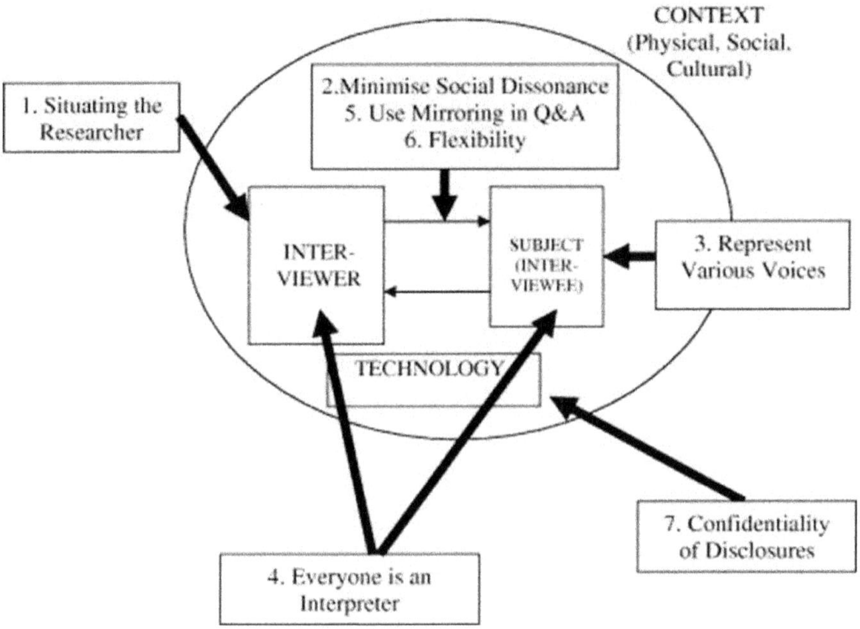

Figure 6.1: Guidelines for thc qualitative research interview

Sources: Myers and Newman (2007)

These guidelines were reinforced with the following suggestions by Easterby-Smith et al. (2008, p.146):

- *The basic probe*: the interviewer repeats a question to get the interviewee back on track; this technique is frequently used when the interviewee is going off tangent.
- *The explanatory probe*: this is used to achieve clearer understanding by completing the incomplete statements of the respondent; the interviewer asks questions such as 'Can you give an example?' or 'Can you explain that?'
- *The focused probe*: this is used to reach particular details of a topic – for example, 'What type of ... did you use?'

- *The silent probe*: here, the interviewer maintains silence and waits for the interviewee to break it; this technique is generally used when the interviewee is taking lot of time to respond or is hesitant.
- *Drawing out*: this is used when the interviewee has stopped responding; the interviewer restates or rephrases the last question or topic (e.g. 'So, the question was ... What else can you tell me about that?'), which helps the interviewee to start talking again.
- *Giving ideas or suggestions:* here, the interviewer makes suggestions or ideas for the interviewee to think about – for example, 'Have you thought about ...?'
- *Mirroring or reflecting:* here, the interviewer repeats what the interviewee has just said but in different words; this helps the interviewee to think about what he or she has just said.

These guidelines (see figure 6.1) and suggestions (Easterby-Smith et al., 2008, p.146) were instrumental in the interviews process which elicited participants' views about the role of privacy in e-government implementation.

As a novice researcher these were printed on a small card to ensure that everything was covered as expected. The card was read every time as a reminder before an interview.

For instance, using the *situating the researcher* guideline, the researcher was able to solicit the interviewees' *experience, position or status, job responsibilities, educational and professional background.* Myers and Newman (2007) recommend that this information is useful in writing up. This was in fact made used of in the writing up. Also, *minimise social dissonance* guideline, came very handy, in terms of dressing appropriately for the occasion. For instance, the researcher was formally dressed for interviews with the Members of Parliament, whereas in the case of the students, a pair of jeans and a t-shirt was appropriate.

A sample of questions that were asked during the interviews is presented in table 6.3 (see a full version at Appendix G). The questions were designed in such a way that there was possibility for the participants to raise issues that had not been captured in the frame.

Question	Purpose of question
1. In your own words what is e-government?	To explore stakeholders understanding of e-government
2. In your opinion do you think e-government implementation is necessary in Ghana? Why?	To explore how e-government implementation can enable the electronic provision of services to citizens
3. Are you aware of any obstacles that are impeding the e-government implementation? If yes, what are they?	To explore and identify the barriers related to successful e-government implementation
4. In your opinion what do you think needs to be done for the public to embrace the e-government implementation?	To explore and identify impediments that might limit the full potential usage of e-government services in particular Internet access, education etc
5. Are there citizen concerns regarding the implementation/use of e-government? If so what are these concerns? And can they be addressed?	To identify the central concerns for citizens with respect to e-government implementation, in particular concerns related to privacy, security, trust
6. In your own words can you briefly explain what is meant by privacy?	To explore stakeholders understanding of privacy
7. In your opinion do you think the Ghana Government should implement privacy legislation alongside e-government? If yes why? If no why?	To explore the necessity of regulatory frameworks dealing with e-government usage
8. Are you willing to lose your privacy in order to obtain e-government services? If yes why? If no why?	To explore whether individuals are ready to give up their personal privacy for e-government benefits
9. Is there anything else about privacy and data protection and e-government implementation in Ghana that you would like to share with me?	To provide interviewees with an opportunity to discuss other factors associated with privacy and data protection in e-Government implementation

Table 6.3: Sample of interview questions

As shown in table 6.3 participants were asked questions about their views on e-government implementation; the state of e-government implementation in Ghana; the main obstacles (i.e. Government commitment, organisational, technological infrastructure, human resources/IT experts, public education etc.) that might impede the successful implementation of e-government in Ghana; the public attitude towards change in the likelihood of e-government being finally implemented; ideas of privacy and data protection; awareness of privacy issues in Ghana; perceptions of the effect of implementation of e-government on personal data of the public; suggestions of priorities/strategies that should be in place for successful implementation of e-government in Ghana; and suggestions for future implementation of privacy law in Ghana. This enabled stakeholders' views in relation to e-government, privacy and data protection implementation to be elicited.

It must be emphasised that all participants are from Ghana, where English has been adopted as an official language. English is a second language of all the participants however, the interviews were conducted in English due to the fact that they speak as many as ten different languages. On average each interview lasted 60 minutes.

6.4.2 Focus group

As explained in detail in Chapter 4 - Research Methodology, focus group is "a group of individuals selected by researchers to discuss and comment on, from personal experience, the topic that has been a subject of the research" (O'Connor, 2012). It has the ability to help the researcher in identifying quickly a full range of perspectives held by research participants. It was employed in this study to expand details that might have been overlooked in the in-depth interviews (Powell and Single 1996 p. 499). It was particularly used to understand and explore how people think and feel about issues (Krueger and Casey, 2000) relating to e-government implementation. Bertot et al. (2010), Verdegem and Verleye (2009) and Scholl et al. (2009) have used this technique effectively in e-government research. Alsaghier and Hussain (2012) for instance, used this technique in their study to gain an in-depth understanding of the citizen's perception of e-government adoption.

In a country where around the time of the first phase of fieldwork a third of the population do not know what the Internet is; and half do not know how to use it (Bowen, 2010), and *"e-government implementation is still in its embryonic stage"* (Participant P24, a top civil servant), it is necessary to employ a focus group technique as a complement to the in-depth one-to-one interviews to explore further the perceptions of the "bulk of web surfers [who] are young urban [dwellers]...and highly educated" (Bowen, 2010). For this reason, the lecturers and students from the universities' ICT departments were seen as an important source of knowledge as their research and academic studies require familiarity with the developments in the field of electronic services and online privacy. They were selected to form the focus groups. The composition of the focus groups satisfies the criteria set in the selection of participants as highlighted in section 6.3.

After a letter of confirmation to participate in the research was received (see Appendix B), a convenient date was arranged for the focus group interviews to take place. Due to the large number of students that were available, random purposeful sampling was employed to choose the focus group participants. In this type of technique, the researcher chooses cases at random from the sampling frame consisting of a purposefully selected sample. Miles and Huberman (1994, p. 28), point out that this technique "adds credibility to sample when potential purposeful sample is too large". The introduction of the researcher as a fellow student collecting data for research facilitated trust and confidence which put the participants in a relaxed mood.

Fontana and Frey (2005, p.704) identify one limitation to using focus group technique, which is the possibility that one or two participants could dominate the proceedings and others may not have the chance to contribute at all. There is also the possibility of one or two individuals being too shy to express their views.

There was an instance in one of the focus group interviews where a participant tried to dominate the discussions. It was observed that this particular participant was trying to act the "best brain" amongst the group by not giving others the chance to contribute to the discussions. With no reference to anybody in particular the moderator politely stopped proceedings and reiterated the ground rules, stressing on the need to allow other participants to also share their opinions. This brought the recalcitrant participant in check. Every effort was taken to ensure that no one person or small coalition of persons dominated the group in the subsequent interviews. All respondents were encouraged to participate which thus facilitated obtaining responses from the entire group to ensure the fullest coverage of the topic as recommended by Fontana and Frey (2005, p.704). The number of participants in each focus group was limited to six. In all three focus groups were conducted.

6.5 Research ethical consideration

Attention was given to the ethical conduct of the research. As required by the research institution, an application to gain ethical approval was submitted to the Human Research Ethics Committee and was approved. The strict code of conduct of The Chartered Institute for IT, Social Research Association Ethical Guidelines, and Economic and Social Research Council Ethics Framework were also followed.

Before the interview, a consent form (see Appendix E), that had been approved by the Human Research Ethics Committee was given to each participant to read and sign if they were willing. The form, among other things, specified: the aim of the study; duration of the interview; confidentiality of participants; and their right to refuse to answer any question or withdraw from the interview at any stage. How the responses/data collected would be protected, secured, stored and who has access to the data was also communicated to them. Most of the research participants provided their contact details for follow-up interviews. As mentioned in section 6.2 a follow-up was undertaken to ascertain if there had been any changes since the previous fieldwork trip.

6.6 Field notes

A notebook was used to record the place, date and time of the interview. The notebook was also used to write down responses of two participants who declined to have the interviews recorded. These did not make any significant contribution to the data analysis so they were later discarded. Observations and emerging themes were also noted in the book. These notes were later expanded and typed onto a laptop after each day's interviews. The notebook itself was helpful in remembering the participants and it was also useful during the data analysis process especially in transcription of the interview data.

6.7 Data transcription

After the data collection, the recorded responses were transcribed for analysis. Due to time constraints the services of a volunteer was engaged. The volunteer transcribed eleven individual face-to-face interviews data and the rest were completed by the researcher. The transcripts (including the ones typed by the volunteer) were all checked against the digitally recorded interviews for accuracy.

6.8 Conclusion and summary of data collection

A purposive sampling method was chosen to select the participants who had a stake in the e-government project; and whose responses would be to answering the research questions. In total fifty-three identified stakeholders selected from various government departments, agencies and private organisations took part in this research.

The study drew on the expertise of persons involved in electronic government implementation, end-users, as well as academics and students with ICT background.

Participants were selected on the basis that they have access to the Internet or e-government services. Participants who were also likely to be involved in the e-government project were selected using purposeful sampling technique. For instance, members of the Select Committee of Communications in Parliament were purposely selected for the study interview to gain an insight to government ICT policy, e-government and privacy and data protection implementation in the country. They were selected from both sides of the political divide and their diverse views illuminated the privacy and data protection and e-government phenomena. Accessibility to the Internet or e-government services was a factor to the selection of participants for the focus group participants. A random purposeful sampling technique was used in selecting the students due to their large number.

Data was collected from the above stakeholders through the use of face-to-face individual interviews and focus groups. Interviews and focus group techniques made it possible to ask the reasons behind participants' responses. Thus in-depth knowledgeable data was collected for analysis to enable the research questions as outlined in Chapter 1 to be answered.

Purposeful sampling was useful in selecting the research participants for data collection. Such an approach restricts the generalisability of the results, but does not necessarily weaken the conclusions (Stahl and McRobb, 2007).

This study could be the basis for future research which will involve rural participants and non-Internet/e-government users as well.

A more detailed description of the data analysis procedure and data analysis of the fieldwork data are presented in the subsequent two chapters.

7

Data Analysis Procedure

7.1 Introduction

Having collected the data required by the research questions, according to techniques outlined in Chapter 6, in this chapter, the strategy used in analysing the data is explained. It discusses how the data analysis technique, borrowed from the Straussian version of Grounded Theory, was employed to create the codes, categories and their associated concepts.

The fieldwork data used in creating the codes and categories are a set of responses to semi-structured questions asked during in-depth interviews and focus groups. As mentioned in section 6.4.1, all participants are from Ghana, where English has been adopted as an official language. The interviews were conducted in English due to the fact that the participants speak as many as ten different languages. Since English is not their first language some of the quotations from the participants' responses may not be grammatically correct. However these grammatical errors did not distort the meaning of the participants' responses. It must be stated that terms used by the participants themselves in their responses were used in labelling the concepts, codes and categories.

A grounded theory approach (Straussian version) was borrowed to analyse the fieldwork transcribed data. Documentation[32], for instance, the participants from the implementing agency (NITA) made available to the researcher some reports which were used to update the literature review. Also, individuals' comments on media reports of the Ghana DPA 2012 enactment were accessed online. These were used in the analysis and discussion of the research findings in section 8.6.

As discussed in Chapter 4, this study adopted an interpretive approach to investigate stakeholders' views on the role of privacy and data protection in e-government implementation. Borrowing from grounded theory

[32] Also, as mentioned in 3.10.2, a draft copy of the Data Protection Act, which had not yet been posted online, was made available to the researcher.

the fieldwork data was coded using: open coding, axial coding and selective coding - as recommended by Strauss and Corbin (1990, 1998).

Table 7.1 highlights the procedure recommended by Creswell (2013, pp.190-191) when using grounded theory approach to analyse qualitative data. This recommendation has been adapted to discuss how the fieldwork data was analysed in this chapter and Chapter 8.

Data analysis and representation	Grounded theory approach
Data organisation	• Create and organize files for data
Reading, memoing	• Read through text, make margin notes, form initial codes
Describing the data into codes and themes	• Describe open coding categories
Classifying into codes and themes	• Select one open coding category for central phenomenon in process • Engage in axial coding – causal condition, context, intervening conditions, strategies, consequences
Interpreting the data	• Engage in selective coding and interrelate the categories to develop a "story" or prepositions
Representing, visualizing the data	• Present a visual model or theory • Present propositions

Table 7.1: Grounded theory approach in analysing qualitative data

Source: Creswell (2013, pp.190-191)

This chapter encompasses *data organisation; reading and memoing; describing the data into codes and themes;* and *classifying into codes and themes* whiles Chapter 8 focuses on *interpreting the data;* and *representing and visualizing the data.*

7.2 Data analysis procedures

The data analysis process of this study commenced with the verbatim transcription of fieldwork data. Necessary precautions were taken to ensure that participants' anonymity was preserved. The transcribed data was organised into individual interviews and labelled P1 (Participant 1), P2 (Participant 2), P3 (Participant 3)...P29 (Participant 29) as shown in table 7.2 below. The focus group participants were also labelled FG1, FG2, FG3... FG24.

Participant label	Profession	Qualification	No of Interviews
P1-P3	Academics/Lecturers	Postgraduate degree	3
P4-P10	Students	Undergraduates	7
P11-P14	Members of Parliament	Graduates	4
P15	Civil servant/Engineer	At least first degree	1
P16-P17	Self-employed	At least first degree	2
P18-P20	Civil servants	MSc	3
P21-P22	Internet service provider staff	BSc	2
P23	IT/IS Professional	BSc	1
P24-P25	Directors – Ministries	MSc	2
P26-P27	Bankers	BSc	2
P28	NGO staff	BA	1
P29	Unemployed graduate	BSc	1
FG1-FG6	IT students	Undergraduates	6
FG7-FG12	Informed citizens	At least first degree	6
FG13-FG18	Ordinary citizens	At least secondary school education	6
FG19-FG24	Internet cafe users	At least secondary school education	6
Total			53

Table 7.2: Summary of the fieldwork participants with their labels

The individual transcripts, fieldwork notes and documents collected during the fieldwork were reviewed. The transcribed data was read through at the same time with the playback of the recorded interviews. This was done to make the necessary corrections to mistranscribed data and also have a general idea of participants' responses. Where there was no clear understanding of participants' responses on specific issues and they had indicated they were willing to be contacted again they were called by phone for clarification. For instance, participant P20, a Civil Engineer, stated that, *"if the citizens could trust the government they would readily give out their personal data when using the e-government services"*. Clarification was sought to find out whether he meant *"trust in government"* or *"trust in e-government"*.

The transcribed data was imported into Nvivo software for coding. Borrowing from grounded theory the interview data was taken through three stages of coding: open, axial and selective coding.

7.2.1 The use of Nvivo in data analysis

As stated in section 4.12, in qualitative research, a qualitative researcher is more often than not faced with large volume of data. Previous researchers (Hoover and Koerber, 2011; Bringer et al., 2006; Weitzman, 2000) therefore recommend the use of CAQDAS, for example Nvivo, in data analysis in order to save time. It must however be be stated that the use of CADQAS do not entirely do the data analysis which results in research findings. They only facilitate the data analysis process. It has a unique feature of "increasing efficiency of data analysis, facilitating multiplicity in research methodologies, and enabling transparency of the process as a whole" (Hoover and Koerber, 2011).

Weitzman (2000) advises researchers who intend using CAQDAS to first of assess their computer literacy/skills. Following this advice this researcher completed the following three training programmes with the DMU Graduate School Office: *Creating and Managing Large Documents; Introduction to NVivo for Qualitative Data Analysis*; and *Advanced NVivo for Qualitative Data Analysis.* The successful completion of these training programmes was also influential factor in the choice of Nvivo as a computer software tool to facilitate the data analysis process which is discussed below.

7.2.2 Open coding

According to Strauss and Corbin (1998, p.101) open coding is "the analytic process through which concepts are identified and their properties and dimensions are discovered in data". It is the initial phase of the data analysis process. In order to capture the essence of the views of the participants, conceptual labels were employed in coding every phrase that has relevance to the research questions:

- ***To what extent is privacy and data protection crucial to e-government implementation in Ghana?; and***
- ***What current issues or challenges, regarding Ghana's e-government implementation do stakeholders consider particularly significant issues?***

The main aim of the study as highlighted in Chapter 1 was to analyse the role of privacy and data protection in e-government implementation. Using opening coding, initial concepts were developed based on the research topic and questions. Caswell (2013, p.184) explains coding as involving aggregating fieldwork data "into small categories of information, seeking evidence for the code from different databases being used in a study and then assigning a label to the code". Even though he recommends that regardless of the size of fieldwork data, not more than 25-30 categories of information [initial concepts] should be developed'. However, in this study, when it reached the point when coding of the data no longer contributed further initial concepts, 36 concepts[33], as presented in table 7.3, had been developed. This was achieved by using *in vivo* to code excerpts from participants' responses that seemed to have the same meaning. *In vivo* coding refers to using "terms used by [research participants] themselves" (Strauss, 1987, p.33) to label concepts. In other words, it uses the "research participants terms as codes to uncover their meanings and understand their emergent actions...[and] studying these codes and exploring leads in them allows you to develop deeper understanding of what is happening and it means" (Charmaz, 2014, pp.134-135). Not only that, "names the researcher composes that seem to best describe the information" (Creswell, 2013, p.185) were also used to represent the concept labels. Pidgeon et al. (1991) suggest that the "label should fit the phenomenon described in the data exactly, so that the terms chosen provide a recognizable description of the item, event or activity under consideration".

For example, the following excerpts, as shown on table 7.3 (point 3) have connotations of potential benefits of e-government implementation:

> *"e-government makes government information more readily available and it improves upon democracy",*
>
> *"it encourages openness and reduces or eliminates corruption",*
>
> *"it saves time and improves upon the way things are done".*

They describe the things that both the government and citizens are likely to benefit from when e-government is successfully implemented. They were therefore grouped together under the concept label *benefits of e-government*. *In vivo* coding was not used in developing the concept label; rather it was a label the researcher composed that seemed to best describe the information.

However in the case of point 12 on table 7.3, for example, the concept label *corrupt government officials* was open coded using *in vivo coding* – that is, using the participants own phrases to represent the concepts. This concept label depicts the corruption in government and its impact in e-government implementation.

[33] These 36 label concepts were developed from responses of all the stakeholders' (both providers and users) who participated in the fieldwork data collection.

Employing the aforementioned coding techniques, the excerpts were coded and grouped under the same concept label as recommended by Strauss and Corbin (1998).

	Concept label[34]	Excerpts from participants' quotes
1	Meaning of e-government	"E-government is government trying to implement its services and functions to the public electronically, in other words, digitalising government functions to achieve a better supervision, a better co-ordination and a better governing process"
2	Lack of technical experts	"even if the government gets all the money [funds] to acquire the computers needed for this [e-government] project they still need the human resource, I mean, the technical people to handle and manage them"
3	Benefits of E-government	"e-government makes government information more readily available and it improves upon democracy", "it encourages openness and reduces or eliminates corruption", "it saves time and improves upon the way things are done"
4	Lack of resources	"we don't have the resources, both human and the technological know-how"; "I think we lack the resources to implement the e-government project"
5	Digital divide	"there is a big divide between the 'haves' and 'have-nots' in terms of computer and Internet access, which means, e-government can only be used by a small number of people"

[34] It must be stated here that based on recommendation by Creswell (2013, p.185), the number of participants who contributed to each concept label were not counted. He explains that, "counting conveys a quantitative orientation of magnitude and frequency contrary to qualitative research." He adds that, "a count conveys that all codes should be given equal emphasis, and it disregard that the passages coded may actually represent contradictory views."

6	Internet access	"make computer and Internet access available to the people to motivate them and they will use it [e-government services]"
7	Internet readily accessible	"It [Internet] is the technology that drives the e-government services and should therefore be readily accessible; it should be available 24/7"
8	Internet affordability	"those who want to subscribe to the Internet should get it at an affordable rate"
9	Challenges of e-government	"the challenge that the government is currently facing is human base"; "our challenge to this e-government project has been low Internet access penetration"
10	Infrastructure	"I think infrastructure in itself cannot be overlooked...that many of the past projects that the government had tried carrying out, they failed because the infrastructure was not put in place before implementing them"
11	Corrupt government officials	"in Africa [and that matter Ghana] we do usually have a corrupt government officials, so we will like to know who will ensure the government does not use or manipulate our personal information anyhow"
12	Meet stakeholders	"the first thing to do address this problem [lack of IT experts] is to meet all the stakeholders especially the university lectures [academics] to develop the higher level computer science education in the country"
13	Public education	"We can do a lot of education in the media, radio, TV whatever...a lot can also come from the youth teaching their parents how to use computers, how to browse the Internet and most importantly how to access e-government services online"

14	E-government awareness	"for the e-government [implementation] to work the government has to create awareness by educating the people"
15	Privacy and data protection awareness	"there is the need for public education to make the people aware of the e-government implementation and more especially their privacy rights as well"
16	Knowledge about latest technologies	"I know there are these sophisticated technologies out there that ensure that you cannot escape the notice of the security services "
17	Use of new technology	"making the ordinary people know about the new technology and bringing it down to their level and showing them how to use it"
18	Meaning of privacy	"Privacy is protecting your data from being misused"; "Privacy is having control over my personal information"
19	Meaning of data protection	"It's got something to do with the law protecting privacy"; "it is about those who collect my personal details ensuring that they are secure and they don't get into the hands of wrong people"
20	Importance of privacy legislation	"privacy legislation is very important; it will ensure the unit that collects our personal data when we use the e-government services protects and secures it"
21	Privacy concerns	"if you are using e-government services, your personal data will be collected and if you don't know what is going to happen it, you will get worried"
22	Lack of privacy legislation	"the absence of privacy law will be harmful to the citizen's personal data": "there is no law to protect the data that would be collected from being misused or identity theft"

23	Scared to put personal information online	"I worry about the latest technologies available that make it possible for people to hack into a computer database; it makes me scary to put my information"
24	Worried about personal details	"I worried about this new age where right form birth till death, information is stored about me in a database...data mining and processing power is so vast that someone gets to profile me so well and someone can easily assume my identity"
25	Need for privacy legislation	"Privacy is a human right and it is the responsibility of Government to respect and protect it"
26	Privacy laws in other countries	"our laws need to move with times, we shouldn't be left behind the rest of the world"
27	Privacy as a human right	"since privacy is a right we need a law to protect it"
28	Motivation to use e-government services	"people will go online and use the services freely once they know that they are protected"; "Privacy legislation will motivate people to use the e-government services"
29	Measures taken in the absence of privacy law	"We don't have privacy law however we do our best to protect and secure our customers personal data using latest security technology available"; "we have invested in high-quality security to protect our customers' personal details"
30	Confidence to use the e-government service	"it will give people confidence to use the e-government service, in the sense that, they know whatever personal information they submit online there is a law backing [protecting] it"
31	Motivation to go online	"knowing that your personal information is secured, protected and that no one is going to misuse it will motivate you to go online"

32	Trust in government	"if the citizens can trust the government they will readily give out personal information when using e-government services"
33	Mistrust in Government	"because we don't trust the system it will be very, very difficult to get people to give their personal details online")
34	Government commitment to privacy legislation	"Government should be committed to privacy legislation"
35	Unwillingness to provide personal information online	"If I can be sure of a law to protect my personal data then I will be more than willing to provide my personal information online"
36	Politicisation of e-government implementation	"we should also not politicise the implementation of important projects like e-government. The opposition should support the government to make it successful"

Table 7.3: Conceptual labels

These labels as captured in table 7.3 were coded making use of 'In vivo coding'. In Vivo coding refers to using "terms used by [research participants] themselves" (Strauss, 1987, p.33) to label concepts.

7.2.3 Axial coding

Axial coding refers to the process of making connections and links between the categories (Strauss and Corbin 1998). Remenyi (2013b, p.148) explains that it "involves grouping open codes to constitute more comprehensive constructs". The intention is to combine the initial concepts into "concepts of greater breadth and depth" (Remenyi, 2013b, p.21). It is essentially about shifting from lower codes to broader categories, and building a more theoretical or conceptual analytic take on the [fieldwork] data" (Braun and Clarke, 2013, p.239). Considering the above and bearing in mind the phenomena being studied, some concepts which share the same property were merged to form categories[35] as discussed below and presented in table 7.4. As recommended by Braun and Clarke (2013, p.239),

[35] Crewell (2013, p.186) recommends 5-7 categories at this stage, that is, the researcher reducing the data to a small, manageable set of themes (categories) to write the final narrative.

the definition of each category has been given to make it more meaningful and relevant to the phenomena.

The concept labels *"e-government awareness" "privacy and data protection awareness"* and *"benefits of e-government"* were merged to form *"awareness of e-government and privacy and data protection"*. The concepts in this category described individuals' awareness of e-government implementation and the potential benefits both the government and citizens would tend to derive as well as privacy concerns and data protection issues.

The codes *"digital divide" "Internet access", "Internet affordability"* and *"Internet readily accessible"* were merged to form the category *"Digital divide"*. Digital divide represents the gap between those who have access to digital technologies (computers and Internet) and those who do not. As mentioned in the literature review, Chapter 2, Internet entity is the major access to e-government services. It is the enabler of the e-government project, however, Bowen's (2010) survey report highlights significant variations in Internet access between rural and urban communities, as found out in Chapter 2.

The concepts *"use of new technology" "computer illiteracy" and "lack of technical experts"* were merged to form a new category *"information and communication technology"*. This category was initially considered to be merged under *digital divide* however further analysis showed that they had distinctive concepts which could be explored to answer the research questions. Whereas, *"digital divide"* (as previously discussed) is about the gap between those *who have* or *have no* access to the technology, the category *"information and communication technology"* deals with the development of basic telecommunication and ICT infrastructure.

The merging of *"trust in government", "mistrust in government"* and *"corrupt government officials"* concepts resulted in the category *"trust in government"*.

In this study, trust is taken in the context of citizens' willingness to use e-government services with a confidence that the government and its departments and agencies will not misuse their personal data.

Carter and Belanger (2005) in a study found out that *trust* was an important factor in citizen's acceptance of e-services. E-government involves online transactions which raise privacy concerns for the citizen and make trust a condition for exchange (Ribbink et al., 2004). Citizens would therefore like to trust the service provider as well as the service provided before using it.

The concepts *"motivation to go online"* and *"confidence to use the e-government service"* were merged under the category *"trust in government"*.

They described the willingness and or tendency of individuals to access the e-government services. Belanger et al (2002) defined trustworthiness as "the perception of confidence in the electronic marketer's reliability and integrity". A citizen confidence to use a new technology is imperative to e-government implementation (Bélanger and Carter, 2008). That confidence is a motivation factor for an individual to go online and access the e-government services.

Privacy concerns emerged as the category to represent the initial concepts: *"unwillingness to provide personal information online"*, *"scared to put personal information online"* and *"worried about personal details"*. As previously explained in section 2.8, *privacy concerns* relate to issues or concerns over how the citizens personal detail are collected, processed, stored and even the possibility of disclosure to a third party without their consent.

The category *"privacy and data protection legislation"* was obtained by merging the codes *"privacy laws in other countries", "privacy as a human right", "importance of privacy legislation", "lack of privacy legislation", "need for privacy legislation", "measures taken in the absence of privacy law" and "government commitment to privacy legislation"*. This category depicted the necessity of the law that protects personal data and its crucial role in the implementation of e-government.

The category *"Privacy concerns"* was further merged into *"Privacy and data protection legislation"*. The relationship between these two categories stems from the fact that privacy concerns of e-government users require data protection legislation to address them.

As explained above, through the axial coding, the concepts developed in the open coding stage were explored further and five categories emerged as shown in table 7.4 below.

Initial concepts	Emerging categories	Relevant literature
• *E-government awareness* • *Knowledge of privacy and data protection* • *Benefits of e-government*	Awareness of e-government and privacy and data protection	Carter and Weerakkody (2008)
• *Digital divide* • *Internet access* • *Internet affordability* • *Internet readily accessible*	Digital divide	Sipior and Ward (2009)

• *Computer illiteracy* • *Lack of technical experts* • *Use of new technology*	Information communication technology	Mossberger (2009), Bertot et al. (2010)
• *Trust in government* • *Mistrust in government* • *Corrupt government officials* • *Motivation to go online* • *Confidence to use the e-government service*	Trust in government, motivation, confidence to go online	Alsaghier et al. (2009), Bélanger and Carter (2008), Carter and Bélanger (2005)
• *Importance of privacy and data protection legislation* • *Lack of privacy legislation* • *Need for privacy legislation* • *Measures taken in the absence of privacy law* • *Government commitment to privacy legislation* • *Privacy concerns* • *Willingness to provide personal information online* • *Privacy laws in other countries* • *Privacy as a human right* • *Scared to put personal information online* • *Worried about personal details*	Privacy and data protection legislation in e-government	Bansal and Chen (2011), Arenesen and Danielsson (2007)

Table 7.4: Emerging categories

Using selective coding the relationships between these five emergent categories were further explored to identify the links among the categories.

In the process the main (core) category was also identified. How this was done is discussed in the next section.

7.2.4 Selective coding

Selective coding is "the process of integrating and refining the theory" (Strauss and Corbin 1998, p.143). It is the process of selecting a focal core category which is the central phenomenon that has emerged from the axial codes and relating it to other categories in addition to validating those relationships (Strauss and Corbin, 1990). The relationships between the categories identified in section 7.2.3 were further investigated and privacy and data protection legislation in e-government emerged as the core category.

7.3 Memo writing

Throughout the data coding process, memo writing took place to list the emerging ideas that occurred to the codes. Memos are "sites of conversation with ourselves about our data" (Clarke, 2005, p.202). They capture the thoughts of researchers as they progress through their work (Fernández, 2004).

In this study, memos were produced constantly from the beginning of the analysis process until reaching closure. For instance, the initial stage of the data analysis process commenced with the following memos written to reflect on the study's research questions and the emerging ideas:

Thoughts arising[36] *from fieldwork data:*

- *Participants*[37] *are aware of the concepts e-government and privacy and data protection;*
- *Participants are aware of the benefits of e-government but a few would prefer using the traditional services for fear of misuse of their personal data;*
- *Fieldwork participants seem to be less concern about their privacy than the pilot study participants (why – has it got anything to do with their geographical location or the sample size?).*

Furthermore, attention was given to the literature search on *"the role of privacy and data protection in the implementation of e-government in developing countries"* which is very close to the title of the research. This facilitated the

[36] These were interim notes made during the research - each only referred to small parts of the research.

[37] This memo was written about the focus group (FG1-FG6) made up of IT undergraduate students – they may possibly have learnt about the phenomena in the lecture room.

comparison of emergent concepts with the results of the literature search as recommended by Eisenhardt (1989). For example the following memo was written and later used in the discussion of findings: *while research participants are unlikely to use e-government services for lack of privacy and data protection legislation which could possibly hinder e-government successful implementation, in UK, BBC (2003) reports the Data Protection Act is hampering e-government project.* The memos kept the data analysis process on track with the study aim and objectives.

7.4 Summary

Borrowing from the Straussian version of grounded theory, the three stages of coding: *open, axial and selective coding* were used to identify the concepts and categories. The outcome of these processes is all codes which did not have any meaning or provide insight into the research questions (outlined in section 1.7) were discarded. Similarly, all concepts with the same meaning were grouped under one category as illustrated in section 7.2.3. Additionally, categories with similar meanings were merged under one category to minimise the number of categories used in the data analysis. The process was repeated many times until all the categories were identified. The emergent categories were: ***awareness of e-government and privacy and data protection, trust in government, motivation and confidence to go online, information and communication technology, digital divide,*** and ***privacy and data protection in e-government.***

A detailed account of the qualitative data analysis of the fieldwork data is presented in the next chapter under these emerged categories and their associated concepts. The interrelationships between them are also discussed using the empirical data.

8

Data Analysis

This chapter reports the interpretations arrived at using the methods described in Chapter 7 to analyse the accounts of interview participants, taking into consideration the research questions, aim and objectives as highlighted in Chapter 2.

The emergent categories are as follows:

- Awareness of e-government and privacy and data protection
- Trust in government, motivation and confidence to go online
- Information and communication technology
- Digital divide
- Privacy and data protection in e-government

Even though the study sought to investigate the role of privacy and data protection in the implementation of e-government in Ghana, some categories as shown in the previous chapter (see tables 7.3 and 7.4) emerged alongside the core category of *privacy and data protection legislation*.

A review of e-government literature shows that the categories which emerged in this study have been identified as challenges to successful implementation of e-government in other research, notably, Dwivedi et al., (2012), Jaeger and Bertot (2010) and Ndou (2004).

8.1 Awareness of e-government and privacy and data protection

The data analysis shows that many of the participants were not acquainted with the concepts of e-government and privacy and data protection. Throughout the individual face-to-face interviews and focus groups it was difficult soliciting clear and understandable meanings of the study phenomena from many of the participants.

In some of the interviews for instance, when it became clear that a few of the participants did not *seem* to have knowledge of the phenomena under discussion, the interviewer used cues. For example, the interviewer asked: *"have you thought about what will happen to your personal information when you submit it in exchange for e-government services?"*. In this instance, the cue was to get the participants to talk about online privacy risks and also whether they are aware of privacy violations such as *identity theft*. It was found out that these few participants had no clue of the phenomena; however they participated in the interviews because they satisfied one of the criteria used in the selection of participants. That is, they *had knowledge of the Internet or had been using the Internet to send email and access information.*

Many of the participants though exhibited some knowledge of the phenomena. The participants from Parliament, universities and the implementing government ministry showed a better understanding, knowledge and experience of the phenomena. Some excerpts of the responses are captured below in this section to illustrate some participants' understanding and knowledge of the research phenomenon *privacy*.

Overall, contributions to the discussion of privacy and data protection show lack of understanding and awareness of the phenomena. As shown in section 8.1.1 below, many of the participants understand privacy and data protection as private life and protection of one's reputation and integrity.

A few though explained *privacy* separately from *data protection*. They had an idea about the relationship between the two and their role in e-government implementation. Examples of some of their responses are as follows:

> *"Privacy is protecting your data from being misused"*, P1, a university lecturer.
>
> *"Privacy is getting to know the purpose for which my personal data is being collected"*, (FG6, undergraduate student).

These responses show that many of the participants from the universities, the implementing sector ministry and Members of Parliament are conversant with personal information privacy. They also have an idea about data protection as Participant FG3, an undergraduate IT student explained:

> *"I think data protection is about how those who collect my personal details ensure that they are secured and not misused"*

Participant FG2, another undergraduate IT student, added that:

> *"It [data protection] means protecting individuals' personal data from being used without their concern"*.

The explanations given by these participants show their knowledge of the phenomena. Similarly, participants from e-government implementation project team and members of the select committee on communication also show that they have knowledge of the concepts of the phenomena. In the case of the lecturers and students, their knowledge and understanding of the phenomena seems to have come from their discussion of the concept in class. They appear to have a meaning near to those as given by authorities in privacy, for example Westin (1967). It captures the western concept of privacy, which is "the right to be left alone" (Warren and Brandeis, 1890). This concept has been the basis of privacy legislation (Sheehan, 2002) in most countries, including Ghana.

Basically, the Ghanaian concept of privacy is articulated by Warren and Brandeis (1890), that is, to "protect the privacy of private life". As explained by the following participants:

> *"Privacy as I understand it is keeping my private life secret" Participant P19,*

When prompted for further explanation he explained that:

> *"If I have some terrible sickness, like say AIDS, it is a private matter and I would hate for it to become by the public"*

Participant P29, an unemployed graduate, said:

> *"What privacy means to me is, my private life is not made public. I consider the things that I do privately as personal matter and so far as those things are not criminal offenses I resent them being made public. "* Participant P29

Others also, especially some politicians from the other side of the political divide, too view privacy as freedom from government surveillance. A Member of Parliament, Participant P12, remarked that, privacy is:

> *"...to be free from security agencies following you around, even to your bedroom".*

Participant P12's remarks suggest government surveillance of the citizens. As was explained in section 2.4.3 "the use of the material monitored by the government for unauthorized purposes, the danger to political expression and association" (Fried, 1968) can lead to mistrust in both government and e-government, which in a way can negatively affect citizens' usage of online services.

It can be inferred from these participants' responses that many Ghanaians concept of privacy is non-intrusion into their personal private life. Privacy to them is *"dignity, honor...and respect* [for] *one's private life and* [the right] *to keep certain things secret,"* (Werro, 2009) from society. People have more concern and are particular about protecting their private matters than online personal privacy. In essence, a common Ghanaian concept of privacy and data protection is the need to protect one's reputation and prevent anything that might bring shame to their family. This has a cultural connotations and Hofstede's model of cultural dimensions (Hotstede et al., 2010, p.31) are used to discuss it further in section 8.8.

8.1.1 Awareness of privacy issues in e-government

The analysis of the fieldwork data shows many of the participants are aware of privacy and its impact on e-government. These were revealed from the participants' responses in the interviews with them:

"Privacy is protecting your data from being misused" P23, computer programmer.

"Privacy is having control over my personal information" FG1, IT student.

"Privacy is a human right and it is the responsibility of Government to respect and protect it" P13, Member of Parliament.

"There is the need for public education to make the people aware of the e-government implementation and more especially their privacy rights as well" P21, IT manager.

"If you are using e-government services, your personal data will be collected and if you don't know what is going to happen it, you will get worried" P1, Lecturer.

"If I can be sure of a law to protect my personal data then I will be more than willing to provide my personal information online" FG20, Businessman.

Some participants knew about privacy risks inherent in accessing e-government services. Participant FG5, an undergraduate ICT student, raised the issue of privacy concern in using e-government services by saying that:

> *"When accessing e-government services I would be afraid to give my details online, because it is possible for it to be misused".*

None of the participants had been victims of privacy breach before; however, their knowledge of privacy issues in e-government comes from the reported cases in the media, both local and international. Participant FG21, a technician, indicated that:

> *"even in the so called developed countries that already have privacy laws, there are reported cases of people's personal data being lost, stolen and online credit card fraud, how much more Ghana which has nothing [privacy legislation] at all" Participant FG21*[38].

[38] As already mentioned in Chapters 1 and 5, this interview fieldwork took place (in November 2010) before the passing of the Data Protection Bill into an Act in February 2012. However, Participant FG21's statement, just like the many

The participant's comparison devalues the need for privacy and data protection in the country and for that matter its role in the e-government implementation. It seems to suggest that if there are privacy breaches in even developed countries which already have established privacy and data protection legislation then the legislation is not so necessary in Ghana.

The plausible reason for the participant and many other people's indifference towards privacy and data protection legislation, as discussed in detail in section 8.7 below, is the low privacy concerns among them, which are influenced by the national culture, specifically collectivist cultural society.

While the participant, just like many others, maybe making a reasonable comparison in his response, he demonstrates lack of awareness and understanding of privacy and data protection issues. He seems not to value the importance of privacy and data protection in e-government implementation.

There are a few participants though who share a contrary view; that is privacy and data protection legislation is necessary in e-government implementation. They even share a view of how the privacy legislation can be enforced. They are of the view that the punishment and fines to be imposed on violators by the privacy law may have deterrent effect and possibly allay individuals' fears to access online services.

Participant P15, a civil servant and a civil engineer by profession said:

> *"I want to be assured that at least there is a privacy law to protect my personal information whenever I go online to use e-government services" Participant P15.*

The interpretation of their responses is that these participants (few though) are aware of the privacy risks that result in using e-government services and they want guarantees for the protection of their personal data when they use online services.

8.1.2 Awareness of potential benefits of e-government implementation

Apart from the privacy and data protection issues raised in the previous section, participants are aware of the potential benefits of e-government implementation. Interviewees were asked questions like: ***"why do you think e-government implementation is necessary in Ghana?"*** to explore how e-government implementation can enable the electronic provision of services and its potential benefits. Participant P17, a self-employed graduate, responded that:

---

others, is still currently relevant to the study.

> *"E-government is very necessary. I have used the services before in abroad and it is very convenient and saves a lot of time. For example, I didn't have to go to any office to apply for a driving licence. I completed the application form online. You don't have to pay bribe to anyone as has been happening here [in Ghana]" Participant P17.*

This response, and many other similar ones, exposes the presumption of corrupt practices by government officials which are dealt with in the next section. The Participant's phrase *"You don't have to pay bribe to anyone"* seems to suggest a potential benefit of e-government implementation to citizens. It suggests citizens' adoption of the online service will eliminate or minimise bribery and corruption. In other words it will eliminate or at least reduce physical contact with corrupt government officials/workers who may want a financial inducement before offering government services to the public.

While Participant P17's response illustrates potential benefits of e-government to citizens, specifically its *convenience of use, time saving* and *elimination of corruption,* it was found that most of the participants hardly use e-government service in its current state. The student participants, in particular, stated that, they occasionally use the government website to search for information (specifically government statistical figures) for their project work. Participant FG4, an IT student, said:

> *"The few times I have visited the government website was to look for information to do my coursework;* [he added mockingly] *there is nothing much to see there anyway, apart from the picture of the President"* Participant FG4.

The demeanour of Participant FG4 when he made the last statement shows that, he finds the state of the Ghana Government portal disappointing. The phrase *"nothing much to see"* can be interpreted to mean the website is not very functional and developed.

However, it had been useful to a few citizens though. For example, Participant P18, a secretary, has been using the Government portal to access information. She shared her experience thus:

> *"I used the government portal once to search for contact details of one of the government agencies, I think, Immigration Services...when I was applying for my passport"* Participant P18.

There are other participants who are of the view that browsing the Government portal is a waste of time and money. For instance, Participant P16, self-employed, said,

> *"I wouldn't pay so much money at the Internet café just to go browse government website. I would go on facebook instead"* Participant 16.

This interviewee response indicates that he does not find the Government website useful. It also brings to the fore the high cost of Internet access to citizens. Probably if Internet access was cheaper or even free then citizens like Participant 16 would be motivated to browse the portal.

Despite of the fact that most of the participants hardly access the government website they are aware of the potential benefits of e-government. The following are listed as some of the potential benefits of e-government:

- Time saving on the part of citizens and government departments and their various agencies (Participant P17);
- Very convenient, due to the fact that the services can be accessed anytime and anywhere (Participant FG5);
- No need to bribe any corrupt government official to obtain a service (Participant FG17).

To reinforce the above, the interviewer asked: *Are you willing to lose your privacy in order to obtain e-government services? If yes why? If no why?* This question was asked to explore whether individuals are ready to give up their personal privacy for e-government benefits. Almost all of the participants responded that these potential benefits are enough incentive for them to access the e-government services without considering their personal privacy. As pointed out by Participant FG17, an administrative staff member with a secondary education:

> *"I wouldn't mind giving out my personal details if it means not going to the ministries [government offices] to join a long queue and also not paying bribe to those people [corrupt government officials]"* Participant FG17.

It appears from this participant and many others that they have little or no concern over possible misuse of their online personal information by the government. To find out she was further asked whether she was not concerned about her personal privacy, she responded:

> *"I am concerned about my privacy, but I need the e-government services, it is convenient and as I said earlier, I don't have to pay bribe to anybody before using it. Besides, of what value is my personal information to anyone? None, I think"* Participant FG17.

This participant's understanding of privacy, just like many others, is limited to private matter. Online personal information does not seem to mean anything to her. The use of the phrase *"of what value is my personal information to anyone?"* shows the low level of privacy concern and lack of awareness of potential privacy violations or misuse of her personal information by *"corrupt government officials"*. It can be deduced from this participant's statement and many other similar responses from other participants that either they are not aware of the privacy risks involved in submitting personal information online or they just cannot be bothered.

On the other hand, the participant use of the phrase *"None, I think"* seems to suggest that probable due to her low income status anyone who steals her identity will not have value for it. Therefore there is no need to show concern or protect personal information which has no value to any interested third party or for which she has nothing to lose if it is stolen. This suggests that income directly affects levels of their privacy concerns.

In addition, the above response can also be interpreted as the potential benefits to be derived from using the e-government service supersede the privacy concerns: *"I need the e-government services,* [since] *it is convenient"*

There are a few other participants though, who in spite of the potential benefits to be derived from accessing e-government services are wary about their personal privacy and data protection. Participant FG8, a self-employed graduate (ICT consultant), had this to say:

> *"While we are aware of the benefits of e-government implementation [however] we don't want our personal data to be misused as a result of accessing the services"* Participant FG8.

This participant's view suggests that the potential benefits must not take the attention from the privacy concerns that arise out of using e-government services.

The privacy concerns are evident in participant FG18's response as well:

> *"we are aware of the benefits of e-government implementation, but we are also worried for our personal data. We want our personal data to be secured and not misused when we use the service"* Participant FG18 (a technician).

These few participants are aware of the potential benefits to be derived from e-government implementation but wary and doubtful about the protection and security of personal information to be submitted in exchange for the service. It highlights the value just a few of these participants attached to privacy and data protection legislation in e-government implementation.

Linking the findings of section 8.1.1 to that of this section it can be concluded that there is lack of awareness of privacy issues and low privacy concern among Ghanaians. As discussed in detail in section 8.7 below, cultural dimension of the Ghanaian collectivist society could be a factor to this finding. Also e-government use is not influenced by privacy and data protection regulation but rather the potential benefits of the online service.

A few participants, though, are aware of the potential benefits of e-government; but due to privacy concerns they are less likely to access the services. They are of the opinion that the presence of privacy and data protection legislation to safeguard their online personal data will let them have trust in government and for that matter the e-government system, which would in turn give them the confidence and motivation to go online.

Overall, it can be concluded from sections 8.1.1 and 8.1.2 that only a few of the participants seem to understand the role of privacy and data protection role in e-government implementation. There is lack of awareness, understanding and misconception of the phenomena among most of the people. Many of the participants are more likely to use the e-government service for its potential benefits without worrying about the potential privacy risks. There is low privacy concern among the participants. The low income status is a possible factor for low privacy concern.

8.2 Trust in government, motivation and confidence to go online

The category *trust in government, motivation and confidence to go online* is relevant to this study. The major source of mistrust comes *"from the need to collect data on individuals as the basis for providing services and fears of data surveillance or the inappropriate secondary use of personal information in computer databases."* (Germanakos et al, 2007).

Participant FG24, a retired civil servant, makes an interesting comment which captures the concept of this category:

> *"You can't trust something you've not used before, something you don't know much about…and if people are around, you won't even go near it [the Internet] for fear of being laughed at when you mess up"* Participant FG24.

The participant's use of the phrase *"something you've not used before"* indicates the new technology, the main enabler of e-government. It shows individuals inability or lack of skills to use the new technology can result in mistrust. As can be inferred from the response, low trust discourages individuals from the use the new technology to access the e-government service. According to Bélanger et al. (2002) trust is significant in determining whether or not an individual would access an online service.

The concept of trust can be captured in the words of Baier (1986),

> *"Trust involves the belief that others will, so far as they can, look after our interests, that they will not take advantage or harm us. Therefore, trust involves personal vulnerability caused by uncertainty about the future behavior of others, we cannot be sure, but we believe that they will be benign, or at least not malign, and act accordingly in a way which may possibly put us at risk."*

In the context of e-government trust is citizens believing in government to protect their online personal information (free from violations by government officials/workers) The lack of trust in government (as result of corrupt practices of government officials) as expressed by some of the participants could give individuals low motivation to access e-government services. Participant P17, a self-employed graduate, remarked that:

> *"E-government is very necessary. I have used the services before in abroad and it is very convenient and saves a lot of time. For example, I didn't have to go to any office to apply for a driving licence. I completed the application form online. You don't have to pay bribe to anyone as has been happening here* [in Ghana]*"* Participant P17.

Participant P17's use of the phrase *"pay bribe to anyone as has been happening here"* seems to expose an on-going bribery and corruption among government workers and officials in the country. It suggests a norm of people having to pay bribes to them before accessing government services. This perception may cause a low level of trust in Government. The phrase *"I completed the application form online"* also suggests e-government eliminates direct contact with corrupt government workers and thereby can remove the occurrence of paying bribes to them.

Participant P8, an IT student, who also expressed corruption among government officials and a privacy concern said:

> *"In Africa [and for that matter Ghana] we do usually have a corrupt government officials, so we will like to know who will ensure the government does not use or manipulate our personal information anyhow"* Participant P8.

In the above response, there is an element of mistrust in e-government due to government officials' corrupt malpractices which brings to the fore privacy concern in e-government use. The interviewee seems to be questioning the security and protection of citizens' online personal information in the face of the on-going corruption among government officials. He therefore seems to asking for guarantees for privacy, security and protection of their personal information.

Participants P17 and P8 thus make contrasting comments which are worth examining further. The former's response suggests mistrust in government as a result of known corruption and bribery practices among public officials and civil servants. Furthermore the participant seems to suggest e-government implementation will eliminate these malpractices which has hitherto lowered trust in the government. The latter's response also suggests mistrust in e-government as a result of corrupt government officials which raises a privacy concern.

It is interesting to note that whilst Participant P17's response suggests that e-government may eliminate or minimise corruption, participant P8 however seems to believe the e-government implementation is a catalyst for more corrupt practices, that is, possible privacy violations of people's online personal information by government officials. What the latter seems to be suggesting is that, these government officials who until e-government implementation collect bribes before rendering services to the citizens are the same ones that will be processing citizens' personal data in any e-government transaction. This means that, the potential financial loss that these officials may lose as a result of e-government implementation may be made up (for example) in identity theft, cyber fraud or even copying the citizens' personal data and selling to an interested third party. Participant P8's mistrust for e-government is reinforced by Participant FG6, an IT student. The participant shares knowledge of how people are tracked when they go online:

> *"I know there are these sophisticated technologies out there that ensure that you cannot escape the notice of the security services and they are also done and coordinated in such a way that no one hold the government accountable for privacy violation"* Participant FG6.

As seen from this response *trust* captures the privacy concerns citizens have or perceive to have about e-government implementation. The participant seems to be suggesting the government will have an ulterior motive, that is, surveillance of citizens whiles they are online browsing government portal.

Participant P1, university lecturer, expressed this concern by stating that:

> *"If you are using e-government services, your personal data will be collected and if you don't know what is going to happen to it, you will get worried"* Participant P1.

This view, like many others, expresses the citizens' privacy concern. The phrase *"you don't know what is going to happen to it"* suggests the participant has doubts about the privacy and security of the online personal data. This concern is as a result of lack of trust in the government to protect the online personal data.

Worrying over possible misuse of their personal data; corrupt government officials; tracking of citizens' online browsing; and lack of privacy and data protection are causes of public mistrust in e-government. These could influence citizens' willingness to use e-government services. Participant FG5, an IT undergraduate student, pointed out that:

> *"If the citizens can trust the government they will readily give out personal information when using e-government services. Because we don't trust the system it will be very, very difficult to get people to give their personal details online"* Participant FG5.

It can be concluded from the views expressed by the participants in this section that trust is a factor in citizens' willingness to access e-government services. The public mistrust in government is as a result of reported cases of corruption among government officials. This section further suggests that since e-government reduces physical between citizens and government officials it can minimise bribery and corruption. E-government through "Information and communication technologies (ICTs) are [therefore] seen by many as a cost-effective and convenient means to promote openness and transparency and to reduce corruption" Bertot et al. (2010).

8.3 Information and communication technology

The *information and communication technology* category emerged as one the category that encompasses a group of potential challenges that can hamper the successful implementation of e-government. Many participants are of the view that the newness of technology and individuals' inability to use it are also potential challenges that can hamper successful implementation of e-government. Participant FG17 is emphatic on this issue:

> *"Even if the government gets all the money [funds] to acquire the computers needed for this [e-government] project they still need the human resource, I mean, the technical people to handle and manage them"*

The lack of technical experts within a project (like the e-government implementation) team has been found to be an important factor likewise the shortages of qualified technical personnel (Gil-Garcia and Pardo, 2005).

In section 8.1.2, it was found out that a few individuals may not use the e-government services due to privacy concerns. As indicated in section 8.4 below, there are others who may not access the e-government services not for the reason just aforementioned, but rather because of lack of knowledge and skills to use the new technology; and access to the enabling technology (the Internet). As expressed by Participant P11, a member of the Select Committee on Communication in Parliament:

> *"There is a big divide between the 'haves' and 'have-nots' in terms of computer and Internet access, which means, e-government can only be used by a small number of people"* Participant P11.

This suggests, there are individuals, who in spite of the potential benefits to be derived from using the online service, would traditional government offices for reasons such as inaccessibility to computers and Internet. In other words, the existence of a digital divide may challenge e-government implementation. This is analysed further in the next section.

Almost all the participants emphasised the importance of this category in e-government implementation in Ghana. They were of the view that a digital divide and for that matter lack of access to the Internet is a major challenge and barrier to Ghana's e-government implementation project. This category emerged from answers to questions like ***"what do you think needs to be done for the public to embrace the e-government implementation?"*** This question was asked to explore and identify barriers that might limit the full potential usage of e-government services.

Participant P28, an NGO Project Manager, had this to say:

> *"It [Internet] is the technology that drives the e-government services and should therefore be readily accessible; it should be available 24/7"* Participant P28.

Participant FG17 suggested:

> *"Make computer and Internet access available to the people to motivate them and they will use it [e-government services]"* Participant FG17.

Participant FG13, an unemployed secondary school dropout emphasised the difficulty in accessing the Internet:

> *"I would like to use the e-government service but it is difficult and expensive to have access to the Internet. When you go to the Internet Café, they charge you so much per hour and even that it is so slow that it takes a long time for you to browse"* Participant FG13.

Almost all the participants' responses suggest that that they are more willing to use e-government services if they have access to the Internet. Currently there is low patronage of the government portal as found out in section 8.1.2. The reason for this was attributed to the current state of the website, that is, its lack of functionality and just the fact that it is only displaying information.

However, the low patronage could also be attributed to low Internet penetration, low rate of adult literacy and no effort on the part of the government to create awareness of the presence of the portal to the citizens. As Participant P5 pointed out:

> *"Many Ghanaians do not even know there is a presence of government website"* Participant P5.

It may be that the policy makers do not realise that if a service is available online but in practice cannot be found by the citizens, it is rendered useless.

It is evident from the analysis that even for the privileged citizens, who have easy access to the Internet, only a few browse the government portal. This does not contribute to government services improvement that e-government implementation seeks to achieve.

Participant FG24, a retired civil servant, makes interesting responses which are worth being analysed in this section to bring out the connections between *awareness, trust, information and communication technology* and *digital divide* categories (see table 8.1). The mistrust, low Internet penetration and lack of skills issues raised below are views shared by many of the participants as illustrated in this section and sections 8.1, 8.2 and 8.3.

> *"You can't trust something you've not used before, something you don't know much about…and if people are around, you won't even go near it [the Internet] for fear of being laughed at when you mess up."*

The participant talked about his preference for traditional government service and also his experience at Internet café as follows:

> *"…I would prefer going to the ministries where I can always get someone to explain it to me. I only use the Internet to send emails to my son in America. Even with that it's very difficult. I don't know how to use the computer so I always write my message on paper and get someone to type it for me. The last time I tried it myself I spent the whole day at the Internet café and they charged me more"* Participant FG24.

Just like this participant, there are a few more who have some basic computer skills but they still employ the services of people to help them send an email. The participant's negative perception of e-government service and hence his preference to go to the government offices where he *"can always get someone to explain it"* to him was largely influenced by his two experiences of lack of skills to use the computer/Internet and also the high cost accessing the Internet.

Phrase		**Concept/category**
something you've not used before	Indicates	new technology
something you don't know much about	Indicates	lack of awareness and digital divide (lack of skills)

something you don't know much about	influences	Trust
you won't even go near it	Indicates	lack of trust, motivation and confidence to go online
don't know how to use the computer	Indicates	Digital divide
charged me more	Indicates	high cost of Internet access (digital divide)
prefer going to the ministries	Indicates	prefer manual traditional government services to e-government

Table 8.1: Interpretation of participant FG24 responses

These experiences are shared by most of the participants and they capture the relationship between findings of sections 8.1, 8.2, 8.3 and 8.4. That is, *lack of awareness, access and skills* to use the *new technology* results in *digital divide* which directly influences *trust, motivation and confidence* to use the e-government services.

8.4 Privacy and data protection in e-government

Having established above that a digital divide, new technology and trust directly influence the use of e-government, the study now investigates the crucial role of the core category, *privacy and data protection* in e-government implementation.

In section 8.1 it was established that a few of the participants were conversant with *privacy and data protection* and as such most of them show low privacy concern and lack of awareness of privacy and data protection issues.

This section analysis focuses on the role of privacy and data protection in e-government implementation. This was done with the consideration of the research question: ***"To what extent is privacy and data protection crucial to e-government?"***

To answer the research question, participants were asked the interview question *"To what extent are you willing to lose your privacy in order to get e-government services?"*

Participant FG5 made a significant comment:

> *"No, never! That will be a risky thing to do; someone can easily steal your identity"* Participant FG5.

This view does not necessarily mean the Ghana Government would steal citizens' data when they submit it in exchange for electronic services. However, as literature search revealed in Chapter 2, instances of cyber fraud cases (Ghana News Agency, 2011b; Guermazi and Satola, 2005, p.42) including reported cases of identity theft among Ghanaians (MailOnline, 2013) and corruption among Government officials (Transparency International, 2012) may make e-government users lose trust in the electronic service and hence be less willing to submit their personal data online.

To increase trust in the e-government implementation to enable users adopt the electronic service, Participant P22, a network engineer, who works for a private Internet Service Provider, suggests Government must ensure protection and security of citizens' personal information:

> *"If the government really wants the e-government project to be successful then there should be measures in place to secure and protect citizens personal details collected when they are online"* Participant 22.

Participant P26, a personal assistant in a private, financial organisation, says that:

> *"I won't be afraid to use the e-government once I know there is a law to protect my personal information"* Participant P26.

Participant P26 seems to suggest privacy legislation as of one the measures that can be taken to address users privacy concerns and thereby increase trust in the e-government implementation.

It is evident from the participants' responses that privacy and data protection must not be sacrificed in order to achieve the benefits of e-government. They tried to justify why privacy and data protection is significant in e-government implementation; and this was evident in participant P28 statement:

> *"I will lie about the personal information I put online if there is no law to protect it"* Participant P28.

Apart from the question of privacy legislation, the only other probable reason why Participant P28 may want to falsify his online personal information is he does not seem to trust either the government or the e-government. His response does not indicate any reason for his mistrust; but as found in section 8.2, Participants P8 and P17 mistrust in government or e-government can be attributed to evident widespread corruption among government officials. This may also be the reason why P28 may want to falsify his online personal information while accessing e-government services.

These few participants are aware of the potential benefits of e-government however they are more likely to continue using the traditional face-to-face services due to privacy concerns. To these participants, privacy and data protection is a possible influential factor to their accessing government online services. This makes privacy and data protection appear quite influential to these citizens' decision to access e-government services. This shows that in spite of the collectivist cultural characteristic of the society, there are a few who care about their privacy and would want to protect it.

As mentioned in Chapter 6, the fieldwork was undertaken before the Ghana Privacy and Data Protection Act 2012 was enacted, it seems from the interviewees' (P22, P26 and P28) responses that if the Act is not enforced it might negatively affect the adoption of the e-government services by a few individuals.

These few individuals' views on privacy and data protection regulation were supported by no less a person than, Participant P14, a Member of Parliament, who stated emphatically that:

> *"Privacy and data protection legislation is very important that is why government is doing everything possible to pass the Data Protection Bill"* Participant P14.

The need for privacy and data protection legislation to address privacy concerns were expressed by other participants.

The enactment of the Ghana Data Protection Act 2012 vindicated these participants. However, as pointed out by Anderson (2003) privacy law may not entirely eliminate privacy violations, It may though at least allay individuals' fears and concerns over their personal data which will in turn develop trust in the government (the service provider).

As mentioned in Chapter 2, before the Data Protection Act was enacted there have been existing cyber laws but none of them deals with privacy and data protection issues. This means that before the passing of the law there were no privacy regulations to deal with any privacy violations.

Interestingly, in such an environment many participants were not bothered by any possible privacy risks. They were willing to access e-government services even in the absence of privacy and data protection legislation. This is evident in Participant FG17's response:

> *"I wouldn't mind giving out my personal details if it means not going to the ministries [government offices] to join a long queue"* Participant FG17.

Here, the assumption deduced from the participants' responses is that many individuals tend to be more willing to sacrifice their personal privacy for needed public services. These responses suggest that accessing the e-government services and appreciating its potential benefits of convenience and time saving supersede any privacy concerns. Accessing e-government service (due to its potential benefits) seems a better option to Ghanaians than rejecting it and having one's privacy.

Participants who gave similar responses do not seem to have any privacy concerns over their personal information. They do not realise the risk implications of having low privacy concern over their personal information. This could be explained in the light of the data analysis findings in section 8.1. It was found out in that section that there is lack of awareness of privacy issues and low privacy concern among Ghanaians.

Further investigation was carried using Hofstede's cultural dimension model (see section 8.8 below). It was found out that Ghana as a collectivist society could be a factor to the public having low privacy concern.

In conclusion to this section, it must be stated that the use of e-government in Ghana is not influenced by privacy and data protection. The potential benefits of e-government motivate people to use the service and except in a few cases not privacy and data protection legislation. There are a few individuals though who may not want to use the e-government services due to absence of privacy and data protection legislation. Fortunately for these individuals, their privacy concerns have been addressed with the enactment of Data Protection Act in February 2012. It is yet to be seen how the Act will be enforced to protect users' online personal information.

8.5 Findings and discussions

This section discusses the research findings. This is done in relation to the research questions (see section 1.6) and the existing knowledge found in literature search (Chapter 2).

Based on the data analysis of the fieldwork interviews and the review of documents collected this study findings are as highlighted below:

- Finding 1: Privacy and data protection does not affect individuals' use of e-government, except in a few cases (see section 8.5.1).
- Finding 2: There is a low privacy concern and a lack of awareness of e-government and privacy and data protection issues (see section 8.5.2).
- Finding 3: New technology is positively associated with digital divide which directly influences e-government use (see section 8.5.3).
- Finding 4: Citizens have low trust in the government however it does not influence their willingness to access e-government services (see section 8.5.4).

8.5.1 Finding 1: Privacy and data protection does not affect individuals' use of e-government services, except in few cases

Privacy concerns over personal information have been identified as one of the challenges in the e-government implementation in previous studies (Carter and McBride, 2010; Belanger and Hiller, 2006). However, this research shows that, in Ghana, individuals have low privacy concern and as such *privacy and data protection does not affect individuals' use of e-government services except in few cases.*

A few of the participants are of the view that privacy legislation would ensure the protection of their personal data and minimise identity theft or fraud. However many shared an opinion that the potential benefits, for instance, the convenience and the desire to save time are reasons and motivations for them to access the e-government services irrespective of presence or absence of privacy and data protection legislation.

This suggests that Ghanaians are prone to be less concerned about their online personal privacy in exchange for e-government services (that is, if the services rendered are beneficial to them)[39]. Similarly, Ghanaians are more likely to give up privacy in exchange for government services if they have no option. This was evident from the SIM card registration directive by the Ghana Government in 2010 (Malakata, 2010), where subscribers had no option other than to register their personal details with network providers. Failure of individuals to comply with the directive resulted in the disconnection of their mobile phone lines.

Also civil servants have been directed to register their biometric personal details for the payroll database. Even though it raises privacy concern, that is, a possible misuse of their personal information, the benefit of civil servants receiving their salaries promptly and regularly, through this system, has overshadowed any privacy concern any individual may have.

Even though a few of the participants were of the view that they would not use e-government services in the absence of privacy and data protection legislation it could still be concluded from this section that many Ghanaians are prepared to lose their privacy to benefit from e-government services.

---

[39] However, considering the collectivist nature of the Ghanaian society where, as mentioned in section 3.8.1, individuals are more likely to safeguard personal private matters, for example, adultery, robbery, corruption and despicable ailments like HIV. These are things that the society disapprove of and are likely to bring shame to the family if an individual is afflicted with any of them. Further research is recommended to find out if an individual would sacrifice any of these private matters in exchange for e-government services and hence warrant worry about PDP.

The data analysis shows that passing privacy and data protection law in Ghana does not have much impact on the citizens' usage of e-government services. As Participant FG6 stated:

> *"I think the public is more likely to use the e-government services if they have access to the internet and they know how to use it. While privacy legislation is necessary, I'm not sure whether for now it [the legislation] would make any difference to the citizens"* Participant FG6.

The phrase *"not sure whether for now it [the legislation] would make any difference to the citizens"* seems to downplay the significance of privacy and data protection legislation in e-government. It seems to suggest that citizens are more likely to use e-government services even in the absence of any legislation. To Ghanaian citizens, Internet access is more important to their using the e-government services than privacy and data protection legislation.

There are a few others though who due to concerns over personal information misuse may lose the confidence and motivation to go online in the absence of privacy regulation. Their concerns may be justified due to reported instances of cyber fraud cases in the country, even though the victims were mainly foreigners, (see Chapter 2).

The reported cases of bribery and corruption among government officials (section 8.2) can also be a contributing factor to their concerns while at the same time being a reason to nonetheless use e-government rather than face-to-face transactions.

8.5.2 Finding 2: There is low privacy concern and lack of awareness of e-government; and privacy and data protection issues

The analysis shows that when it comes to violation of personal privacy in Ghana, individuals' main concern is not about identity theft or an organisation's misuse of their personal data, but rather the damage to their reputation (see section 8.1).

As shown in section 8.1.2, many participants doubt the value of their personal information and question its significance to any interested individual or organisation. They have a perception that they have nothing to lose if their personal identities are stolen. In other words they are assuming because of their low income there is no financial gain for any third party who might be interested in stealing their personal details. They are ignorant of the fact that someone can assume their identity and use it to commit fraud as was recently reported by MailOnline (2013) and mentioned in Chapter 2. This suggests low privacy concern as well as lack of awareness of privacy and data protection issues. It also suggests that people of low income have low privacy concern for their personal information.

The suggestion of low value of privacy concern for personal information is supported by Participant FG19, a university administrative staff, example of how people's personal records are managed in some public institutions:

> *"In Ghana it is of no news to find patients and bank customers' personal details printed on papers in public bins. If you like go to Korle Bu [Teaching Hospital], you will see what I'm talking about"* Participant FG19.

One of the possible consequences of such blatant privacy violations is identity theft. It can "have several negative consequences for individuals, including financial, social, and emotional impacts" (Belanger and Van Slyke, 2011) however these seem not to be concerns of the participants and for that matter the Ghanaian populace.

Apart from lack of awareness of privacy issues as identified from the participants' responses, there could be other reasons for the public apathetic attitude towards privacy and data protection. Individuals may not have experienced any privacy violations and there has not been any reported case of misuse of any individual's personal information, therefore people take their right to privacy for granted. Likewise, limited usage of debit and credit cards among the Ghanaian populace could also be a likely factor. Many individuals do not have access to credit cards, thus online payment for goods and services is not widespread at the moment. If they hardly use online services, they are hardly going to worry about identity theft. The public is therefore tempted to have a perception that there is no privacy risk. There have been reported cases of cyber fraud (Internet Crime Complaint Center, 2010), however, the victims have mostly been foreigners (Warner, 2011). It is possible these reported cases could have influenced them into having a perception that cyber fraud and identity theft are targeted only at foreigners and the rich in the society (the affluent).

It could be that e-government implementation is in its initial (non-transactional) stage and the potential privacy risks for using the service, for instance identity theft and fraud, have not manifested yet. There is no empirical evidence to show that there has been any threat to individuals' personal privacy information in the country. Likewise, non-usage of credit cards among the Ghanaian populace could also be another reason. Individuals do not have access to credit cards, thus online payment for goods and services is non-existent at the moment for the general public. For these reasons there is the tendency for the public to have a perception that there is no risk of identity theft or cyber fraud to them personally; and even government surveillance targets only political opponents.

This research suggests that the aforementioned reasons might have contributed to the unconcerned attitude towards privacy and data protection. As mentioned in section 8.1 there may also be a cultural factor which is discussed in detail in section 8.8 below.

According to the UN (2012) e-government survey report, Ghana e-government readiness is at an early stage with 30% development. Privacy may not be a problem at this stage due to its non-transactional functionality, however, if Snowden's revelations, as mentioned in section 2.4.1, are anything to go by then the privacy concerns of the few individuals who use the government website cannot be ignored at this stage. As seen in sections 8.1 and 8.2, participants P12 and FG6 articulated their concerns of possible tracking of citizens by Ghana government.

In spite of possible tracking of individuals by government, it is worth noting that respondents are more willing to use the e-government services due to its potential benefits, however, the current patronage of the government portal is very low (see figure 1.2). As indicated on the figure, only 6% of the Internet users access information from the government portal. The low patronage may not necessarily mean users do not want to access the portal. The reason may be due to the low Internet penetration and high cost of its usage. As already mentioned in Chapter 2, the cost of Internet access is beyond the reach of many Ghanaians.

Analysis of the interviewees' responses in section 8.1.2 suggest that, apart from high cost of Internet access, the low patronage of Government website could be attributed to its current state of limited functionality and non-transactional. The website only displays government news, policies and information for businesses and investors, and contact details of ministries, departments and agencies.

Studies have shown that "high quality e-government websites do matter in building citizen trust towards public e-services" (Tan et al. 2008); likewise, ''the use of government Web sites may lead to positive attitudes toward e-government, which, in turn, may encourage improved trust or confidence in government generally'' (Tolbert and Mossberger, 2006, p.358). It is therefore necessary for government to develop its portal to the required standard that would attract more people to use it.

The results of the analysis in section 8.1.2 show that if government portal provides the needed online services, very many people are likely to use the services even in the absence or presence of privacy and data protection legislation. They will access the e-government services for its convenience of time and cost saving. To these individuals, privacy and data protection is not an issue, but rather the potential benefits to be gained from the electronic service as end-users. The convenience of usage of e-government services (for example its availability anytime, 24/7) as compared to the traditional brick and mortar offices, not to mention the elimination of middlemen and corrupt government officials, may have superseded any privacy concerns these individuals may have. An excerpt from Participant FG17 supports this assertion:

> *"I am concerned about my privacy, but I need the e-government services"* Participant G17.

This reflects Hann et al.'s (2007) finding that individuals are willing to disclose personal information for benefits.

This study concluded in section 8.5.2 that the lack of awareness of privacy issues (for instance, the possible misuse and violation of their personal data); non-usage of credit cards among the Ghanaian populace; non-transactional stage of the e-government implementation (where there is no online payment of e-government services); and the Ghanaian collectivist cultural society could be possible reasons for the low concern for privacy and data protection.

Most of the participants were of the view that privacy and data protection legislation does not affect their personal privacy in any way. This assertion can be attributed to the fact that some government projects, notably biometric voters register, biometric passport application and the SIM card registration were implemented, even though they raised privacy concerns. They have been implemented in the absence of privacy and data protection legislation thus these participants could not envisage any significant effect whether positive or negative that the enactment of privacy and data protection legislation could have on their personal privacy.

Participant FG8 revealed that:

> *"When the government directed that all mobile phones' SIM cards in circulation should be registered, otherwise they would be deactivated, I guess I was one of the first people to do it…I wasn't even thinking about what they were going to do to my personal information"* Participant FG8.

When asked to explain further he stated:

> *"I needed the service and I didn't want to be disconnected...I didn't want to lose contacts with my business partners, family and friends" Participant* FG8.

This suggests that when citizens do not have a choice or any options to a particular service they are more likely to compromise their personal privacy in order to use or benefit from the service. This has positive implications for e-government implementation. The public may be more likely to use e-government services when it is implemented. Privacy concerns of users over their personal information may not be a barrier or a challenge to the implementation. This was evident in the successful registration of SIM cards of mobile phone subscribers.

Additionally, the participant complied with the SIM card registration directive mainly because he *"didn't want to be disconnected...didn't want to lose contacts with my business partners, family and friends"*. For this reason he relegated whatever concern he may have over the registration of his personal details to the background. This supports the earlier suggestion in this section that, the convenience (potential benefit) of usage of a service supersedes any privacy concerns individuals may have. It supports Hann et al.'s (2007) finding that individuals are willing to disclose personal information for benefits as well.

8.5.3 Finding 3: New technology is associated with digital divide which directly influences e-government use

The results of the analysis show that the newness of technology and individuals' inability to use it are potential challenges that could hamper successful implementation of e-government. As can be seen from table 1.4, low level of Internet penetration (14.1%) as well as less than 1% broadband subscription definitely limits the use of e-government services. Low literacy rate is also a limitation, in the sense that the citizens' inability to read and understand will make the usage of e-government a difficult task.

Moon (2003) points out that information and communication technology (which is the main enabler of e-government) can offer potentially useful tools to governments and help them to restore public trust by enhancing transparency, cost efficiency, effectiveness, and policy participation. However it must be pointed out if the technology is not well executed it ends up undermining the very purpose for which it was implemented.

This was evident in the Ghana 2012 presidential and parliamentary elections. In this instance, biometric technology was employed to ensure the detection and removal of multiple registrations of voters and hence produce a more accurate and reliable register for the December 2012 elections. However, on the election day, malfunction and lack of knowledge about the usage of the technology by the polling officials disenfranchised some voters. The outcome of these glitches is, a supposedly one-day election was extended to another day, and the election results were challenged in the Supreme Court by the losing political party.

The glitches with the new biometric identification technology in the 2012 elections raise concerns about the use of new technology in Government's e-projects. For instance, the aftermath of the elections, in terms of the new technology glitches, can possibly result in Ghanaians losing trust in any new technology (e-government inclusive) to be implemented by government. When that happens the citizens would like to go back to the traditional services that they are familiar with, and which seem to yield better results than the new technology.

Participants' responses brought to the fore the limited, and high cost of, access to the Internet and computers hence creating digital divide among citizens in the country. This is evident in the literature which shows that Ghana has low penetration of Internet access.

According to a survey report by Bowen (2010), a third of Ghanaians do not know what the internet is; half say they do not know how to use it. The low Internet penetration suggests only a few privileged people would have access to e-government services, thus the potential benefits as highlighted by participants in section 8.1 will be accessible to a privileged few if the digital divide is not bridged.

Participant FG17's response (see section 8.1.2), emphasizes the fact that making Internet access available to the citizens can heighten their motivation to access e-government services. Participant P25, a top civil servant pointed out that, *"Government is aware of the digital divide and it is working towards solving that problem by building CIC [Community Information Centres] in every district"*. The construction of the Community Information Centres (CIC) is a major policy initiative of the Ghana Government to provide information and communication technology infrastructure and services to under-served and un-served communities (Awotwi, 2011; Awotwi and Owusu, 2009),. The idea is to increase the low Internet/computer penetration of citizens, especially in the rural areas. This is a worthy cause which will lower the high computer illiteracy rate and improve the well-being of citizens.

Some participants suggested the use of the media (especially the FM stations) and the mobile phones as an alternative means to access government information and the e-government services. Participant FG2, an IT undergraduate student, has this to say:

> *"Although we might make a case for infrastructure being an obstacle, I think we don't have to wait to get everything before we start the [e-government] project. We have to start from somewhere, then move on and gradually add on things that will facilitate the project. For instance, we can make up for the low Internet penetration with using mobile phones,*

text messages FM radio stations and so on to disseminate government information to the people."

As stated in Chapter 1 while internet accessibility is low mobile phone subscriptions have gone up significantly. According to Bowen (2010) survey report, mobile phone use among Ghanaian people is widespread and even use rate (about 70%) is high in rural areas. Mobile phone technology is seen as an enabling and general purpose technology, with a "potential for pervasive use in a wide range of sectors in ways that drastically change their modes of operation" (Helpman, 1998, p.3). Therefore mobile phones with their ease of use and widespread subscription could be used as a familiar technology and as an alternative medium to access the e-government services.

An increase in Internet access would not be enough incentive or motivation to use the online services if other factors like the citizens' digital skills, their awareness and trust of the e-government service and its inherent privacy issues are not considered, as explained in the next sub-section.

8.5.4 Finding 4: Citizens have low trust in the government however it does not influence their willingness to access e-government services

Trust plays a crucial role in citizens' confidence and motivation to access e-government services. According to Germanakos et al. (2007) lack of trust both in government organisations and in the Internet has been cited as one of the critical impediments to the widespread acceptance and adoption of e-government. The data analysis revealed that some participants were concerned about the possibility of government and its agencies putting cookies on their websites which can track their "movement over the internet". They are justified in their concern since by this means it is possible to monitor behaviours and preferences without their consent or knowledge (Olivero and Lunt, 2002). This of course raises privacy concern. There are reported cases which justify the participants' lack of trust in the government, for example the Snowden revelation about how American government has been tracking people on the Internet, reading their emails and keeping tags of their Internet browsing (The Guardian, 2013).

In Ghana, the recent SIM card registration and voters' biometric data registration have heightened the mistrust citizens have in the government. The reason for the SIM registration was to address criminal activities being aided with the use of mobile telephones. Kidnapping for ransom, mobile theft, SMS scam and illegal threatening phone calls were among some of the criminal activities cited as reason for the registration. This clearly shows the government placing national security above privacy and personal data protection of the Ghanaian people.

IMANI Ghana, a pressure group, was at the forefront raising awareness about the downside of the SIM card registration. It also led to protests from a few political activists who questioned the "ethics and motivations" of the registration. This did not deter the government and it went ahead with the registration. A top National Communication Authority (NCA) official is reported to have said that despite the privacy concerns a few people expressed about the SIM card registration exercise, the fact that 85 percent of mobile phone subscribers had registered in the first few days of the exercise showed that they had accepted the new order and that this was encouraging (Cellular News, 2011). On the contrarily, it could be said that subscribers were more inclined to register because they did not want their mobile phones to be disconnected. This is evident in Participant FG8 response as quoted in section 8.6.2.

For government to have gone ahead and enforced the SIM card registration without due regard to privacy concerns raised by a few individuals, and the involvement of Bureau of National Investigations (BNI) could have been a possible cause of mistrust in government.

Corruption was also cited as one of the causes of people's mistrust in government. It "severely affects a country's development because it takes resources away from the economy" (Garcia-Murillo, 2013) and influences citizens' trust in government. As discussed in 2.7.1, "stories of political corruption are constantly in the media" (Richey, 2010) and citizens tend to trust less when they perceive that corruption in the country is high (Uslaner, 2004). This leads to ineffective government (Mauro, 1997, p.5) which consequently affect e-government implementation.

The aforementioned suggest that Ghanaians have low trust in government. Instances have been cited as evidence to support this. However, on the whole there seems to be some trust in institutions in the country as has been shown in the Bowen's (2010) national survey of Ghana report (see figure 8.1 below).

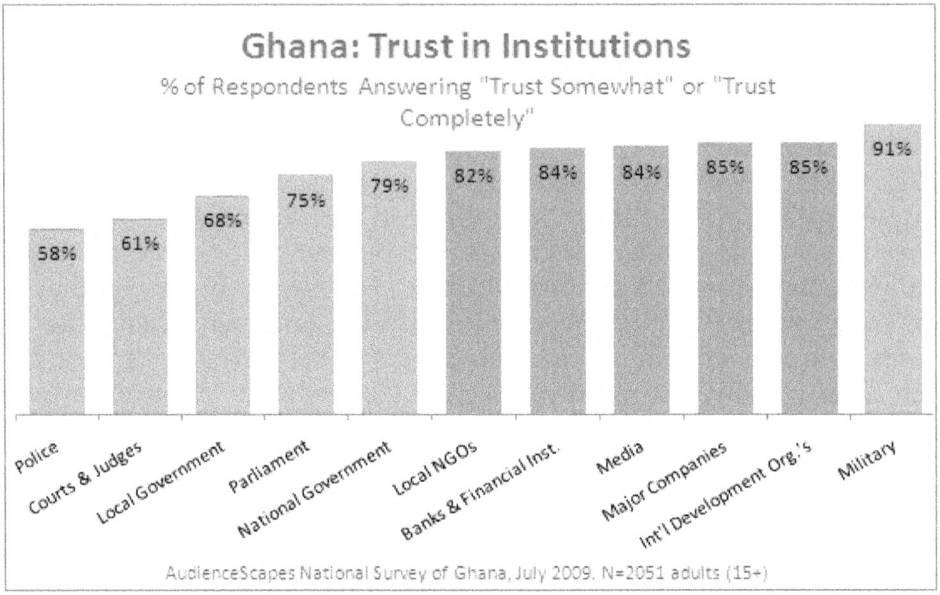

Figure 8.1: Trust in institutions in Ghana

Bowen (2010)

The contrast with this study finding could be due to the sampling population. While this study employed purposive sampling to select participants from only urban dwellers by using a criteria that also limited the inclusion of certain urban people, especially, non-Internet users, the InterMedia survey, using random sampling, selected respondents from all over the country, rural dwellers inclusive (see figure 8.2 below).

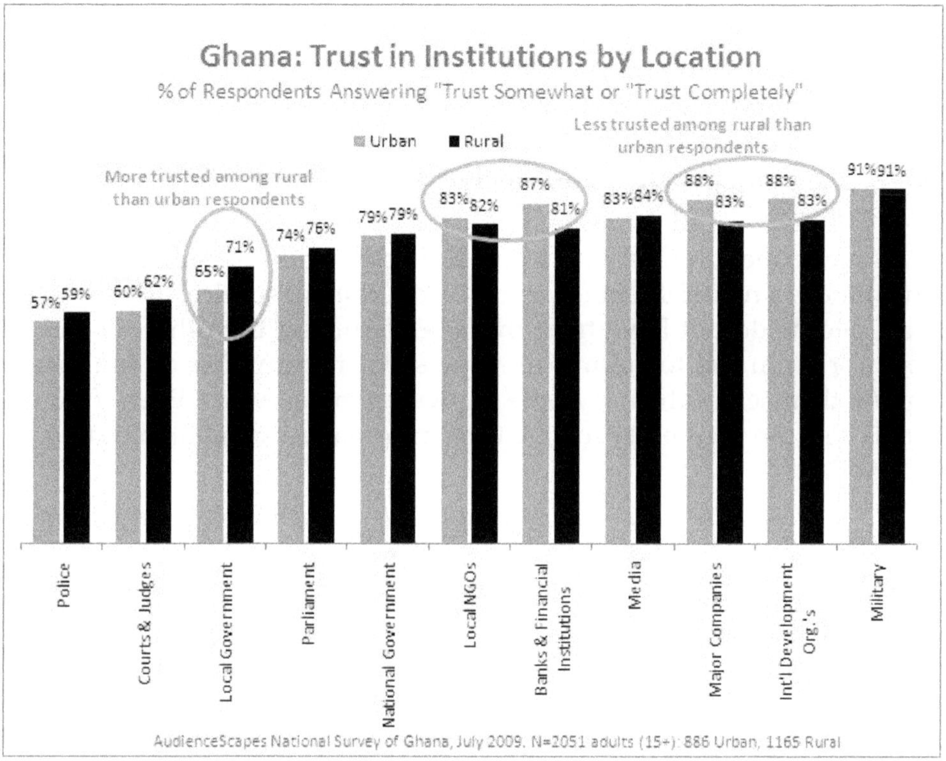

Figure 8.2: Trust in institutions in Ghana - by location

Source - Bowen (2010)

The differences in trust levels between urban and rural respondents, as shown in figure 8.2, could be attributed to people trusting, believing and having faith in things that they see, experience and have physical contact with. For example, as can be seen from the figure 8.2, the rural respondents have more trust in Local Government, because of its activities in the rural community than the urban. Similarly, the urban dwellers have higher trust in major companies, banks and International development organisations due to their predominantly presence in urban areas. This implies that e-government services are more likely to be used by the urban dwellers who have more access to the ICT infrastructure and hence trust it.

Ghana's score of 15 in the Hofstede's cultural dimensions (section 3.5) which makes it a collectivist society confirms the Bowen's (2010) report that the people of Ghana have trust in government and its institutions.

Mistrust in government can possibly make individuals "more concerned about personal privacy and to react by being unwilling to disclose personal information" (Olivero and Lunt, 2004) when using e-services. Ghanaians may have low trust in government yet the data analysis findings show they would still disclose their personal details in order to use e-government services. There are reasons for this: this study has found out in section 8.5.1 that Ghanaians have low privacy concern and thus are more willing to submit personal information in order to benefit from e-government services.

As mentioned in Chapters 1 and 2, disclosing one's personal information online is a requirement for using e-government services. This suggests that if people do not have trust in the government then there is the tendency for them not to submit their personal information online thereby denying themselves the use of the e-government services. Even if they do there is also the possibility to give false information as pointed out by participant P28:

> *"I will lie about my personal details if I don't trust the government [the service provider]"* Participant P28.

One other issue that also came out of the data analysis (and which will be discussed in much detail in the next section) was lack of privacy and data protection legislation to safeguard the citizens' personal information. If citizens are of the opinion that the government is not protecting the privacy of their individual personal information, it may cause mistrust for government. The outcome of this situation is citizens may be either less willing to provide this information or alternatively will provide false information. This suggests that while there is not much concern about PDP directly, there may be a link between trust and privacy and data protection legislation.

It can be concluded here that since the government is the service provider, trust in it encompassed trust in the e-government project as well as trust in the reliability and ease of use of the enabling technology (the Internet).

In conclusion to the discussions of the study findings, Hofstede culture dimension model (Hofstede et al. 2010) will further be used to explain in section 8.8 why Ghanaians comply with Government directives and easily adopt government's implementation projects, even though such projects raise privacy concerns.

As mentioned in section 8.6.2, when the Ghana government directed mobile network operators in the country to register all SIM card subscribers, the people complied, even though their personal information privacy was at risk. Radwanski, a former privacy commissioner of Canada warns against such situations and states that:

> *"we must guard against the tendency of governments to create new databases of privacy-invasive information on justified, exceptional grounds of enhancing security, and then seek to use that information for a whole range of other law enforcement or governmental purposes, simply because it's there and available." (The New York Times, 2003)*

Concerns about privacy and data protection are often cited as an important factor that may influence use of e-Government, however this study suggests otherwise. While privacy and data protection maybe necessary in the implementation of e-government, it is not a condition for some individuals to access e-government services in Ghana. To the Ghanaian populace there are more crucial factors than privacy and data protection which play significant role in the implementation and use of e-government. The research models in the next section show the relationship between the categories of the findings. As it was found out in the data analysis, if the digital divide among the Ghanaian populace is bridged by providing adequate access and necessary skills to use the new technology then the citizens would adopt the e-government service, irrespective of the mistrust they may have in government.

8.6 Research models discussion

In this section the relationships between the factors that influenced the study findings are discussed using the research models in figures 8.3, 8.6 and 8.7. Using Grounded Theory to analyse qualitative data is "typically about seeking an explanation, and to this end, models can be useful tool" (Braun and Clarke, 2013, p.262). The models, as presented below, are the result of the study which seeks to investigate the role of privacy and data protection in the implementation of e-government in Ghana.

The proposed research models have been influenced by the data analysis findings and literature search as highlighted in Chapter 2. The categories and the concepts that emerged in the analysis, as mentioned in the introduction of this chapter, have been identified as challenges to successful implementation of e-government in other research, notably, Dwivedi et al., (2012), Jaeger and Bertot (2010) and Gil-Garcia and Pardo (2005), and they together form the constructs of the research models.

As found in the literature search in Chapter 2, e-government can be classified as one instance of e-commerce (Schneider, 2008, p.236). It is "the application of e-commerce technologies to government and public services" Cheffey (2009, p.28). Both phenomena primarily involve users (citizens and consumers) submitting their personal details online in exchange of services which raises privacy concerns and data protection issues. Since studies on privacy and data protection in e-government are relatively limited this study employs the findings of prior studies on privacy and data protection in e-commerce as well in the comparative discussion of the research models.

The models show the relationships among privacy and data protection, privacy concerns, corruption, digital divide, trust, technology, potential benefits and culture on the implementation of e-government.

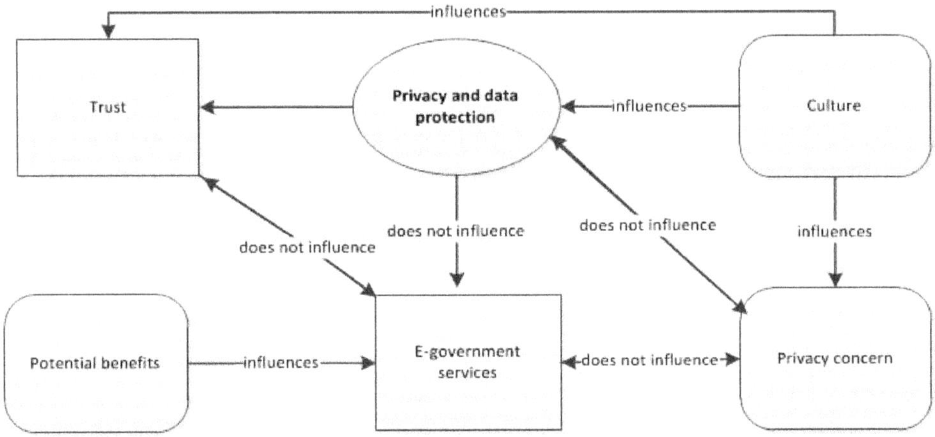

Figure 8.3: PDP does not influence e-government implementation in Ghana

The research model, figure 8.3, suggests that privacy and data protection does not have effect or influence on the use of e-government services by the citizens in the context of this study. The study finding which shows that the people have low privacy concern is an influential factor to this suggestion. It is also a possible reason for the delay in the enactment of Data Protection Act. This suggestion is supported by Milberg et al. (1995, 2000) and Bellman et al. (2004).

Milberg et al. (2004) for instance posit that "as privacy concerns among the populace increase, a natural reaction among legislators is to put in place more restrictive structures". Considering the study finding and also the fact that there is no empirical evidence to the knowledge of this study to show that there have been increased concerns among Ghanaians over their information privacy; this study suggests that the enactment of the Data Protection Act 2012 is not as a result of the people's concerns over their privacy.

While privacy concerns may not become much of an issue in the e-government implementation in Ghana, there is a still a possibility of government tracking online activities of people as was empirically evident in the fieldwork data. This has the potential to lead to mistrust in government.

However as show in figure 8.3, many of the participants would use the e-government services regardless of level trust of they have for the government.

The lack of privacy awareness as empirically shown in the data analysis is a possible reason why the people do not see privacy and data protection as crucial or influential to their adoption of e-government services. This is evident in the comments posted by Ghanaians to media websites when the DPA was reported as passed. For example, on Ghanaweb (2012), a commentator writes:

> *"We are wasting time and precious resources passing laws when we don't enforce them. That is our greatest problem: our laws are never enforced."*

Another commentator adds:

> *"I think there are other more pressing/important things the parliament could work on"* Ghanaweb (2012).

While the former suggest lack of trust in the government and also lack of commitment on the part of the supervisory body, such as the Data Protection Commission, to enforce the DPA 2012, the latter devalues the role of privacy and data protection legislation. The comments portray how both the government and the citizens attach little importance to privacy and data protection issues and for that matter a privacy law. The second commentator comments are similar to Participant FG21's (and many others) captured in section 8.1 and may be attributed to lack of privacy awareness. It is possible that the lack of privacy awareness is an influential factor to the citizens' willingness to adopt e-government services without any concerns for privacy risks and data protection of personal information.

Literature revealed in Chapter 2 that "as government agencies move through the stages of e-government, the level of data collection and constituent privacy concerns increase" (Hiller and Belanger 2001). As the study already suggests, privacy and data protection does not play crucial role in e-government implementation in Ghana. This suggestion is in contrast with previous studies (Carter and McBride, 2010; Belanger and Hiller, 2006; Ebrahim and Irani, 2005). For instance, Ebrahim and Irani (2005) in a study identify security and privacy as significant barrier to the adoption of e-government in the UK.

Similarly, whereas, Carter and McBride (2010) found privacy and data protection to be a critical factor that influences the adoption of e-government in the developed countries such as the US, this study finds the opposite for Ghana in ways that are likely to apply to other developing countries, especially Sub-Saharan African countries. The distinct privacy concerns among various nationals may the reason for the contrast. The privacy concerns among the people are known to be influenced by the national cultural dimensions of the society (Hofstede et al., 2010).

Using Hofstede's dimensions of national culture to compare Ghana with developed countries, for example, UK and US, show distinct privacy concerns for online personal information. For instance, as can be seen from figure 8.4, a score of 89 for UK in the individualism score makes the country a very highly individualistic society and for that matter a very highly privacy risks conscious people. Ghana on the other hand with a score of 15 is considered a collectivistic society. As explained in Chapter 2, this depicts Ghana as a country or society with a low value of concern for privacy.

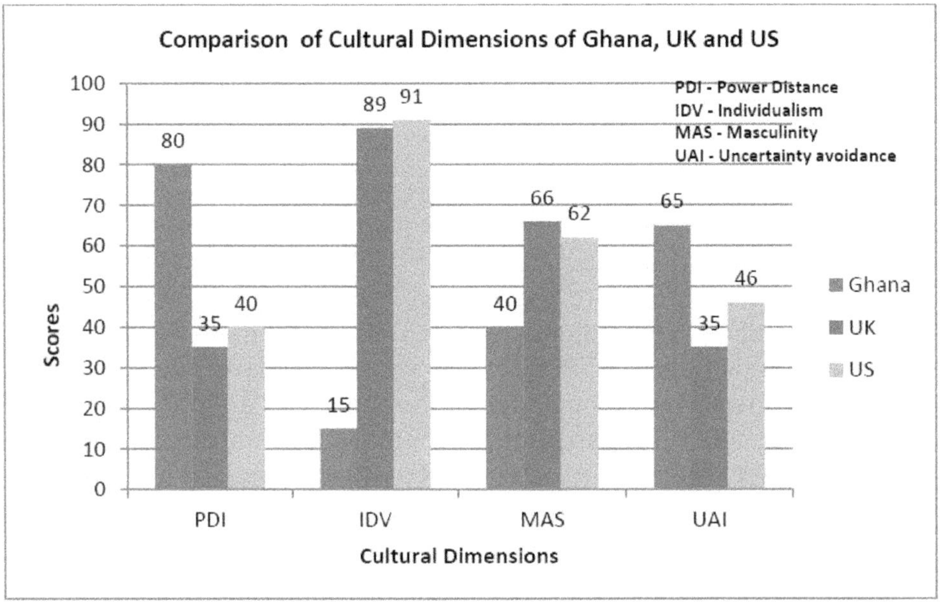

Figure 8.4: Comparison of national cultural dimensions of Ghana, UK and US

Adapted from Hofstede (2014)

A further examination of figure 8.4 shows that UK and US have almost near scores and therefore depict both countries as highly privacy concern society.

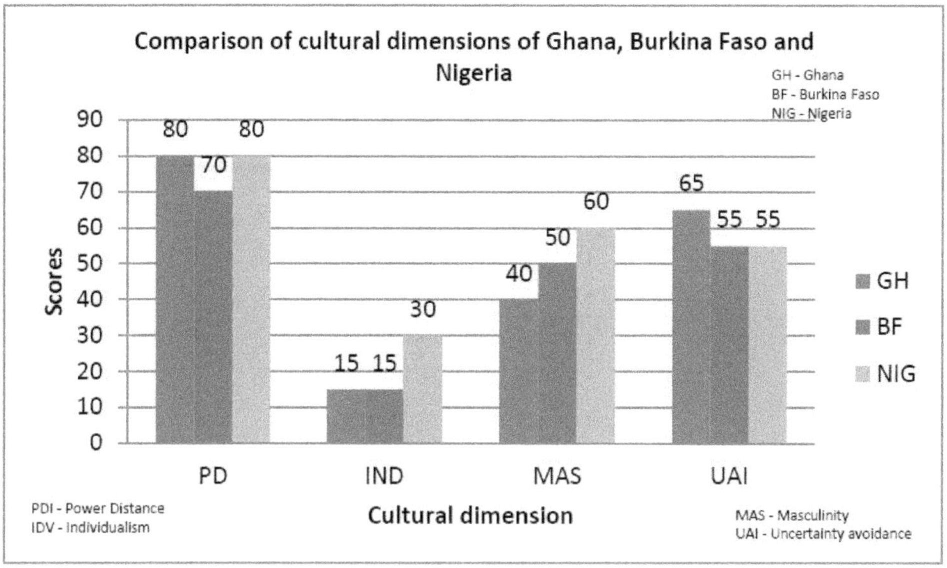

Figure 8.5: Comparisons of cultural dimensions of Ghana, Nigeria and Burkina Faso

Adapted from Hofstede (2014)

Likewise, examining Ghana, using figure 8.5, shows a profile similar to other sub-Saharan African countries, for example, Burkina Faso and Nigeria, two of its West African neighbours. It therefore suggests that the research model might be applied to these countries.

It is interesting to note how Ghana, with a distinct conception of privacy, passes a DPA along the line of the EU's Data Protection Directive – a directive whose principles are based on western conception of privacy.

The research model, figure 8.6, shows that the use of e-government services is influenced significantly by the potential benefits. It suggests that if the citizens are of the conviction that e-government services are beneficial to them they are more likely to use them irrespective of the potential privacy risks concerns.

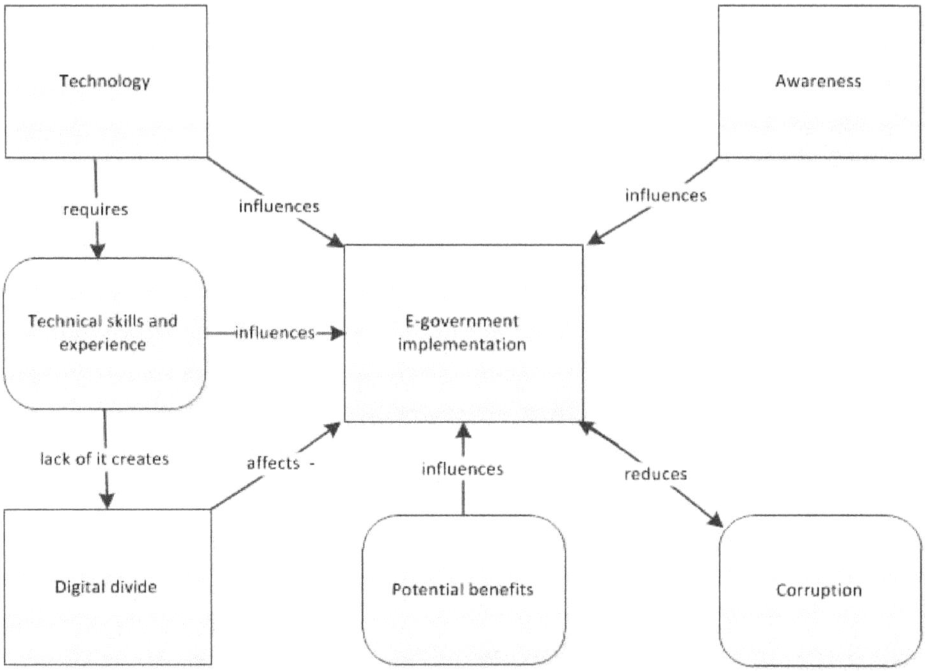

Figure 8.6: Factors that affect or influence e-government implementation

It was also shown that e-government use is associated with the new technology (ICT). Inadequate provision and accessibility of the technology couple with lack of technical skilled staff to handle and maintain it creates digital divide.

As shown in the research model digital divide is related to the use of e-government services. The study finding that digital divide influences citizens' motivation and confidence to use e-government supports the finding of Jaeger and Thompson (2004) which maintained that the gap in "Internet usage, naturally, have a significant impact on e-government usage".

Figure 8.6 shows a link between e-government and technology (ICT/Internet). "An effective e-government program requires successful and seamless integration of appropriate ICT" (Lee et al, 2005), which can be used by the citizens with ease and also be maintained by the technical staff without a problem.

As shown in figure 8.7, lack of e-skills and knowledge creates digital divide which in itself negatively influences individuals' intention to use the e-government services. This is evident in many participants' responses with examples captured in section 8.4.

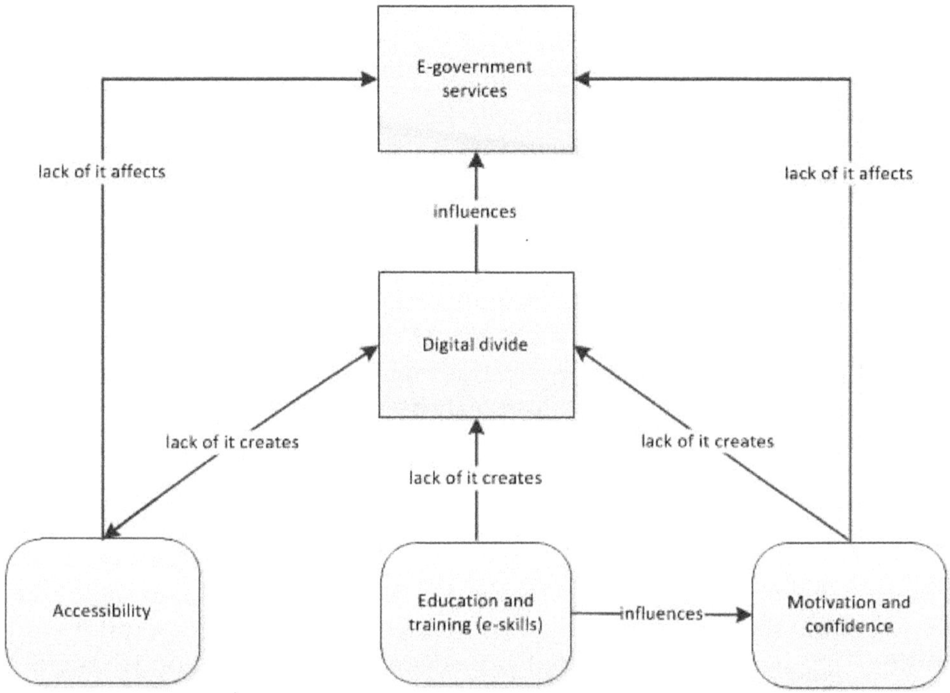

Figure 8.7: Digital divide influences e-government implementation

The construction of Community Information Centres (CICs) by the Ministry of Communications across the country, to bridge the digital divide between urban and rural dwellers in the country (Awotwi and Owusu, 2009), have generally improved information access and the wellbeing of citizens, though in small way. Despite the progress being made, the CIC project is hampered with inadequate computers, a very slow Internet connectivity and lack of trained staff (IICD, 2012).

As already shown Internet (technology) has a strong link to e-government implementation. It is an enabling tool in the e-government implementation to facilitate citizens' access to information and service delivery. However, if it is used by government to surveil citizens it may create mistrust. For example, the study participants are aware of how governments use cookies and advanced technology to collect personal data of their citizens; and this is a privacy concern that "reduces the level of trust" (Olivero and Lunt, 2004). However the low trust in government does not affect Ghanaians motivation to use e-government services.

It was revealed in the analysis that low trust in e-government was possible to discourage a few individuals from using the service altogether or influence potential users to submit false personal information online.

'When conducting transactions over the internet it is necessary for [government departments and] agencies to collect data from citizens, therefore collection is integral to the success of e-services' (Carter and McBride, 2010). This personal data must be accurate to help government offer effective and efficient service. Therefore, measures must be taken to avoid situations where citizens will provide false information when using the service.

Low trust in government is not limited to only corrupt practices of government officials, but also governments using cookies and high-technology to collect online personal information of citizens' which raises privacy concerns. The latter puts in doubt the trustworthiness and reliability of the enabling technology (Internet), the main point (medium) of access to e-government services. Technology can be used efficiently if it is trusted (Gatautis, 2008).

8.6.1 Pilot study finding

As mentioned in section 5.3, only three participants were available to take part in the pilot study. A sample size of 3 is too small and may possibly affect the data quality. However, it is worth discussing the pilot study finding because it suggested that privacy and data protection is crucial to e-government implementation and was found to be consistent with previous studies but contrary to the main study.

The analysis of the fieldwork data revealed that issues relating to corruption in government and e-government came up many times in the participants' responses without the interviewer asking any specific corruption questions during the data collection. It is worth mentioning that all the fieldwork participants who shared views on corruption in government are all non-government officials or workers. It confirms the suggestions made in section 5.7 that government workers/officials were uncomfortable answering corruption related questions.

There is an element of globalisation in the pilot study finding. Globalisation is increasing the rate of cultural change in people as evident among the staff of Ghana High Commission who participated in the pilot study. Their conception of privacy is distinct from that of the fieldwork data. This reveals how western culture and its advanced technology have influenced the cultural values of these Ghanaian professionals. It confirms Allwood (1990) suggestion that, the cultural environment people live in is assumed to have a strong effect on how they conceptualise reality. Likewise the "nationality and national culture significantly influenced internet users' privacy concerns to the extent that...internet users from an individualistic culture were more concerned about online privacy than their counterparts" Cho etc al. (2009).

Globalisation factor is possible to influence the cultural dimensions scores of Ghana. The scores as shown in figure 8.4 might change to be similar to that of the western world. The implication of this is that Ghanaians will have high privacy concern which will in turn influence their adoption of e-government. This is an assumption based on previous studies findings that sought to suggest privacy and data protection is significant in e-government adoption in countries with high perception of privacy concerns.

8.7 The influence of culture on privacy and data protection

As revealed in Chapter 3, culture affects people's attitudes towards privacy (Kumaraguru and Cranor, 2006). This section is therefore a further discussion of the data analysis findings (section 8.6) in relation to the role of privacy and data protection in e-government implementation. It discusses the influence of culture on the findings as highlighted in the next paragraph.

Ghana being a collectivist society suggests the people are likely to have low value of privacy concern (section 3.8.1). This is discussed further in this section in the light of the study finding (see section 8.5.1) that, except in few cases *Ghanaians have low privacy concerns* and do not value their privacy.

There seems to be a link between low privacy concern and absence of privacy and data protection legislation. The absence of privacy and data protection law until recently may be attributed to the low privacy concern of the country. Most probably, due to the low privacy concern of the society privacy and data protection legislation was an issue that did not necessarily need priority attention of the policy makers. Milberg et al. (1995) point out that "regulatory responses usually occur in reaction to a growing level of discontent within the populace, which is transmitted to legislators in some form". This could be a possible explanation why most collectivist societies, such as countries of Sub-Sahara Africa do not have privacy legislation (for example Nigeria) or did not have one until recently (for example Ghana). The aforementioned also suggest that if there was not any level of discontent (in terms of privacy concerns) among the Ghanaian people yet the government passed the 2012 DPA law then it was for economic reasons. The motive could well have been to satisfy the EU Directive that prohibits trans-border flows of personal data without adequate protection. It allows EU companies to setup customer service call centres or to outsource personal data to Ghana for processing. In turn this could help reduce unemployment and increase foreign exchange in the country. This fits with Makulilo's (2013) statement that "those few African jurisdictions which have so far adopted data protection legislation have largely done so for economic motivations".

Also, as suggested in section 3.8.1 Ghanaian people are more inclined to be concerned with their personal life or private matters than their online personal privacy. As was pointed out in sections 2.8 and 3.8.1. Ghanaians by virtue of their collectivist society tend to understand privacy as matters that intimately concern them that they do not want others to have anything to do with to be accorded the needed distance (Dagbanja, 2014).

This was confirmed in the data analysis. For instance, in response to the question *"what is privacy?"* Participant P29, an unemployed graduate said:

> *"What privacy means to me is, my private life is not made public. I consider the things that I do privately as personal matter and so far as those things are not criminal offenses I resent them being made public."* Participant P29

This and many other responses explain why Ghanaians are more concerned with their private life than online privacy. Individuals would strive harder to protect personal, private matters from being published in the media than protecting online personal information. This suggests that people would have low value of their online personal information privacy than their private life.

The above confirm the findings of other empirical studies (Bellman et al., 2004; Milberg et al., 1995, 2000) that the level of individualism-collectivism influences the privacy concerns of personal information submitted online.

Considering the ***power distance*** dimension, Ghana's score of 80 means Ghanaians have lower levels of trust and are expected to have higher levels of privacy concerns (Hofstede et al., 2010) and less willingness to share personal information online. This is inconsistent with this study finding where Ghanaians are more willing to share their personal information online in order to access e-government services. However, Ghana's score of 15 in the masculinity dimension suggests low levels of privacy concern. This is consistent with the study finding that people would have low value of their online personal information privacy than their private life.

It can therefore be concluded that the four dimensions of Hofstede's model that were employed to examine the influence of culture on privacy and data protection in e-government implementation in Ghana, cannot all predict the exact privacy concerns of the Ghanaian society. In view of this, further research is suggested to investigate the inconsistencies.

8.8 The influence of culture on e-government

Considering the discussion in the above section, Ghana as collectivist society has an implication in the context of e-government implementation. It implies that many Ghanaians are more likely to access e-government services without having too much concern about their privacy, as evident in most of the responses of the participants. For example, as Participant FG17 said in section 8.1.2:

> *"I need the e-government services…*[so]*…I wouldn't mind giving out my personal details"* Participant FG17.

Apart from the low privacy concern it was evident that online personal data protection would not significantly influence their willingness to use e-government services. Participant FG6 has this to say about this issue:

> *"I think the public is more likely to use the e-government services if they have access to the internet and they know how to use it. While privacy legislation is necessary, I'm not sure whether for now it [the legislation] would make any difference to the citizens"* Participant FG6.

The phrase *"any difference to the citizens"* can be interpreted as the presence or absence of privacy and data protection legislation would not significantly influence the people use of e-government services. The public's main concern in this field is Internet (ICT) access and the skills to use the service, not privacy and data protection.

One of the findings of this study indicates that some individuals in spite of the potential benefits of e-government would still want to access the traditional, manual government services. This can be attributed to the *high or strong uncertainty avoidance* culture of the Ghanaian society. From figure 3.3, Ghana scored 65 in the uncertainty avoidance dimension, which is relatively high. High uncertainty avoidance cultures have the tendency to view new, unfamiliar things being introduced into their community as threatening and try to avoid them. This was evident from the response of Participant FG22, a self-employed trader, and many others:

> *"I don't know how to use it. I always get the [Internet] café staff to help me send my emails. Honestly, I prefer the old school way of writing letters and posting them. Even though this new email thing is fast, it frustrates me. I feel stupid asking these young boys for help everyday"* Participant 22

This is an indication of individuals' *hesitancy toward new products and technologies* (Hofstede et al., 2010). Even though, the participant is aware of the convenience of using the Internet technology, he lacks the motivation and confidence to use it, and therefore prefers the old traditional service.

The finding of this study, that is, some *individuals would still want to use the traditional government services regardless of the benefits of accessing e-government services*, can also be explained using the *individualism versus collectivism dimension*. Ghana as a collectivist society is characterised by long-lasting, strong relationship between people. "Face-to-face dependence relationship" (Crozier, 1964, p.222) is a significant trait in this society and people look up to others in assisting them to get task done. In a collectivist society, "relationship prevails over task [and]…only natural persons are worthy of trust" (Hofstede et al., 2010) but not computers or the Internet. Also, "consumption patterns show dependence on others", that is, the use of government services is done with face-to-face assistance from public officials. This is evident in the response of Participant FG24:

> *"…I would prefer going to the ministries where I can always get someone to explain it to me. I only use the Internet to send emails to my son in America. Even with that it's very difficult. I don't know how to use the computer so I always write my message on paper and get someone to type it for me. The last time I tried it myself I spent the whole day at the Internet café and they charged me more"* Participant FG24.

These traits are more likely to hamper the successful implementation of e-government, especially where for instance, individuals, fear of getting things wrong (Participant FG24) and/or are comfortable with face-to-face transaction with government workers, would still prefer to go to offices to transact business with government. This was evident in the data analysis findings and consistent with Jaruwachirathanakul and Fink (2005) study, which indicate that face-to-face interaction is a barrier to Internet banking (an electronic service just like e-government) among collectivist and high uncertainty avoidance society.

8.9 Conclusion

This research revealed that, privacy and data protection is not crucial to the implementation of e-government. There are other challenges such as digital divide, the newness of technology and individuals' inability to access it and even lack of technical experts to handle it and also mistrust in government.

The role of privacy and data protection in e-government implementation is not as significant as the pilot study and previous studies findings suggested. While the study finding suggests that privacy and data protection does not play a crucial role in the e-government implementation the pilot study finding suggested otherwise. However the pilot study finding is consistent with previous studies findings. The inconsistency maybe due to the national cultural dimension of the society the participants are from or they live in. In other words, the perceived privacy concerns of the participants in relationship to whether the society that they live in is individualistic or collectivist influenced the outcome of the finding.

To many Ghanaians (who predominantly come from collectivist society), privacy and data protection is not relevant and does not pose any challenge or barrier to their adoption of e-government. However, there is still the need to protect the citizens' online personal information when then they are using the e-government services. This is reinforced by Participant P12, a Member of Parliament:

> *"Whilst we fully recognise the fact that the public needs to adopt the new technology, we do not want to see their personal data misused"* Participant P12.

The need for enforcement of the Data Protection Act is relevant as has been revealed in section 8.6.2. The data analysis shows ignorance of privacy rights, issues and in particular, the privacy risks associated with e-government usage. It suggests there is lack of understanding and awareness of privacy issues among individuals and as a result there is little public concern over privacy and personal data protection.

Even though the government portal is limited in its functionality it has been beneficial in its small way to a few individuals in terms of information search. This study suggests that, Government portals should "be seen not only as channels for providing government information" (Sandoval-Almazan and Gil-Garcia, 2012), but providing functional, transactional online services such as citizens' application for driving licence, passport, jobs and filing of taxes by businesses.

Considering the current Internet penetration rate of 14.1%, it means should the government portal become more functional and operational, more than half of the citizenship will not have access to the e-government services due to digital divide.

The government should redesign its website to make it more appealing and functional. As this study finds out in section 8.1.2, the Ghanaian public hardly visits the Government portal. This is consistent with the results in Bowen's (2010) survey report which indicated only 6% of Internet users actually access information from the Ghana government portal. As already mentioned in Chapter 1, 14.1% of the Ghanaian population has access to Internet.

Considering the study finding that Ghanaians are more willing to adopt the e-government implementation if adequate provision is made for ICT infrastructure, the low rate of the public accessing the government portal is more likely to increase if the e-government implementation should move to a stage where people can downloads applications, file tax returns and apply for passports, driving licences and birth and death certificates online.

Considering the low privacy concerns, lack of privacy awareness of Ghanaians and the low patronage of the government portal as found out in this study; and also the low literacy rate (see table 1.4) it seems to suggest that only a few individuals are aware of the existence of the new Privacy and Data Protection Act and their rights under the law.

It is concluded that the findings of the study went against the literature from which this study assumed that privacy and data protection is crucial to e-government implementation; and for that matter individuals concerns over personal information affects their use of e-government services.

This study suggests a survey should be conducted to find the awareness level of the public of the Data Protection Act. It also suggests future research of the impact of increased privacy awareness of e-government adoption in Ghana.

The next chapter makes recommendations highlights recommendations for policy makers based on the study findings discussed above.

9

Research Recommendations and Conclusions

This chapter presents discussions of the implications, contributions and limitations of the research and makes recommendation for future research.

The findings show that privacy and data protection does not currently play a significant role in e-government implementation in a developing country such as Ghana. Other factors such as access to information and communication technologies (Internet accessibility) and e-skills were found to be challenges which significantly impact on the citizens' use of e-government.

The study also finds that there is low privacy concern among Ghanaian citizens which is linked to a lack of awareness of privacy issues and also to the cultural dimension of the society. The concepts of privacy and data protection and e-government are new to many Ghanaians.

9.1 Policy implications and recommendations

The findings of this study have several policy implications. These are discussed in this section and appropriate recommendations suggested.

The study finds that privacy and data protection does not currently play a crucial role in e-government implementation in Ghana and as such it is not an impediment to the citizens' adoption of e-government services. It rather identifies the following as more likely to have effect on the citizens' intention to adopt e-government services:

- lack of accessibility to enabling technology, especially, the Internet;
- lack of knowledge and skills to use the technology;
- lack of awareness of e-government service and its consequences (i.e. potential benefits and privacy risks);
- non-functionality of government portal;
- lack of skilled technical personnel to handle and maintain the technology; and

- mistrust in government as a result of corrupt government officials/ workers;

The fact that privacy and data protection did not make it onto the list above implies it is not considered an important issue by the citizens in the e-government implementation in Ghana. It is not an impediment to the citizens using e-government services contrary to previous studies have found in developed countries.

It must however be pointed out to the policy makers that PDP issues, though not influential in citizens adoption of e-government, must still not be relegated to the background. This is due to the fact that citizens must submit their personal data in exchange for the online services. Government needs to have access to data in order to provide effective and efficient services. This carries potential risks to the citizens. These potential risks seem more real and are heightened in the light of the revelation as found in Chapter 2 that the country is among the top ten countries in the world involved in cyber fraud; media reports of rampant bribery and corruption cases against government officials, not to mention that some Ghanaians are known to be involved in identity theft cases.

The aforementioned suggest there are high potential risks for e-government users, in terms of online identity theft and fraud. However, in the light of the study finding that, Ghanaians have low privacy concern, it can be concluded that they are more likely to overlook these potential privacy risks as the empirical data suggests in section 8.1.2.

It therefore behoves on the government, as the service provider, to take the necessary measures to safeguard individuals' personal data. This study recommends the need to enforce the 2012 Data Protection Act and also to create awareness among the public on the need to secure their personal details such as installing anti-virus software on their computers and also using secure passwords.

The Government must task the Data Protection Act oversight body, the Data Protection Commission, with ensuring that all departments and agencies which collect online personal data about individuals post privacy policies/statements on their website.

Also there is the need to create awareness in civil servants who are tasked with the responsibility of e-government transactions that the privacy of every Ghanaian citizen is important, irrespective of whether the citizens are aware of that human right or not. Civil servants should therefore be reminded that any attempt on their part to breach the Data Protection Act can result in dismissal and possibly prosecution in a law court.

Public education must also be used to raise awareness among the public and to change their perception of privacy and data protection issues. This recommendation is made in the light of the study findings as already mentioned that there is a low privacy concern and lack of awareness and understanding of privacy issues among citizens. Acknowledging the literature finding that Ghana is a collectivist society, which is an influential factor in the citizens low privacy concerns, reinforces the need to raise privacy awareness.

Government must therefore take the necessary steps to create awareness and sensitise the public about the Data Protection Act 2012. An abridged version (in leaflets) of the Act in simple English and local languages must be published and circulated among the citizens. The leaflet must highlight citizens' rights in the light of the DPA.

The citizens must also be made aware of the presence of e-government services and the potential benefits to be derived from their usage - not forgetting the privacy issues involved as already mentioned. This recommendation is made in the light of the study finding that only a few Ghanaians use the Government portal which supports Bowen's (2010) survey results that only 6% of Internet users access the government portal.

If a service is available online but in practice cannot be found by citizens, it is rendered useless and will neither be used nor contribute to government improvements. The Government Ministries of Information, Education and Communication should therefore be tasked to come together and draw up a privacy and data protection and e-government awareness public education programme. The aim is to launch a public education and training programme designed to raise privacy and data protection and e-government awareness, encourage computer literacy (e-skills) and improve access to information and communication technologies for the digitally disadvantaged citizens.

The study suggests that the Ministry of Communication, as the sector ministry in-charge of the e-government implementation, should coordinate all the programme activities and also see to the provision of and access to information and communication technologies infrastructure. The Information Ministry should see to the raising of public awareness aspect. The training of the digitally disadvantaged citizens in e-skills too should come under the supervision of the Ministry of Education.

According to Bowen (2010) survey report, ninety percent of Ghanaians listened to the radio and they use it (radio) to receive news and information on at least a weekly basis. It is also therefore one of the best platforms to educate the public.

Zaller (1996) argues that when lawyers, academics and other related professionals discuss an issue and media cover this discussion, people learn about the issue being raised. It is therefore incumbent on policy makers to involve stakeholders in the public education of the citizens. Government officials, in collaboration with other stakeholders, for example, university lecturers can hold seminars, workshops and radio talk shows to educate citizens on using e-government services and also about potential risks in submitting their personal details online and how to secure these details. This is a necessary measure to create privacy awareness among citizens, since the study findings suggest that Ghanaians do not care about their online personal information.

Based on the study findings that the Ghanaian society has low privacy concern and that there is lack of privacy awareness among them; it is also recommended to the government to undertake a survey or an opinion poll to ascertain the level of awareness of e-government services and the privacy and data protection issues involved. The results will inform the government how well citizens are accepting e-government services and also their level of awareness of associated privacy risks.

This information will help the government to determine how much effort they have to put into public education to increase public awareness for successful e-government implementation. Literature search reveals that awareness creates citizen satisfaction, likewise trust. Every effort must therefore be made to let citizens have trust in the government and for that matter, the e-government implementation project.

Even though the study finds that the citizens have low a level of trust in the government for reasons already mentioned, they are more likely to use the e-government services for their potential benefits. However, these potential benefits may be stalled by low penetration of Internet access. As it was revealed in the previous chapter, the citizens' need for ICT (Internet) access in e-government implementation is stronger and more crucial than privacy and data protection. Governments should therefore make it a priority by providing adequate ICT infrastructure as well as bringing down the high rate of computer illiteracy through training to bridge the digital divide.

As identified in the literature search, larger numbers of Ghanaians access the Internet through mobile phones than computers (Bowen, 2010). In the light of this, the high penetration of mobile phone subscriptions (see table 1.4) can be taken advantage of and be adopted as an alternative to access government information and e-government services.

In addition, the government must re-design its website to make it more appealing and functional. This study's empirical data analysis reveals that the public hardly visit the website. As already indicated only 6% of Internet users access information from the government portal. This low percentage is not an encouraging indicator of successful e-government implementation. Probably, it is likely to increase if the implementation moves to a stage where there are more online services and the citizens can transact business with the government, for example filing tax returns, applying for passports, driving licences and birth and death certificates.

9.2 Research contribution

This section highlights and discusses the study's contribution to knowledge. Previous research (Carter and McBride, 2010; Belanger and Hiller, 2006) have been undertaken to investigate privacy in e-government, however, there is no empirical evidence to show any of these studies were carried out in developing countries, especially sub-Saharan African countries, which are predominantly collectivist societies.

The research findings and model are therefore major contributions to knowledge. The research contributes to the effect of privacy and data protection issues which arise when e-government is implemented in a developing country such as Ghana.

One key finding that has emerged is that, privacy and data protection does not at the moment play a crucial role in e-government implementation in developing countries such as Ghana. This is a major contribution to knowledge in the sense that the findings of previous studies have shown otherwise. The inconsistency suggests the role of privacy and data protection in e-government implementation is different in different cultural societies. In other words, its significance depends on whether the society is individualistic or collectivist.

Even though this study's recommendations are based on the findings from the analysis of the fieldwork data from Ghana, they are applicable to developing countries, especially sub-Saharan African countries, because of their common background (see section 8.7).

This thesis contributes to a better understanding of privacy and data protection issues in e-government implementation in developing countries, especially sub-Sahara African countries. These countries have been found to have very similar cultural dimensions, especially collectivism, (Hofstede et al., 2010) which influence their online privacy concerns. Similarly, the UN (2012) e-government survey identified these countries as having almost the same barriers and challenges in their e-government development, that is "widespread lack of infrastructure and functional literacy... and [they] remain at the tail end of the digital divide". The study findings suggests that in the implementation of e-government in Ghana, privacy and data protection is not currently the major challenge or barrier but rather digital divide, that is, the lack of access to ICT infrastructure (Internet) and lack of e-skills. This supports the UN e-government survey results on African countries and therefore the recommendations made herein are applicable to them.

9.3 Research limitation

As stated in Chapter 1, studies on privacy and data protection in e-government are limited. Therefore this study employed the findings of previous studies on privacy and data protection in e-commerce as well, in the comparative discussion of the findings and the research model. In other words there is a limited number of previous studies on privacy and data protection in e-government implementation for which the findings of this study could fit in.

Furthermore, the criteria used in selecting the participants excluded some sections of the public from being part of the study, especially citizens who do not use internet or are not involved in e-government implementation. The fieldwork was therefore undertaken in urban areas in Ghana, which excluded the rural community. It is recommended that in future research, criteria for the selection of participants is widened to include rural dwellers and non-Internet users.

Future research to investigate the impact of privacy awareness on e-government adoption in Ghana should be undertaken; and the sample frame should encompass all potential e-government users.

9.4 Research implication

There are implications to be drawn from the study findings. While previous studies have found privacy and data protection to be crucial in the implementation of e-government, it is not an influencing factor (or motivation) for individuals to access the electronic services in Ghana. The evidence from this research suggests that individuals are more willing to use e-government services without paying attention to privacy and data protection issues, particularly, concerns of privacy risks.

Similarly, Ghanaians may have a low trust in the government but will still use e-government services. Much of the citizens' mistrust in government is as a result of media reports of bribing and corruption among government officials. Interestingly, this social menace is one of the reasons more likely to influence the citizens' willingness to adopt e-government.

The following excerpts of the empirical data are worth repeating here to support this claim:

> *"I completed the [driving licence] application form online [in UK]. You don't have to pay bribe to anyone as has been happening here [in Ghana]"* Participant P17.

> *"I don't have to pay bribe to anybody before using it [e-government service]"* Participant FG17.

The main concern that emerged, which has the potential to affect e-government implementation is the new technology. That is, the lack of accessibility and the inability to use it due to e-skills deficiency may hinder citizens' usage of the online services.

The study concludes that while concerns about privacy and data protection are often cited as an important factor that may influence use of e-Government in previous studies it does not currently play a significant role in e-government implementation in a developing country like Ghana. The citizens are more concerned, in particular, about access to ICT infrastructure and e-skills (bridging the digital divide). They may not trust the government, the service provider, but for the fact that, e-government service eliminates or reduces the reported problem of paying bribes to corrupt officials, they may be more than willing to adopt it.

This study suggests future research to investigate the impact of privacy awareness on e-government adoption in a collectivist society such as Ghana.

9.4.1 Implication of research findings in the light of the Ghana DPA 2012

In this section, the implication of the research findings, specifically the low privacy concerns of the citizens, is discussed with regard to the enactment of the new Data Protection Act 2012.

According to Long and Quek (2002), some countries have adopted new privacy and data protection regulations mainly to trade with the EU. Ghana can be said to be no exception to this assertion. The study findings show that there are low privacy concerns among people. Previous studies have also shown that "regulatory responses usually occur in reaction to a growing level of discontent within the populace, which is transmitted to legislators in some form" (Melberg et al., 1995). Since there is no evidence to show or even suggest that people of Ghana might have been agitated about their personal data, it can be concluded that the privacy concerns of the citizens did not influence the passing of the 2012 Data Protection Act. The Act "may have little relationship with the privacy preferences" (Bellman et al., 2004) of citizens, since the EU DP directive upon which the Act is based was made for countries with distinct national cultural dimensional scores. This is illustrated in section 8.7.

Even though the Ghana News Agency (2012) reports the then Minister of Communication, Mr. Haruna Iddrisu, as saying that, the Data Protection Act was enacted to protect Ghanaians privacy and personal data, it seems to this study that the primary objective of the new legislation is probably to facilitate and boost trade with the western countries, especially the EU. As mentioned in Chapter 2, the eighth principle the EU Data Protection Directive states that:

> *Personal data shall not be transferred to a country or territory outside the European Economic Area unless that country or territory ensures an adequate level of protection for the rights and freedoms of data subjects in relation to the processing of personal data.*

The implication of this is that, subject to ratification by the EU, it is now possible for member states to outsource personal data to Ghana for processing. This is likely to reduce unemployment and boost the Ghanaian economy.

Despite the conclusion drawn, regarding why the new Act was passed, this study is of the view that the Data Protection Act is appropriate. This statement is made in the light of reports of Ghana being among the top ten countries involve in cyber fraud. It will at least send a signal to the international community that the country has a law to deal with this problem, specifically, *the Sakawa menace* (Warner, 2011). The new Data Protection Act is therefore timely and might allay the fears of foreign investors and visitors from individualist Western countries.

It must be added that while the passing of the Data Protection Act may not eliminate the widespread of reported cases of cyber fraud, it will at least be a useful opportunity to salvage the country's international image. It may possibly enhance or restore foreigners and investors trust and confidence in the country to some extent.

Locally, there are positive implications to the enactment of the Data Protection Act 2012. It is going to change the way educational institutions collect, process and store students' personal data. Hitherto, students' personal data (including examination results) were displayed on notice boards without due regard to possible privacy violations. Patients' medical records and bank customers' personal information is going to be protected and secured in a manner which is unprecedented in the country, since the Act requires the institutions and organisations to protect personal information of data subjects. Any breach of the Data Protection Act is punishable in a court of law and this may be an effective deterrent to would-be privacy violators.

It has been established in this study that the low privacy concern among the citizens has cultural connotations. However it must be pointed out that culture is dynamic. The government must not lose sight of the fact "culture itself changes over time…[It] change[s] by coming into contact with another culture, through international trade [and] migration" (Erez and Gati, 2004). The extent of privacy concerns among Ghanaians is therefore likely to increase through globalisation and foreign cultural influences. This is evident in the findings of the pilot study.

The participants in the pilot study have a strong view on privacy issues. They are all Ghanaians and their high value of privacy concerns can be attributed to influence of foreign culture. In other words, working and living in a highly individualist country has influenced their perception of privacy.

While the passing of the Data Protection Act 2012 is commendable, policy makers must go beyond the enactment to enforce it and create awareness. As already suggested in section 8.1, public education should be mounted to sensitise the people of their privacy rights under the Act. This is necessary in view of the research finding that Ghanaians have low privacy concern and as such there is lack of privacy awareness among them.

9.5 Research conclusion

This research sought to investigate the privacy and data protection issues which arise when e-government is introduced in developing countries. It specifically explored the crucial role of privacy and data protection in the implementation of e-government in Ghana.

Literature searching and analysis of fieldwork data revealed that, through e-government implementation, governments are able to provide better, effective and efficient services to their citizens. It is convenient, time saving and can minimise bribery and corruption among government workers/officials; however, it carries potential privacy risks to the citizens. The potential for online identity theft, cyber fraud and even possible misuse of citizens' personal information by government officials/workers raise privacy concerns.

Previous studies have found privacy concerns, and for that matter privacy and data protection issues, crucial to e-government implementation. However, these studies have been undertaken in developed countries; without any empirical evidence to show for developing countries, especially sub-Saharan-African countries.

To bridge the research gap and contribute to knowledge, this study sought to examine privacy and data protection issues which arise when e-government is introduced in developing countries such as Ghana.

Ghana was chosen for the investigation of the research phenomena, considering its unique position as being among the top ten countries in the world involved with cyber fraud; news media reported cases of identity theft among Ghanaians; and rampant corruption among government officials. All these have links with privacy concerns and trust which pose challenges to e-government implementation. It is therefore justified for it to have been chosen as the place for the investigation.

The study employed a qualitative approach, interviews and focus groups to gain an in-depth understanding of data protection issues in e-government implementation in Ghana. In spite of the country's involvement in cyber fraud, identity theft and high level of corruption, the findings from this study show that citizens' awareness and understanding of privacy and data protection issues are limited and individuals have low value privacy concerns for their online personal information.

The implication of the study finding is that privacy and data protection is not a major issue or challenge in the country's e-government implementation project. Many people have little or no idea about what privacy is. This situation therefore means their conception of privacy is different from the western concept of privacy found in literature search. From the analysis of the empirical data, Ghanaians concept of privacy is someone using their personal information to damage their reputation which might bring shame to their family. The western culture of privacy concerns regarding how their personal information is accessed online is therefore alien to many Ghanaians.

The analysis reveals that, privacy and data protection does not play any crucial role in the e-government implementation in Ghana. In other words, it has no effect on citizens' intention to use e-government services. Similarly, privacy concerns will not impede e-government use and that the majority of the citizens are more likely to access government online services for their potential benefits.

While many Ghanaians find e-government convenient and cost saving (among other potential benefits) and prefer its services to the traditional way of government service delivery, there are a few who would still want to go to government departments and offices to transact business face-to-face. The study finds that the reason behind this is due to these individuals fear of using new technology; or they may need someone to assist them if anything goes wrong; or inaccessibility to new technology (Internet). This brings to the fore the issue of *digital divide*: a category which the study found to be crucial to the e-government implementation in the country.

The study finds that digital divide, inadequate ICT infrastructure (computer and Internet access) and lack of e-skills, is rather crucial to e-government implementation, but not privacy and data protection. It also finds that people have low trust in government due to rampant reported corruption cases among government officials in the media. However, Bowen's (2010) survey reports on Ghana, which is supported by Hofstede's (2014) individualism low dimensional score contradicts this finding. Ghana, with a score of 15 is considered a collectivistic society. According to Hofstede et al. (2010), a collectivist society has the tendency to have trust in institutions.

Trust in public institutions is positively associated with e-government implementation. Previous studies (Carter and Bélanger, 2005; Tolbert and Mossberger, 2006, Bélanger and Carter, 2008) findings have shown that it is significant in citizens' intention to use an e-government service.

It was also found that mistrust in new technology is likely to affect the willingness of individuals to use the e-government services. However, mistrust in government as a result of media reports of corruption and bribing among government officials does not negatively affect citizens' willingness to use the e-government services. They are rather of the view that e-government will reduce bribing and corruption if not eliminate it.

Even though Internet access availability is limited (14.1% penetration), the widespread of mobile phone subscriptions could make up for this digital divide to enable citizens access to e-government services.

This study finds that privacy and data protection do not currently play any significant role in e-government implementation in Ghana as previous studies suggest. Rather access to information and communication technologies (Internet) and e-skills barriers are found to be significantly related to e-government usage.

Low privacy concern among the Ghanaian citizens is related to the cultural dimension of the society and the lack of awareness of privacy issues. The study concludes by emphasising the importance of government investing in ICT infrastructure. Public education to raise awareness of e-government services and privacy and data protection issues is also essential. Public education to create awareness "to increase participation among groups that are not yet heavily involved in e-government can prevent whole social groups from becoming disenfranchised in this new manifestation of the democratic process" (Jaeger and Thompson, 2004).

Currently e-government implementation is at a 'cataloguing stage,' where the government simply makes information available to citizens on its website (Hiller and Belanger, 2001, p.15). The study finding has shown that e-government is more likely to be adopted by the citizens due to its potential benefits. The low value of privacy concern among the citizens as found out in the study findings may possibly increase due to factors such as globalisation and probably public education awareness campaign. The Data Protection Act should therefore be enforced to neutralise any possible negative effect that an increased privacy concern might have on the citizens' adoption of the e-government service.

Data Protection Act enforcement is necessary in the light of media reports (see Chapter 2) and previous studies (Warner, 2011) citing Ghana as among the top ten countries leading in cyber crime. Even though privacy and data protection is not currently salient in e-government implementation in Ghana, its issues, particularly potential privacy risks to citizens, it must not be relegated to the background. The study therefore suggests future research to investigate the impact of privacy awareness on individuals' adoption of e-government in a collectivist society such as Ghana.

In conclusion, this research finds that in developing countries, especially sub-Saharan African countries, such as Ghana, with their inherent collectivist societies, privacy and data protection does not currently play a crucial role in the implementation of e-government. Other factors such as digital divide (that lack of Internet access and e-skills), culture, potential benefits of e-government services and mistrust through perceived corruption of government officials are influential factors in individuals' intention to access e-government services. It was noted however that, mistrust in government is not a strong influential factor to inhibit individuals' intention to use e-government services, perhaps because mistrust in face-to-face is even greater.

Finally, since developing countries, especially those in sub-Sahara Africa share common cultural dimensions and challenges in e-government implementation, the study findings and recommendations can reasonably be expected to be applicable to these countries as well.

9.6 Summary

It is essential to understand that the idea behind the implementation of e-government in countries across the world is to make delivery of government services to citizens, businesses and other government departments or agencies electronically. Currently, in Ghana, if an individual wants to apply for a passport or driving licence he/she has to go to the appropriate department or agency in person. In an attempt to eliminate this manual way of transacting business with the public and also to cut down the paperwork, the Government of Ghana has initiated an e-government implementation project. However the implementation of e-government carries potential risks to users. The potential for online identity theft and fraud raises privacy concerns.

There is no available evidence to show how concerned Ghanaian citizens are with their personal data. It is therefore essential to explore the extent to which privacy and data protection will affect the e-government implementation in Ghana in due course a country reported to be among top ten countries in the world involved in cyber fraud; rampant bribery and corruption cases among government officials; and known identity theft cases.

The study employed a qualitative approach, interviews and focus groups to gain an in-depth understanding of the role of privacy and data protection in e-government implementation Ghana. The Straussian version of Grounded Theory was borrowed to analyse the fieldwork data that took place in Ghana. The emergent categories were as a direct result of participants' responses to the interview questions. Many of the participants for this study showed lack of awareness and knowledge of e-government, privacy and data protection issues. Individuals' mistrust in government was identified as not being a hindrance to the use of e-government though.

Many of the participants were emphatic about their mistrust of the government. This low level of trust had arisen due to news media reports of cases of corruption against government officials. Another issue that has heightened the mistrust is the government directive to all mobile phone subscribers to register their SIM cards. The mistrust is due the public perception that the "SIM card registration will give authorities the ability to monitor people wherever they may be, examining conversations, text messages and Internet activity" (Malakata, 2010). For this reason, the public seem not to have trusted the government on the motive behind the mandatory SIM card registration directive.

The research questions as outlined in Chapter 2 were answered. Privacy and data protection was found not to have any significant influence on the implementation of e-government in Ghana at the moment. As was found in section 8.2, the citizens have mistrust in the government and e-government services through perceived corruption of government officials. However as shown in the research model, the mistrust does not suggest any negative influence on individuals' intentions to use the e-government services. In other words, individuals are more likely to use the e-government services in spite of their mistrust in government. Influential factors such as potential benefits, digital divide (in terms of lack of Internet accessibility and e-skills) and national cultural dimensions significantly influence an individual's intentions to use the e-government services.

The study recommends that the government provides more information on the e-government implementation through public education; enforces the Data Protection Act and educates the citizens on their privacy rights. The government must also endeavour to bridge the digital divide through the provision of adequate ICT infrastructure and necessary e-skills to use the new technology.

Access to e-government services and for that matter the government portal should not be limited to Internet alone. Considering its high subscription (see table 1.4), mobile phones should be encouraged for use as a complement to the rather low internet penetration.

The research had a limitation in the sense that the study population was limited to only urban dwellers who are Internet users or involved with the implementation of the e-government project. The study recommends future research to investigate the impact of privacy awareness on e-government adoption in Ghana. It proposes that the sample frame should be expanded to include participants from rural areas of the country and non-Internet users as well.

While potential benefits of using e-government services may supersede any perceived potential privacy risks, and thereby make any privacy concerns less significant, digital divide appears to be a crucial challenge and barrier to the e-government implementation in Ghana. The study therefore recommends to the policy makers and for that matter the Ghana government to make accessibility of Internet to citizens a priority. Similarly, there must be an increased public education campaign to create awareness of the presence of the e-government services and its inherent privacy issues.

References

ABC EYEWITNESS NEWS (2014) *2 from Ghana Arrested in Bolingbrook on Fraud Charges*. [Online] Available from: http://abc7chicago.com/archive/9396513/ [Accessed 19/01/14].

AGYEI, D.D. and VOOGT, J. (2011) ICT use in the teaching of mathematics: Implications for professional development of pre-service teachers in Ghana. *Education and Information Technologies,* 16 (4), pp. 423-439.

AILON, G. (2008) Mirror, mirror on the wall: Culture's consequences in a value test of its own design. *Academy of Management Review, 33*(4), 885-904.

AILON, G. (2009) A reply to Geert Hofstede. *Academy of Management Review,* 34 (3), pp. 571-573.

AKKAYA, C., WOLF, P. and KRCMAR, H. (2012) The Surprisingly Low Effect of National Culture on E-Government Adoption: A Cross-Cultural Comparison.

ALGHAMDI, R., DREW, S. and AL-GHAITH, W. (2012) Factors unflinching e-commerce adoption by retailers in Saudi Arabia: Qual Analysis. *ArXiv Preprint arXiv:1211.2404,*.

ALI, M., WEERAKKODY, V. and EL-HADDEDEH, R. (2009) The Impact of National Culture on E-Government Implementation: A Comparison Case Study, AMCIS 2009 Proceedings, San Francisco, California.

ALLWOOD, C.M. and WANG, Z. (1990) Conceptions of computers among students in China and Sweden. *Computers in Human Behavior,* 6 (2), pp. 185-199.

ALRECK, P.L. and SETTLE, R.B. (1995) The Survey Research Handbook: Guidelines and Strategies for Conducting a Survey, 2E.

ALSAGHIER, H. et al. (2009) Conceptualising citizen's trust in e-government: Application of Q methodology. *Electronic Journal of E-Government,* 7 (4), pp. 295-310.

ALSAGHIER, H.M. and HUSSAIN, R. (2012) Conceptualization of Trust in the e-Government Context: A Qualitative Analysis. In: *Digital Democracy: Concepts, Methodologies, Tools, and Applications*: IGI Global, pp. 1524-1553.

ALSHEHRI, M., DREW, S. and ALFARRAJ, O. (2012) A Comprehensive Analysis of E-government services adoption in Saudi Arabia: Obstacles and Challenges. *Higher Education,* 6, pp. 8.2.

AL-SHEHRY, A.M. (2010) *Transformation towards E-government in The Kingdom of Saudi Arabia: technological and organisational perspectives.* Unpublished thesis (PhD), De Montfort University.

ALTINAY, L. and PARASKEVAS, A. (2008) *Planning research in hospitality and tourism*: Routledge.

AMBALI, A.R. (2009) Digital Divide and its implication on Malaysian e-government: Policy initiatives. *Social and Political Implications of Data Mining: Knowledge Management in e-Government,* pp. 267-287.

ANDERSON, P. and DEMPSEY, J. (2003) Privacy and e-government: privacy impact assessments and privacy commissioners–two mechanisms for protecting privacy to promote citizen trust online. *Global Internet Policy Initiative,*.

ANGELOPOULOS, S. et al. (2010) Emerging barriers in e-government implementation. In: *Electronic Government*: Springer, pp. 216-225.

ANING, K. and EDU-AFFUL, F. (2013) *Legal and Policy Frameworks Regulating the Behaviour of Politicians and Political Parties - Ghana.* [Online] Available from: http://www.idea.int/publications/legal-and-policy-frameworks-ghana/loader.cfm?csModule=security/getfile&pageid=58647 [Accessed 09/10/14].

ARMSTRONG, A. (2011). *'Sakawa'Rumours: Occult Internet Fraud and Ghanaian Identity.*

ARNESEN, D. and DANIELSSON, J. (2007) Protecting citizen privacy in digital government. *Encyclopedia of Digital Government,* pp. 1358-1363.

AUGENSTEIN, S. (2013) *Man Claiming To Be From Ghana Arrested For Identity Theft at Linden Walmart, Police Say*. [Online] Available from: http://www.nj.com/union/index.ssf/2013/01/man_claiming_to_be_from_ghana.html [Accessed 19/01/14].

AWOTWI, J.E. (2011) The Ghana Community Network Services Ltd (GCNet): Implementation Challenges. *Global Strategy and Practice of E-Governance: Examples from Around the World*, pp. 209.

AWOWI, J.E. (2010) Ghana Community Information Centers (CiCs) e-Governance Success or Mirage?. *Journal of E-Governance*, 33 (3), pp. 157-167.

BAIER, A. (1986) Trust and antitrust. *Ethics*, 96 (2), pp. 231-260.

BAKAR, A.B.A. (2011) Evaluation of eGovernment Implementation at Federal, State and Local government Levels in Malaysia. In: *The Proceedings of the 11th European Conference on EGovernment: Faculty of Administration, University of Ljubljana, Ljubljana, Slovenia, 16-17 June 2011*: Academic Conferences Limited, pp. 1.

BANK OF GHANA (2011), http://www.bog.gov.gh/ [Accessed on 15/08/2011]

BANSAL, G. and CHEN, L. (2011) If they Trust our E-commerce Site, Will They Trust our Social Commerce Site Too? Differentiating the Trust in E-commerce and S-commerce: The Moderating Role of Privacy and Security Concerns.

BARCLAYS-GHANA (2013) *Privacy Policy*. [Online] Available from: http://gh.barclays.com/ [Accessed 13/07/2013]

BARDHAN, P. (2012) *Awakening giants, feet of clay: Assessing the economic rise of China and India*: Princeton University Press.

BASKERVILLE, R. F. (2003) Hofstede never studied culture. *Accounting, organizations and society*, 28 (1), pp. 1-14.

BASKERVILLE-MORLEY, R. F. (2005) A research note: the unfinished business of culture. *Accounting, Organizations and Society*, 30 (4), pp. 389-391.

BASU, S. (2004) E-government and developing countries: an overview. *International Review of Law, Computers & Technology*, 18 (1), pp. 109-132.

BBC (2012) *Queues to vote in Ghana elections.* [Online] Available from: http://www.bbc.co.uk/news/world-africa-20648367 [Accessed 30/08/2013].

BBC (2013) *Queues to vote in Ghana elections.* [Online] Available from: http://www.bbc.co.uk/news/world-africa-20648367 [Accessed 12/03/13].

BBC NEWS (2007) *Phone calls and texts to be logged.* [Online] http://news.bbc.co.uk/1/hi/uk/7021647.stm [Accessed 17/09/12].

BBC NEWS (2011) *East Surrey Hospital loses confidential patient records.* [Online] Available from: http://www.bbc.co.uk/news/uk-england-surrey-15176343. [Accessed 15/01/13].

BBC NEWS (2013) *Gang attacked police car days before* £105,000 robbery, *court told.* [Online] Available from: http://www.bbc.co.uk/news/uk-england-24068696 [Accessed 24/09/13].

BBC NEWS CHANNEL (2003) *Privacy laws 'hamper e-government'.* [Online] Available from: http://news.bbc.co.uk/1/hi/technology/3033633.stm [Accessed 15/01/13].

BBC NEWS SOUTH EAST (2013) *Catherine Kyie [A Ghanaian] Jailed over Woman's Identity Theft.* [Online] Available from: http://www.bbc.co.uk/news/uk-wales-south-east-wales-23143240 [Accessed 19/01/14].

BBC NEWS TECHNOLOGY CHANNEL. (2009) *Brussels criticises UK on privacy.* [Online] Available from: http://news.bbc.co.uk/1/hi/8337685.stm [Accessed 15/10/2011]

BÉLANGER, F. and CARTER, L. (2008) Trust and risk in e-government adoption. *The Journal of Strategic Information Systems,* 17 (2), pp. 165-176.

BÉLANGER, F. and CARTER, L. (2009) The impact of the digital divide on e-government use. *Communications of the ACM,* 52 (4), pp. 132-135.

BELANGER, F. and HILLER, J.S. (2006) A framework for e-government: privacy implications. *Business Process Management Journal,* 12 (1), pp. 48-60.

BELANGER, F. and VAN SLYKE, C. (2011) *Information systems for business: an experiential approach*: Wiley Publishing.

BELANGER, F., HILLER, J.S. and SMITH, W.J. (2002) Trustworthiness in electronic commerce: the role of privacy, security, and site attributes. *The Journal of Strategic Information Systems,* 11 (3), pp. 245-270.

BELDAD, A., DE JONG, M. and STEEHOUDER, M. (2011) I trust not therefore it must be risky: Determinants of the perceived risks of disclosing personal data for e-government transactions. *Computers in Human Behavior,* 27 (6), pp. 2233-2242.

BELLMAN, S., JOHNSON, E.J., KOBRIN, S. J. and LOHSE, G.L. (2004) International differences in information privacy concerns: A global survey of consumers. *The Information Society, 20*(5), pp. 313-324.

BENBASAT, I., GOLDSTEIN, D.K. and MEAD, M. (1987) The case research strategy in studies of information systems. *MIS Quarterly,* pp. 369-386.

BENNETT, C.J. (2000) An international standard for privacy protection: objections to the objections. In: *Proceedings of the tenth conference on Computers, freedom and privacy: challenging the assumptions*: ACM, pp. 33-38.

BERNARD, H.R. (2012) *Social research methods: qualitative and quantitative approaches.* Thousand Oaks, Calif: SAGE.

BERTOT, J.C., JAEGER, P.T. and GRIMES, J.M. (2010) Using ICTs to create a culture of transparency: E-government and social media as openness and anti-corruption tools for societies. *Government Information Quarterly,* 27 (3), pp. 264-271.

BEYNON-DAVIES, P. (2004). *e-Business.* New York, Palgrave Macmillan.

BIRCH, S. (2012) *Ghana West Africa Still A Hot Zone For Scams, Say Investigators.* [Online] Available from: http://globalinvestigations.blogspot.com/2012/03/ghana-west-africa-still-hot-zone-for.html [Accessed 19/01/14].

BIZTECH AFRICA (2011) Data Protection bill withdrawn, [Online] Available from: http://www.biztechafrica.com/article/data-protection-bill-withdrawn/933/ [Accessed 30/10/2011]

BLOOM, P.N., MILNE, G.R. and ADLER, R. (1994) Avoiding misuse of new information technologies: legal and societal considerations. *The Journal of Marketing,* pp. 98-110.

BOATENG, R. et al. (2011) Sakawa—Cybercrime and criminality in Ghana. *Journal of Information Technology Impact,* 11 (2), pp. 85-100.

BORCH, O.J. and ARTHUR, M.B. (1995) STRATEGIC NETWORKS AMONG SMALL FIRMS: IMPLICATIONS FOR STRATEGY RESEARCH METHODOLOGY*. *Journal of Management Studies,* 32 (4), pp. 419-441.

BOSWORTH, B. and COLLINS, S.M. (2007). *Accounting for Growth: Comparing China and India,.*

BOWEN, H. (2010) *Making Connections: Using data on Ghanaians' media use and communication habits as a practical tool in development work.* [Online] Available from: http://www.audiencescapes.org/sites/default/files/AudienceScapes%20Ghana%20Surve y%20Research%20 Report%202010.pdf. [Accessed 15/09/13].

BRAUN, V. and CLARKE, V. (2013) *Successful qualitative research : a practical guide for beginners.* London: SAGE.

BRINGER, J.D., JOHNSTON, L.H. and BRACKENRIDGE, C.H. (2006) Using computer-assisted qualitative data analysis software to develop a grounded theory project. *Field Methods,* 18 (3), pp. 245-266.

BROOKS, G. (2004) The challenge to Lloyd's in Indian outsourcing. *Privacy and Data Protection Journal,* 5 (1), pp. 10 -11

BRYANT, A. and CHARMAZ, K. (2010) *The SAGE handbook of grounded theory.* Los Angeles [i.e. Thousand Oaks, Calif.]: SAGE Publications.

BUCHELE, S.F. and OWUSU-ANING, R. (2007) The one laptop per child (OLPC) project and its applicability to Ghana. In: *Proceedings of the 2007 international conference on adaptive science and technology,* pp. 113-118.

BURRELL, JENNA,, (2012) *Invisible users youth in the Internet cafés of urban Ghana.* [Online].

BYRNE, M.M. (2001) Linking philosophy, methodology, and methods in qualitative research. *AORN Journal,* 73 (1), pp. 207-210.

CAGLE, S., REINSCH, M. and ZHANG, X. (2006) IT in Developing Nations–A Look at Sub-Saharan Africa. *University of Missouri, St.Louis IS5800 Paper,.*

CARTER, L. and BÉLANGER, F. (2005) The utilization of e-government services: citizen trust, innovation and acceptance factors*. *Information Systems Journal,* 15 (1), pp. 5-25.

CARTER, L. and MCBRIDE, A. (2010) Information privacy concerns and e-government: a research agenda. *Transforming Government: People, Process and Policy,* 4 (1), pp. 10-13.

CARTER, L. and WEERAKKODY, V. (2008) E-government adoption: A cultural comparison. *Information Systems Frontiers,* 10 (4), pp. 473-482.

CASTILLO J. J. (2009) *Convenience Sampling*. [Online] Available from: http://explorable.com/convenience-sampling [Accessed 12/02/13].

CATE, F.H. (1997) *Privacy in the Information Age*. Washington, D.C., Brookings Institution Press

CELLULAR NEWS (2011) *2.5 Million SIM Cards Cut Off in Ghana Over the Weekend*. [Online] Available from: http://www.cellular-news.com/story/48587.php [Accessed 15/10/12].

CHAFFEY, D. (2003) *Business information systems*. Harlow (England): Financial Times/Prentice Hall.

CHAFFEY, D. (2006) *E-business and e-commerce management: strategy, implementation, and practice*. Harlow, FT/Prentice Hall.

CHAFFEY, D. (2007) *E-business and e-commerce management : strategy, implementation, and practice*. Harlow, England; New York: FT Prentice Hall.

CHAFFEY, D. (2007) *E-business and e-commerce management: strategy, implementation, and practice.* Harlow, England; New York: FT Prentice Hall.

CHAFFEY, D. (2009) *Internet marketing: strategy, implementation and practice.* Harlow: Financial Times Prentice Hall.

CHEN, G.M. (2001) Toward transcultural understanding: A harmony theory of Chinese communication. In Milhouse V.H., Asante M.K. and Nwosu P.O. (eds.) *Transcultural Realities: Interdisciplinary Perspectives on Cross-cultural Relations.* Sage, Thousand Oaks, CA, pp. 55-70.

CHEN, Y. et al. (2006) E-government strategies in developed and developing countries: An implementation framework and case study. *Journal of Global Information Management (JGIM)*, 14 (1), pp. 23-46.

CHO, H., RIVERA-SÁNCHEZ, M. and LIM, S.S. (2009) A multinational study on online privacy: global concerns and local responses. *New Media & Society*, 11 (3), pp. 395-416.

CHRAJ (2012) *What we do.* [Online] Available from: http://www.chrajghana.com/?page_id=27. [Accessed 15/09/14].

CIA-THE WORLD FACTBOOK (2013) *Africa: Ghana.* [Online] Available from: https://www.cia.gov/library/publications/the-world-factbook/geos/gh.html [Accessed 15/09/13].

CLARKE, A., (2005) *Situational analysis : grounded theory after the postmodern turn*. Thousand Oaks, Calif.: Sage Publications.

CLARKE, R. (1999) Introduction to dataveillance and information privacy, and definitions of terms. *Roger Clarke's Dataveillance and Information Privacy Pages,.*

COLLIS, J. and HUSSEY, R. (2003) *Business research: a practical guide for undergraduate and postgraduate students.* Houndmills, Basingstoke, Hampshire; New York: Palgrave Macmillan.

COLLIS, J. and HUSSEY, R. (2003) *Business research: a practical guide for undergraduate and postgraduate students*. Houndmills, Basingstoke, Hampshire; New York: Palgrave Macmillan.

COMMONWEALTH NETWORK (2014) *Welcome to Ghana*. [Online] Available from: http://www.commonwealthofnations.org/country/Ghana/ [Accessed 15/09/14].

CORBIN, J.M. and STRAUSS, A. (1990) Grounded theory research: Procedures, canons, and evaluative criteria. *Qualitative Sociology*, 13 (1), pp. 3-21.

CRESWELL, J. W. and PLANO CLARK, V. L. (2007) *Designing and conducting mixed methods research*. Thousand Oaks, Calif, SAGE Publications.

CRESWELL, J.W. (2013) *Qualitative inquiry & research design: choosing among five approaches.* Los Angeles: SAGE Publications.

CRESWELL, J.W. and MILLER, G.A. (1997) Research methodologies and the doctoral process. *New Directions for Higher Education,* 1997 (99), pp. 33-46.

CRESWELL, J.W. and PLANO CLARK,V.L. (2010) *Designing and conducting mixed methods research.* Thousand Oaks: SAGE.

CROTTS, J.C. and ERDMANN, R. (2000) Does national culture influence consumers' evaluation of travel services? A test of Hofstede's model of cross-cultural differences. *Managing Service Quality,* 10 (6), pp. 410-419.

CROZIER, M., (1964) *The bureaucratic phenomenon.* Chicago: University of Chicago Press.

CULLEN, R. (2009) Culture, identity and information privacy in the age of digital government. *Online Information Review,* 33 (3), pp. 405-421.

CULNAN, M.J. and ARMSTRONG, P.K. (1999) Information privacy concerns, procedural fairness, and impersonal trust: An empirical investigation. *Organization Science,* 10 (1), pp. 104-115.

DAGBANJA, D.N. (2014) Privacy in Context: The Right to Privacy, and Freedom and Independence of the Media under the Constitution of Ghana. *African Journal of International and Comparative Law,* 22 (1), pp. 40-62.

DALMIA, V. (2011) *India: New Indian Privacy And Data Protection Rules.* [Online] Available from: http://www.mondaq.com/x/135856/Telecommunications+Mobile+Cable+Commu nications/Indian+Information+Technology+Laws [Accessed 11/08/2011].

DAVIDSON, M. (2009) *Exploring culture in international learning.* Available from: http://www.nottingham.ac.uk/pesl/internationalisation/docs/Internationalisation-Exploring-culture-in-international-learning.pdf. [Accessed 10/01/15].

DAVIS, F. D. (1989) Perceived usefulness, perceived ease of use, and user acceptance of information technology. *MIS Quarterly,* 13(3), p.319–340.

DE LUQUE, M.S. and JAVIDAN, M. (2004) Uncertainty avoidance, in: *Culture, Leadership and Organizations: The GLOBE Study of 62 Societies,* Sage Thousand Oaks.

DE VAUS, D.A. (1993) *Surveys in Social Research* (3rd edn.), London: UCL Press.

DEARDORFF, A.V. (2010) *The Terms of Trade and Other Wonders.* [Online] Available from: http://www-personal.umich.edu/~alandear/glossary/d.html. [Accessed 15/01/14].

DEBENEDICTIS, A. et al. (2002) E-government defined: an overview of the next big information technology challenge. *Issues in Information Systems,* 3 (1), pp. 130-136.

DEMPSEY, J.X., ANDERSON, P. and SCHWARTZ, A. (2003) Privacy and E-Government. A Report to the United Nations Department of Economic and Social Affairs, as background for the World Public Sector Report: E-Government. *Center for Democracy and Technology, Washington, DC,.*

DENSCOMBE, M., (2007) *The good research guide for small-scale social research projects.* Maidenhead: Open Univ. Press.

DENZIN, N. (2000) Introduction: the discipline and practice of qualitative research in Denzin, N. and Lincoln, Y (ed.) Handbook of qualitative research.

DENZIN, N.K. and LINCOLN, Y.S. (1994) *Handbook of Qualitative Research,* Thousand Oaks, CA; Sage.

DEY, I. (2005) *Qualitative data analysis: a user-friendly guide for social scientists.* London: Routledge.

DIX, A. (2005) *Report of the Working Group on Internet Governance.* [Online] Available from: http://www.itu.int/wsis/docs2/pc3/contributions/misc/iwg-data-protection.pdf Available at: [Accessed 30/10/20/11]

DOCSTOC (2013) *Ghana ICTAD Policy.* [Online] Available from: http://www.docstoc.com/docs/158025951/1-Ghana-ICTAD-Policy [Accessed 28/09/14].

DONALDSON, T. and PRESTON, L.E. (1995) The stakeholder theory of the corporation: Concepts, evidence, and implications. *Academy of Management Review,* 20 (1), pp. 65-91.

DONOVAN, K. and MARTIN, A. (2012) The Rise of African SIM Registration: Mobility, Identity, Surveillance and Resistance. *Identity, Surveillance and Resistance (November 7, 2012),.*

DWIVEDI, Y. K., WEERAKKODY, V. and JANSSEN, M. (2012) Moving towards maturity: challenges to successful e-government implementation and diffusion. *ACM SIGMIS Database, 42* (4), 11-22.

EASTERBY-SMITH, M., THORPE, R. and JACKSON, P. (2008) *Management research.* Los Angeles; London: SAGE.

EASTERBY-SMITH, M., THORPE, R. and JACKSON, P. (2012) *Management research.* London: SAGE.

EBRAHIM, Z. and IRANI, Z. (2005) E-government adoption: architecture and barriers. *Business Process Management Journal,* 11 (5), pp. 589-611.

EISENHARDT, K. M. and GRAEBNER, M. E. (2007) Theory building from cases: Opportunities and challenges. *Academy of management journal, 50*(1), 25-32.

EISENHARDT, K.M. (1989) Building theories from case study research. *Academy of Management Review,* 14 (4), pp. 532-550.

EREZ, M. and GATI, E. (2004) A Dynamic, Multi-Level Model of Culture: From the Micro Level of the Individual to the Macro Level of a Global Culture. *Applied Psychology,* 53 (4), pp. 583-598.

EUROPEAN COMMISSION (2011) *Data Protection: Europeans share data online, but privacy concerns remain – new survey.* [Online] Available from: http://europa.eu/rapid/pressReleasesAction.do?reference=IP/11/742&format=HT ML&aged=0&language=EN&guiLanguage=en [Accessed 05/11/2011].

EUROPEAN UNION (1995) *Directive 95/46/EC.* [Online] Available from: http://ec.europa.eu/justice/policies/privacy/docs/95-46-ce/dir1995-46_part1_en.pdf [Accessed 10/10/2011].

FAIRWEATHER, N.B. and ROGERSON, S. (2006) Towards morally defensible e-government interactions with citizens. *Journal of Information, Communication and Ethics in Society,* 4 (4), pp. 173-180.

FERLIE, E., HARTLEY, J. and MARTIN, S. (2003) Changing public service organizations: current perspectives and future prospects. *British Journal of Management,* 14 (s1), S1-S14.

FERNÁNDEZ, W.D. (2004) The grounded theory method and case study data in IS research: issues and design. In: *Information Systems Foundations Workshop: Constructing and Criticising.*

FONTANA, A. and FREY, J. H. (2005) The interview: From neutral stance to political involvement. In N. K. Denzin and Y. S. Lincoln (Eds), *The SAGE handbook of qualitative research* (pp.695-728). Thousand Oaks, CA: Sage.

FOSU, I. (2011) Exploring the potential of wireless technologies to accelerate universal Internet access in Ghana. *Telecommunications Policy,* 35 (6), pp. 494-504.

FREEMAN, R. E. (1984) *Strategic management: A stakeholder approach.* Boston: Pitman.

FREMPONG, G. (2011) Developing Information Society in Ghana: How Far?. *The Electronic Journal of Information Systems in Developing Countries,* 47.

FREMPONG, G.K. (2007) Ghana Telecommunications Sector Performance Review. FRIED, C. (1968) Privacy [A Moral Annalysis]. *Yale Law Journal,* 77, pp. 21.

GARCIA-MURILLO, M. (2013) Does a government web presence reduce perceptions of corruption? *Information Technology for Development,* 19 (2), pp. 151-175.

GATAUTIS, R. (2008) The impact of ICT on public and private sectors in Lithuania. *In¿ Inerin¿ Ekonomika,* 4, pp. 18.

GERMANAKOS, P., CHRISTODOULOU, E. and SAMARAS, G. (2007) A European perspective of e-government presence–Where do we stand? The EU-10 case. In: *Electronic Government*: Springer, pp. 436-447.

GHANA COMMERCIAL BANK LIMITED (2011) *About us.* [Online] Available from: https://www.gcbbank.com.gh/ [Accessed on 15/08/2011]

GHANA INVESTORS GALORE (2011) *About Ghana.* [Online] Available from: http://64.17.137.225/government.html [accessed 16/11/2011].

GHANA INTEGRITY INITIATIVE (2005) *"Voice of the People" survey (Southern Ghana), Project Completion Report* Available from: http://www.afrimap.org/english/images/documents/GhanaVoiceofthe-PeopleSurve y05.pdf [Accessed 09/12/14].

GHANA NEWS AGENCY (2006) *Implementation of e-governance being hampered.* [Online] Available from: http://www.ghanaweb.com/

GhanaHomePage/NewsArchive/artikel.php?ID=9877 0 [Accessed 15/01/13].

GHANA NEWS AGENCY (2009) *Bank of Ghana gets ISO 27001 Certification.* [Online] Available from: http://www.ghananewsagency.org/details/Economics/Bank-of-Ghana-gets-ISO-27001-Certification/?ci=3&ai=5407 [Accessed 05/12/2011].

GHANA NEWS AGENCY (2010) *Data Protection Bill 2010 underway.* [Online] Available from: http://www.ghananewsagency.org/details/Science/Data-Protection-Bill-2010-underway/?ci=8&ai=19674 [Accessed 10/11/2010].

GHANA NEWS AGENCY (2011a) *Child's Rights activist says children's rights being violated.* [Online] Available from: http://www.ghananewsagency.org/details/Social/Child-s-Rights-activist-says-children-s-rights-being-violated/?ci=4&ai=31897 [Accessed 05/12/2011].

GHANA NEWS AGENCY (2011b) *Ghana at unenviable position on internet fraud table.* [Online] Available from: http://www.ghananewsagency.org/details/Science/Ghana-at-unenviable-position-on-internet-fraud-table/?ci=8&ai=29778 [Accessed 27/11/11].

GHANA NEWS AGENCY (2011c) *Human Rights Court to rule on GFA and EOCO's saga.* [Online] Available from: http://www.ghananewsagency.org/details/Sports/Human-Rights-Court-to-rule-on-GFA-and-EOCO-s-saga/?ci=5&ai=25910 [Accessed 05/12/2011].

GHANA NEWS AGENCY (2012) *We have to protect the privacy of the Ghanaian - Iddrisu.* [Online] Available from: http://www.ghananewsagency.org/print/44947 [Accessed 29/03/13].

GHANA STATISTICAL SERVICES (2011) *Total Population.* [Online] Available from: http://www.ghana.gov.gh/census/img8.html [Accessed 25/11/11]

GHANAWEB (2009) *Ghana banned from use of Credit Cards.* [Online] Available from: http://www.ghanaweb.com/GhanaHomePage/NewsArchive/artikel.php?ID=1670 65 [Accessed 27/11/11].

GHANAWEB (2010) *Ghana to implement SIM card registration.* [Online] Available from: http://www.ghanaweb.com/GhanaHomePage/NewsArchive/artikel.php?ID=1854 27 [Accessed 15/11/12].

GHANAWEB (2013) *Mobile subscription hits 26.5m.* [Online] Available from: http://www.ghanaweb.com/GhanaHomePage/business/artikel.php?ID=285236 [Accessed 10/09/14].

GIL-GARCÍA, J.R. and PARDO, T.A. (2005) E-government success factors: Mapping practical tools to theoretical foundations. *Government Information Quarterly,* 22 (2), pp. 187-216.

GILLHAM, B. (2008) *Small-scale social survey methods: real world research*: Continuum International Publishing Group.

GILLWALD, G. AND STORK, S. (2008) *Towards Evidence-based ICT Policy and Regulation: ICT access and usage in Africa - VOLUME ONE 2008 Policy Paper Two.* [Online] Available from: http://www.researchictafrica.net/publications/Towards_Evidence-based_ICT_Policy_and_Regulation_-_Volume_1/RIA%20Policy%20Paper%20Vol%201%20Paper%202%20-%20ICT%20Access%20and%20Usage%20in%20Africa%202008.pdf [Accessed 10/10/14].

GLASER, B.G. and STRAUSS A.L. (1967) *The Discovery of Grounded Theory: Strategies for Qualitative Research.* Chicago: Aldine.

GNA (2008) *Italy to Assist Ghana Implement E-Governance Project.* [Online] Available from: http://m.modernghana.com/mobile/155515/1/italy-to-assist-ghana-implement-e-governance-proje.html [Accessed 14/08/10].

GNA (2012) *Governing Board of Data Protection Commission inaugurated.* [Online] Available from: http://www.modernghana.com/news/427470/1/governing-board-of-data-protection-commission-inau.html [Accessed 12/02/13].

GODFRED, K. and AHUMA, G. K. (2011) *First Ghana Internet Governance Forum* [Online] Available from: http://www.waigf.org/IMG/pdf/Ghana_IGF_Report-_Final.pdf [Accessed 17/11/2011].

GOV.UK (2011) *"The relationship between the UK and Ghana is strong and vibrant".* [Online] Available from: https://www.gov.uk/government/speeches/the-relationship-between-the-uk-and-ghana-is-strong-and-vibrant. [Accessed 19/06/14].

GOVERNMENT OF GHANA (2012) *Ghana's Data Protection Law in the Digital Age.* [Online] Available from: http://www.ifg.cc/index.php?option=com_content&task=view&id=40163 [Accessed 25/03/13].

GOVERNMENT OF GHANA (2013) *Government of Ghana Official Portal.* [Online] Available from: http://www.ghana.gov.gh/ [Accessed 15/0/13].

GRAPHICONLINE (2013) *Govt worried over delay in data centre project.* [Online] Available from: http://graphic.com.gh/business/telecom/13580-govt-worried-over-delay-in-data-centre-project.html [Accessed 12/09/13].

GRAPHICONLINE (2014) *CAC advocates review of SIM card registration.* [Online] Available from: http://www.ghanaweb.com/GhanaHomePage/business/artikel.php?ID=310616 [Accessed 10/10/14].

GREENLEAF, G. (2011) Global data privacy in a networked world.

GRODZINSKY, F.S. and TAVANI, H.T. (2005) P2P networks and the Verizon v. RIAA case: implications for personal privacy and intellectual property. *Ethics and Information Technology,* 7 (4), pp. 243-250.

GRUNDÉN, K. (2012) A Social Perspective on the Implementation of e-Government: A Longitudinal Study at the County Administration of Sweden. *Case Studies in E-Government,* 1, pp. 120.

GUBA, E. G. (1990) The alternative paradigm dialog. In E. G. Guba (Ed.), *The paradigm dialog* (pp. 17–30). London: Sage.

GUBA, E. G. and LINCOLN, Y. S. (1994) Competing paradigms in qualitative research. In N. K. Denzin and Y. S. Lincoln (Eds.), *Handbook of qualitative research* Thousand Oaks. CA: Sage Publications, pp. 105–117.

GUBA, E.G. and LINCOLN, Y.S. (1994) Competing paradigms in qualitative research. *Handbook of Qualitative Research,* 2, pp. 163-194.

GUERMAZI, B and SATOLA D. (2005) Creating the "Right" Enabling Environment for ICT In SCHWARE, R. *E-development: from excitement to effectiveness: prepared for the World* Summit on the Information Society, Tunis, November 2005. Washington, DC, World Bank.

HALAWEH, M., FIDLER, C. and MCROBB, S. (2008) Integrating the Grounded Theory Method and Case Study Research Methodology Within IS Research: A Possible'Road Map'. *ICIS 2008 Proceedings,* pp. 165.

HAMILTON, B.A. (2002) International e-economy benchmarking: The world's most effective policies for the e-economy. *London: Booz Allen Hamilton,.*

HANN, I.H., HUI, K.L., LEE, S.Y.T. and PNG, I.P. (2007) Overcoming online information privacy concerns: An information-processing theory approach. *Journal of Management Information Systems, 24* (2), pp. 13-42.

HEEKS, R. (2001) *Building e-governance for development: A framework for national and donor action*: University of Manchester. Institute for development policy and management.

HEEKS, R. (2002) Information systems and developing countries: Failure, success, and local improvisations. *The Information Society,* 18 (2), pp. 101-112.

HEEKS, R. (2006) Understanding and measuring eGovernment: international benchmarking studies. In: *UNDESA workshop,"E-Participation and E-Government: Understanding the Present and Creating the Future", Budapest, Hungary,* pp. 27-28.

HEEKS, R. and BAILUR, S. (2007) Analyzing e-government research: Perspectives, philosophies, theories, methods, and practice. *Government Information Quarterly,* 24 (2), pp. 243-265.

HELPMAN, E. (1998) *General purpose technologies and economic growth*: The MIT press.

HILLER, J.S. and BELANGER, F. (2001) Privacy strategies for electronic government. *E-Government,* 200, pp. 162-198.

HOBBY, S.P. (2005) EU Data Protection Directive: Implementing a Worldwide Data Protection Regime and How the US Position Has Progressed, The. *Int'l L.& Mgmt.Rev.,* 1, pp. 155.

HOFSTEDE, G. (1980) *Culture's consequences: international differences in work-related values.* Beverly Hills CA: Sage.

HOFSTEDE, G. (2002) Dimensions do not exist – a reply to Brendan McSweeney. *Human Relations,* 55 (11), pp. 1355-61

HOFSTEDE, G. (2003) What is culture? A reply to Baskerville. *Accounting, Organizations and Society,* 28 (7), pp. 811-813.

HOFSTEDE, G. (2009) Who is the fairest of them all? Galit ailon's mirror. *Academy of Management Review,* 34 (3), pp. 570-571.

HOFSTEDE, G., HOFSTEDE, G.J. and MINKOV, M. (2010) *Cultures and organizations: software of the mind: intercultural cooperation and its importance for survival.* New York: McGraw-Hill.

HOFSTEDE, G.H. (2014) *The Hofstede Center - What about Ghana?* [Online] Available from: http://geert-hofstede.com/ghana.html [Accessed 15/03/14].

HOOK, C, (1989) *Data Protection Implications for Systems Design.* NCC Publications

HOOVER, R.S. and KOERBER, A.L. (2011) Using NVivo to answer the challenges of qualitative research in professional communication: Benefits and best practices tutorial. *Professional Communication, IEEE Transactions on,* 54 (1), pp. 68-82.

HOWLEY, R. et al. (2004). *The role of information systems staff in the provision for data protection on privacy-A subjective approach.* CCSR, DMU.

HOWLEY, R. et al. (2002) *The role of information systems personnel in the provision for privacy and data protection in organisations and within information systems.*[Online] Available from: http://www.ccsr.cse.dmu.ac.uk/conferences/ethicomp/ethicomp2002/abstracts/70. html [Accessed 9/12/07].

HUSSEY, J. and HUSSEY, R. (1997) *Business research : a practical guide for undergraduate and postgraduate students.* Basingstoke: Macmillan Business.

IGF (2011) *West Africa Internet Governance Forum* Ghana IGF report and final communiqué. [Online] Available from: http://www.waigf.org/IMG/pdf/Ghana_IGF_Report-_Final.pdf Available at: [Accessed 20/10/11]

IICD (2012) *Community Information Centre Initiative - Ghana.* [Online] Available from: http://www.iicd.org/projects/ghana-cic/?searchterm=None. [Accessed 22/03/13].

INFORMATIONWEEK GOVERNMENT (2011) *India Adopts New Privacy Rules.* [Online] Available from: http://www.informationweek.com/news/government/policy/229402835 [Accessed 12/11/2011]

INTERNATIONAL TELECOMMUNICATION UNION (2011) *Measuring the Information Society.* [Online] Available from: http://www.itu.int/ITUD/ict/publications/idi/2011/Material/MIS_2011_without_annex_5.pdf Available at: [Accessed 25/11/11]

INTERNATIONAL TELECOMMUNICATION UNION (2012) *Measuring the Information Society.* [Online] Available from: http://www.itu.int/dms_pub/itu-d/opb/ind/D-IND-ICTOI-2012-SUM-PDF-E.pdf. [Accessed 15/09/13].

INTERNET CRIME COMPLAINT CENTER (2011) *THE DANGEROUS SIDE OF ONLINE ROMANCE SCAMS.* [Online] Available from: http://www.ic3.gov/media/2011/110429.aspx [Accessed 12/11/12].

INTERNET CRIME COMPLAINT CENTER (IC3) (2010) *2010 Internet Crime Report, Internet Crime Complaint Center,* USA. [Online] Available from: http://www.ic3.gov/media/annualreport/2010_ic3report.pdf [Accessed 20/12//2012].

IRANI, Z., ELLIMAN, T. and JACKSON, P. (2007) Electronic transformation of government in the UK: a research agenda. *European Journal of Information Systems,* 16 (4), pp. 327-335.

ITU (2013) *ICT STATISTICS NEWSLOG - GHANA'S MOBILE SUBSCRIBERS REACHED 26.33M AT END-FEBRUARY.* [Online] Available from: http://www.itu.int/ITU-D/ict/newslog/Ghanas+Mobile+-Subscribers+Reached+2633m+At+EndFebruary.aspx [Accessed 15/09/13].

JAEGER, P.T. (2003) The endless wire: e-government as global phenomenon. *Government Information Quarterly,* 20 (4), pp. 323-331.

JAEGER, P.T. and BERTOT, J.C. (2010) Designing, implementing, and evaluating user-centered and citizen-centered e-government. *International Journal of Electronic Government Research (IJEGR),* 6 (2), pp. 1-17.

JAEGER, P.T. and THOMPSON, K.M. (2003) E-government around the world: lessons, challenges, and future directions. *Government Information Quarterly,* 20 (4), pp. 389-394.

JAEGER, P.T. and THOMPSON, K.M. (2004) Social information behavior and the democratic process: Information poverty, normative behavior, and electronic government in the United States. *Library & Information Science Research,* 26 (1), pp. 94-107.

JAMES, J. (2011) Internet skills in developing countries: how much do we know? *Information Development,* 27 (2), pp. 94-99.

JAMIL, A., RAFIQUE, F. and RIZVI, S. (2014) Evaluating the Impact of IT on University Students of Bahawalpur with Special Reference to

Free laptop Distribution by Govt. of Punjab. *International Journal of Academic Research in Business and Social Sciences,* 4 (6), pp. 233-250.

JANKOWICZ, A.D., (1991) *Business research projects for students.* London: Chapman & Hall.

JANSSEN, M. and BORMAN, M. Critical Success Factors for E-Government Infrastructure Implementation.

JARUWACHIRATHANAKUL, B. and FINK, D. (2005) Internet banking adoption strategies for a developing country: the case of Thailand. *Internet Research,* 15 (3), pp. 295-311.

JOHNSON, R.B. and ONWUEGBUZIE, A.J. (2004) Mixed methods research: A research paradigm whose time has come. *Educational researcher,* 33 (7), pp. 14-26.

JOHNSON, R.B., ONWUEGBUZIE, A.J. and TURNER, L.A., (2007). Toward a definition of mixed methods research. *Journal of mixed methods research,* 1 (2), pp. 112-133.

JONES, M. L. And ALONY, I. (2007) The cultural impact of information systems– through the eyes of Hofstede–a critical journey.

JOSHI, J.B. et al. (2002) Security and privacy challenges of a digital government. In: *Advances in Digital Government*: Springer, pp. 121-136.

KAGITCIBASI, C. (1997) Individualism and collectivism. *Handbook of cross-cultural psychology, 3,* 1-49.

KHAZANCHI, D. and MUNKVOLD, B.E. (2003) On the rhetoric and relevance of IS research paradigms: a conceptual framework and some propositions, *System Sciences, 2003. Proceedings of the 36th Annual Hawaii International Conference on* 2003, IEEE, pp. 10.

KOVAČIĆ, Z.J. (2005) The impact of national culture on worldwide egovernment readiness. *Informing Science Journal, 8,* 143-158.

KRUEGER, R.A. and CASEY, M.A. (2000) *Focus groups: a practical guide for applied research.* Thousand Oaks, Calif.: Sage Publications.

KUMARAGURU, P. and CRANOR, L. (2006) Privacy in India: Attitudes and awareness. In: *Privacy Enhancing Technologies*: Springer, pp. 243-258.

KUNER, C. (2011). *Regulation of Transborder Data Flows Under Data Protection and Privacy Law: Past, Present and Future,.*

LANGE, R. and LAMPE, C. (2008) Feeding the privacy debate: An examination of Facebook. In: *The annual meeting of the International Communication Association, Quebec: ICA*, pp. 26.

LAYNE, K. and LEE, J. (2001) Developing fully functional E-government: A four stage model. *Government Information Quarterly, 18*, pp. 122 -136.

LEE, J. (2010) 10year retrospect on stage models of e-Government: A qualitative meta-synthesis. *Government Information Quarterly,* 27(3), pp. 220-230.

LEE, S.M., TAN, X. and TRIMI, S. (2005) Current practices of leading e-government countries. *Communications of the ACM, 48*(10), pp. 99-104.

LEWIS, I. M. (1985) *Social Anthropology in Perspective*. Cambridge: Cambridge University Press.

LIAMPUTTONG, P. (2005): *Qualitative Research Methods,* 2nd ed. Oxford University Press

LINCOLN, Y.S. and GUBA, E.G. (1985) *Naturalistic inquiry*. Beverly Hills, Calif.: Sage Publications.

LING, S and BAUER. C. (2000) A model of factor influences on electronic commerce adoption and diffusion in small and medium-sized enterprises. In: *Proceedings of the Fourth Pacific Asia Conference on Information Systems*. Hong Kong, June 1, 2000.

LLEWELLYN, G., SULLIVAN, G. and MINICHIELLO, V. (1999) Designing health research: Sampling in qualitative research. In V. Minichiello, G. Sullivan, K. Greenwood, and R. Axford (Eds.), *Handbook for research methods in health sciences.* Sydney, New South Wales, Australia: Addison-Wesley, pp.174-199.

LONG, W. J. and QUEK, M. P. (2002) Personal data privacy protection in an age of globalization: the US-EU safe harbor compromise. *Journal of European Public Policy,* 9(3), pp. 325-344.

Macaulay, L. and Watts, L. (2002) *Best Practice Guidance on Data Protection for Systems Design* (Version May 2002: Draft for Public Consultation) [Online] Available from: http://www.co.umist.ac.uk/research/tech_reports/trs_2002_002_lam.pdf [Accessed 26/6/04]

MAILONLINE (2013) *Illegal immigrant stole dead mother's identity to get into Britain from Ghana before stealing £100,000 in benefits.* [Online] Available from: http://www.dailymail.co.uk/news/article-2353780/Illegal-immigrant-stole-dead-mothers-identity-Britain-Ghana-stealing-100-000-benefits.html. [Accessed 05/07/13].

MAKULILO, A. (2012). *Protection of Personal Data in Sub-Saharan Africa.*

MAKULILO, A.B. (2012) Privacy and data protection in Africa: a state of the art. *International Data Privacy Law,* 2 (3), pp. 163-178.

MAKULILO, A.B. (2013) "One size fits all": Does Europe impose its data protection regime on Africa?. *Datenschutz Und Datensicherheit-DuD,* 37 (7), pp. 447-451.

MALAKATA, M. (2010) *SIM card registration stirs concern in Africa.* [Online] Available from: http://news.idg.no/cw/art.cfm?id=97BAE8AF-1A64-6A71-CE489938A5591ED4. [Accessed 16/08/13].

MAURO, P. (1997) *Why worry about corruption?*: International Monetary Fund.

MCCORT, D. and MALHOTRA, N.K. (1993) Culture and consumer behavior: toward an understanding of cross-cultural consumer behavior in international marketing. *J Int Consum Mark* 6 (2):91–127.

MCROBB, S. and STAHL, B.C. (2007) Privacy as a shared feature of the e-phenomenon: a comparison of privacy policies in e-government, e-commerce and e-teaching. *International Journal of Information Technology and Management,* 6 (2), pp. 232-249.

MCSWEENEY, B. (2002a) Hofstede's model of national cultural differences and their consequences: A triumph of faith-a failure of analysis. *Human relations,* 55 (1), pp. 89-118.

MCSWEENEY, B. (2002b). The essentials of scholarship: A reply to Hofstede' *Human Relations,* 55 (11), pp. 1363-1372.

MCSWEENEY, B. (2003). *Is 'National Culture' A Myth?A critique of the claims of Geert Hofstede.* Available from: http://www.powershow.com/view1/62755-ZDc1Z/Is_National_Culture_A_Myth_A_critique_of_the_claims_of_Geert_Hofstede_p owerpoint_ppt_presentation. [Accessed 10/01/15].

MILBERG, S.J., BURKE, S.J., SMITH, H.J. and KALLMAN, E.A. (1995) Values, personal information privacy, and regulatory approaches. *Communications of the ACM, 38*(12), 65-74.

MILBERG, S.J., SMITH, H.J. and BURKE, S.J. (2000) Information privacy: Corporate management and national regulation. *Organization Science,* 11 (1), pp. 35-57.

MILES, M.B. and HUBERMAN, A.M. (1994) *Qualitative data analysis: An expanded sourcebook*: Sage.

MILLARD, J. (2008a) eGovernment measurement for policy makers. *European Journal of ePractice,* 4, pp. 19-32.

MILLARD, J. (2008b) *User Attitudes to E-Government Citizen Services in Europe, Electronic Government: Concepts, Methodologies, Tools, and Applications,* Information Science Reference, Tampere.

MINTZBERG, H. (1996) Managing government, governing management. *Harvard Business Review,* 74 (3), pp. 75-&.

MOATSHE, R.M. and MAHMOOD, Z. (2011) Strategies for eGovernment Implementation in Developing Countries: A Case Study of Botswana Government. In: *The Proceedings of the 11th European Conference on EGovernment: Faculty of Administration, University of Ljubljana, Ljubljana, Slovenia, 16-17 June 2011*: Academic Conferences Limited, pp. 386.

MOON, M.,WELCH, ERIC, (2005) Same Bed, Different Dreams? A Comparative Analysis of Citizen and Bureaucrat Perspectives on E-Government. *Review of Public Personnel Administration,* 25 (3), pp. 243-264.

MOON, M.J. (2003) Can IT help government to restore public trust? Declining public trust and potential prospects of IT in the public sector. In: *System Sciences, 2003. Proceedings of the 36th Annual Hawaii International Conference on*: IEEE, pp. 8 pp.

MOORE, N. (2000) *How to do Research: The Complete Guide to Designing and Managing Research Projects* (3rd ed), Library Association Publishing

MORGAN, D.L. (1998) *The focus group guidebook*: Sage.

MOSSBERGER, K. (2009) Toward digital citizenship. Addressing inequality in the information age. *Routledge Handbook of Internet Politics,* pp. 173-185.

MOSSBERGER, K., TOLBERT, C.J. and MCNEAL, R.S. (2008) *Digital citizenship: the internet, society, and participation.* Cambridge (Mass.): MIT.

MYERS, M.D. (1997) Qualitative research in information systems. *Management Information Systems Quarterly,* 21, pp. 241-242.

MYERS, M.D. (2009) *Qualitative research in business and management.* Los Angeles: SAGE.

MYERS, M.D. (2013) *Qualitative research in business and management.* Los Angeles: SAGE Publications.

MYERS, M.D. and AVISON, D.E. (2002) *Qualitative research in information systems : a reader.* London: SAGE.

MYERS, M.D. and NEWMAN, M. (2007) The qualitative interview in IS research: Examining the craft. *Information and organization,* 17(1), pp. 2-26.

NCA (2011) *MOBILE NUMBER PORTABILITY – THE FIRST MONTH-END REPORT.* [Online] Available from: http://www.nca.org.gh/downloads/NCA%20News%20Release%20-%20MNP%20End%20July%202011%20110801%20(2).pdf [Accessed 05/01/14].

NCA (2014) *Legislations.* [Online] Available from: http://www.nca.org.gh/128/69/Legislations.html [Accessed 15/10/14].

NDOU, V. (2004) E-government for developing countries: opportunities and challenges. *The Electronic Journal of Information Systems in Developing Countries,* 18.

NIKOLAS, K. (2012) *Fake [Ghanaian] doctor with stolen ID saw 500 patients in South Carolina.* [Online] Available from: http://www.digitaljournal.com/article/331985 [Accessed 19/01/14].

NITA (2013) *Online Services Portal of the Government of Ghana.* Available: http://www.nita.gov.gh/. [Accessed 15t/09/13].

NORRIS, D. (2007) *Current Issues and Trends in E-Government Research,* CyberTech Publishing.

NORRIS, P. (2001) Digital divide: Civic engagement, information poverty, and Internet worldwide. New York: Cambridge University Press.

OATES, B.J. (2006) *Researching information systems and computing*. London: SAGE.

O'CONNOR, R. (2012) Using grounded theory coding mechanisms to analyze case study and focus group data in the context of software process research.

ODURO-FRIMPONG, J. (2012) Popular Media, Politics and Everyday Life in Contemporary Ghana.

OFFICE OF THE PRIVACY COMMISSIONER FOR PERSONAL DATA (2001), *The Ordinance at a Glance*. [Online] Available from: http://www.pcpd.org.hk/english/ordinance/ordglance1.html#dataprotect [Accessed 21/11/2011]

OLIVERO, N. and LUNT, P. (2004) Privacy versus willingness to disclose in e-commerce exchanges: The effect of risk awareness on the relative role of trust and control. *Journal of Economic Psychology,* 25 (2), pp. 243-262.

ORANGE, G. et al. (2007) CARE: an integrated framework to support continuous, adaptable, reflective evaluation of e-government systems. *International Journal of Cases on Electronic Commerce (IJCEC),* 3 (3), pp. 18-32.

ORLIKOWSKI, WANDA J., BAROUDI,JACK J., (1991) Studying Information Technology in Organizations: Research Approaches and Assumptions. *Information Systems Research,* 2 (1), pp. 1-28.

OTLEY, D.T. and BERRY, A. (1994) Case study research in management accounting and control. *Management Accounting Research,* 5 (1), pp. 45-65.

PARDO, T. (2010) Digital Government Implementation: A Comparative Study in USA and Russia.

PARDO, T.A. et al. (2000) New york state central accounting system stakeholder needs analysis. *Center for Technology in Government, Albany, NY,.*

PAROŠKI, M., KONJOVIC, Z. and SURLA, D. (2013) Implementation of e-Government at the local level in underdeveloped countries:

The case study of AP Vojvodina. *Electronic Library, the,* 31 (1), pp. 99-118.

PATTON, M. Q. (2002). *Qualitative research and evaluation methods* (3rd ed.). Thousand Oaks, CA: Sage.

PATTON, M.Q. (1990). *Qualitative Research and Evaluation Methods* (2nd ed.), Newbury Park, CA: Sage

PIDGEON, N.F., TURNER, B.A. and BLOCKLEY, D.I. (1991) The use of Grounded Theory for conceptual analysis in knowledge elicitation. *International Journal of Man-Machine Studies,* 35 (2), pp. 151-173.

POLIT, D.F., BECK, C.T. and HUNGLER, B.P. (2001) *Essentials of Nursing Research: Methods, Appraisal and Utilization.* 5th Ed., Philadelphia: Lippincott Williams & Wilkins

POPE, C. and MAYS, N. (2006) *Qualitative research in health care.* Malden, Mass.: Blackwell Pub./BMJ Books.

POTTER, W. J. (1996) *An analysis of thinking and research about qualitative methods.* Hillsdale, NJ: Lawrence Erlbaum Associates.

POWELL, R.A. and SINGLE, H.M. (1996) Focus groups. *International Journal for Quality in Health Care,* 8 (5), pp. 499-504.

PRIVACY AND DATA PROTECTION LIMITED (2002) *Privacy and Data Protection* [Online] Available from: http://privacydataprotection.co.uk/guide/part1/ [Accessed 25/06/08]

PRIVACY WORKING GROUP (1995) *Privacy And The National Information Infrastructure: Principles For Providing And Using Personal Information.* [Online] Available from: http://aspe.hhs.gov/datacncl/niiprivp.htm [Accessed 19/09/2011]

PRYCE, P. and OIDTMANN, R. (2014) The 2012 general election in Ghana. *Electoral Studies,* 34, pp. 330-334.

RAHMAN, H. (2009) *Social and political implications of data mining: Knowledge management in e-government*: Information Science Reference.

RAPOPORT, R.N. (1970) *Three dilemmas in action Research: with special reference to the Tavistock Experience.* London: Sage.

RECKER, J. (2013) *Scientific research in information systems: a beginner's guide.* Berlin; New York: Springer.

REDDICK, C.G. (2004) A two-stage model of e-government growth: Theories and empirical evidence for US cities. *Government Information Quarterly,* 21 (1), pp. 51-64.

REGAN, P.M. (2008) Privacy in an Electronic Government Context. *Digital Government.* Springer, pp. 127-140.

REILLY, E.D., (2004) *Concise encyclopedia of computer science.* Chichester, West Sussex, England; Hoboken, NJ: Wiley.

REMENYI, D., (2013a) *Field methods for academic research - interviews, focus groups and questionnaires in business and management studies.* Reading, U.K.: Academic Conferences and Publishing.

REMENYI, D., (2013b) *Grounded theory : the reader series.* [S.l.]: Acpi.

REPUBLIC OF GHANA (2003), *The Ghana ICT for Accelerated Development (ICT4AD) policy.* [Online] Available from: http://www.ict.gov.gh/pdf/Ghana%20ICT4AD%20Policy.pdf [Accessed 12/11/2010]

REXHEPI, A., REXHA, B. and DIKA, A. (2012) Assessment of success factors of e-government project implementation: challenges for the Kosovo e-government perspective. In: *Proceedings of the 6th International Conference on Theory and Practice of Electronic Governance*: ACM, pp. 324-331.

RIBBINK, D. et al. (2004) Comfort your online customer: quality, trust and loyalty on the internet. *Managing Service Quality,* 14 (6), pp. 446-456.

RICHEY, S. (2010). The impact of corruption on social trust. *American Politics Research, 38* (4), pp. 676-690.

RITCHIE, J. (2003) The applications of qualitative methods to social research. *Qualitative research practice: A guide for social science students and researchers,,* pp. 24-46.

ROGERS, E. M. (2003) *Diffusion of innovation.* New York: Free.

ROUSE, A. and DICK, M. (1994) The use of NUDIST, a computerized analytical tool, to support qualitative information systems research. *Information Technology & People,* 7 (3), pp. 50-62.

ROWLEY, J. (2011) e-Government stakeholders—Who are they and what do they want? *International Journal of Information Management,* 31 (1), pp. 53-62.

SAMPSON, H. (2004) *Navigating the waves: the usefulness of a pilot in qualitative research*, Qualitative Research, Volume 4, pp.383-402.

SANDELOWSKI, M. (1995) Sample size in qualitative research. *Research in nursing & health*, 18(2), pp. 179-183.

SANDOVAL-ALMAZAN, R. and GIL-GARCIA, J.R. (2012) Are government internet portals evolving towards more interaction, participation, and collaboration? Revisiting the rhetoric of e-government among municipalities. *Government Information Quarterly*, 29, pp. S72-S81.

SANG, S., LEE, J. and LEE, J. (2009) E-Government challenges in least developed countries (LDCs): a case of Cambodia. In: *Advanced Communication Technology, 2009. ICACT 2009. 11th International Conference on*: IEEE, pp. 2169-2175.

SARNAIK, R. (2001) *What Is Civil Society?* [Online] Available from: http://www.bbc.co.uk/worldservice/people/highlights/010705_civil.shtml. [Accessed 15/01/13].

SAUNDERS, M., LEWIS, and THORNHILL, A. (2009) *Research methods for business students*. New York: Prentice Hall.

SAXBY, S. (2014) The 2013 CLSR-LSPI seminar on electronic identity: The global challenge–Presented at the 8th International Conference on Legal, Security and Privacy issues in IT Law (LSPI) November 11–15, 2013, Tilleke & Gibbins International Ltd., Bangkok, Thailand. *Computer Law & Security Review*, 30 (2), pp. 112-125.

SCHNEIDER, G. P. (2008) *Electronic Commerce* (8 ed.). Boston, MA: Thomson Learning Inc.

SCHOLL, H.J. et al. (2009) E-Commerce and e-Government: How do they Compare? what can they Learn from each Other?. In: *System Sciences, 2009. HICSS'09. 42nd Hawaii International Conference on*: IEEE, pp. 1-10.

SECHREST, L. and SIDANI, S., (1995) Quantitative and qualitative methods:: Is There an Alternative? *Evaluation and program planning*, 18 (1), pp. 77-87.

SHEEHAN, K.B. (2002) Toward a Typology of Internet Users and Online Privacy Concerns. *The Information Society*, 18(1), pp. 21-32.

SILVERMAN, D. (2013) *Doing qualitative research: a practical handbook.*

SIPIOR, J.C. and WARD, B.T. (2009) Bridging the digital divide for e-government inclusion: A United States case study. *Asymptotic and Computational Methods in Spatial Statistics,* pp. 167.

SMITH, H.J., MILBERG, S.J. and BURKE, S.J. (1996) Information privacy: measuring individuals' concerns about organizational practices. *MIS Quarterly,* pp. 167-196.

SMITH, S. and JAMIESON, R. (2006) Determining key factors in e-government information system security. *Information Systems Management,* 23 (2), pp. 23-32.

SOBH, R. and PERRY, C. (2006) Research design and data analysis in realism research. *European Journal of Marketing,* 40 (11/12), pp. 1194-1209.

SPINELLO, R.A. (1995) *Ethical Aspects of Information Technology Prentice.* Hall New Jersey.

STONE, E.F., GUEUTAL, H.G., GARDNER, D.G. and MCCLURE, S. (1983) A field experiment comparing information-privacy values, beliefs, and attitudes across several types of organizations. *Journal of applied psychology,* 68 (3), pp. 459-468.

STRAUSS, A.L. (1987) *Qualitative analysis for social scientists.* Cambridge [Cambridgeshire]; New York: Cambridge University Press.

STRAUSS, A.L. and CORBIN, J. (1990) *Basics of Qualitative Research: Techniques and Procedures for Developing Grounded Theory.* Newbury Park, CA: Sage.

STRAUSS, A.L. and CORBIN, J. (1998) *Basics of Qualitative Research: Techniques and Procedures for Developing Grounded Theory* (2ed ed.). Thousand Oaks, CA: Sage.

STURCKE J. (2008) Laptop lapses which embarrassed government [Online] Available from: http://www.guardian.co.uk/politics/2008/jun/12/defence.terrorism [Accessed 12/10/2010].

SUNDQVIST, S., FRANK, L. and PUUMALAINEN, K. (2005) The effects of country characteristics, cultural similarity and adoption timing on the diffusion of wireless communications. *Journal of business research, 58*(1), pp.107-110.

SUTHARSHAN, A (2013) Human factors and cultural influences in implementing agile philosophy and agility in global software development. Unpublished thesis (PhD.), Edith Cowan University.

SZEREMETA, J. (2002) Benchmarking e-government: a global perspective. In: *INTERNATIONAL CONGRESS ON GOVERNMENT ON LINE.*

TAN, C., PAN, S. L. and LIM, E.T. (2008) Managing Stakeholder Interests in E-Government Implementation: Lessons Learned from a Singapore E-Government Project. In Anttiroiko, A. (Ed.), *Electronic Government: Concepts, Methodologies, Tools, and Applications*. pp. 3262-3282.

TAVANI, H.T., (2004) *Ethics and technology : ethical issues in an age of information and communication technology*. Hoboken, NJ: Wiley.

THE CONSTITUTION OF THE REPUBLIC OF GHANA (1992). *THE CONSTITUTION OF THE REPUBLIC OF GHANA 1992.* [Online] Available from:http://www.judicial.gov.gh/constitution/second_schedule/home.htm. [Accessed 15/01/13].

THE GUARDIAN (2013) *Edward Snowden statement: 'It was the right thing to do and I have no regrets'.* [Online] Available from: http://www.guardian.co.uk/world/2013/jul/12/edward-snowden-full-statement-moscow. [Accessed 14/07/13].

THE NATIONAL ARCHIVE. [Online] Available from: http://www.legislation.gov.uk/ukpga/1998/29/schedule/1 [Accessed 21/11/2011]

THE NEW YORK TIMES (2003) *Canadian and Dutch Officials Warn of Security's Side Effects*. [Online] Available from: http://www.nytimes.com/2003/02/28/international/americas/28PRIV.html [Accessed 12/10/13].

THE US DEPARTMENT OF STATE (2011) *2010 Human Rights Report: Ghana.* [Online] Available from: http://www.state.gov/g/drl/rls/hrrpt/2010/af/154349.htm [Accessed 27/11/11]

THE WHITE HOUSE (2013) *Government to Government.* [Online] Available from: http://www.whitehouse.gov/sites/default/files/omb/assets/omb/egov/c-2-govern.html. Last [Accessed 15/09/13].

THE WORLD BANK (2014a) *About Development* [Online] Available from: http://web.worldbank.org/WBSITE/EXTERNAL/EXTSITE-

TOOLS/0,,contentM DK:20147486~menuPK:344190~pageP-K:98400~piPK:98424~theSitePK:95474,00.htm l [Accessed 31/07/14].

THE WORLD BANK (2014b) *Enterprise survey - Ghana* [Online] Available from: http://www.enterprisesurveys.org [Accessed 16/11/14]

TOLBERT, C.J. and MOSSBERGER, K. (2006) The Effects of E-Government on Trust and Confidence in Government. *Public administration review,* 66(3), pp. 354-369.

TOTTERDALE, R.L. (2012) Globalization and Data Privacy: An Exploratory Study. In H. Nemati (Ed.), *Optimizing Information Security and Advancing Privacy Assurance: New Technologies* (pp. 132-149). Hershey, PA: Information Science Reference.

TRANSPARENCY INTERNATIONAL (2012) *Corruption Perceptions Index 2012.* [Online] Available from: http://cpi.transparency.org/cpi2012/results/ [Accessed 06/06/13].

TURNER, B.A. (1981) Some practical aspects of qualitative data analysis: one way of organising the cognitive processes associated with the generation of grounded theory. *Quality and Quantity,* 15 (3), pp. 225-247.

TURNER, M.A., JOHNSON, P.A. and BALLS, D. (2004) *Privacy Rights and Policy Wrongs: How Data Restrictions can Impair Information-Led Development in Emerging Markets* [Online] Available from: http://www.perc.net/wp-content/uploads/2013/09/ild.pdf [Accessed 23/11/07]

UN (2012) *United Nations E-government Development Database.* [Online] Available from: http://unpan3.un.org/egovkb/datacenter/countryview.aspx. [Accessed 15/01/13].

UN (2014) *UNITED NATIONS E-GOVERNMENT SURVEY 2014.* [Online] Available from: http://unpan3.un.org/egovkb/Portals/egovkb/Documents/un/2014-Survey/E-Gov_Complete_Survey-2014.pdf [Accessed 15/10/14].

UNESCO (2005) E-government toolkit for developing countries Available at: http://unesdoc.unesco.org/images/0013/001394/139418e.pdf [Accessed 12/11/2010]

UNIES, N. (2008) *United Nations e-government survey 2008: From e-government to connected governance*: UN.

US DEPARTMENT OF STATE (2011) *2010 Human Rights Report: Ghana.* [Online] Available from: http://www.state.gov/j/drl/rls/hrrpt/2010/af/154349.htm. [Accessed 15/01/13].

USLANER, E.M. (2004) 5 Trust and corruption. *The New Institutional Economics of Corruption,* pp. 76.

VENKATESCH, V., MORRIS, M., DAVIS, G. and DAVIS, F. (2003) User acceptance of information technology: toward a unified view. *MIS Quarterly,* 27(3), p.425–478.

VERDEGEM, P. and VERLEYE, G. (2009) User-centered E-Government in practice: A comprehensive model for measuring user satisfaction. *Government Information Quarterly,* 26 (3), pp. 487-497.

VINOD, H.D. (2008) Fraud and Corruption. *Governance, Risk, and Compliance Handbook: Technology, Finance, Environmental, and International Guidance and Best Practices,* pp. 121.

WALESONLINE (2013) *Ghanaian Couple Who Stole Dead Woman's Identity to Claim False Benefits Are Jailed.* [Online] Available from: http://www.walesonline.co.uk/news/wales-news/ghanaian-couple-who-stole-dead-4809962 [Accessed 19/01/2014].

WALL, D.S. (2010) 'Criminalizing cyberspace: the rise of the internet as a "crime problem"', in Jewkes, Y. and Yar, M. (eds) *Handbook of Internet Crime,* London, Willan Publishing, pp. 88–103.

WALSH, M. (2003) Teaching qualitative analysis using QSR NVivo. *The Qualitative Report,* 8 (2), pp. 251-256.

WALSHAM, G. (1995) The emergence of interpretivism in IS research. *Information Systems Research,* 6 (4), pp. 376-394.

WARKENTIN, M., GEFEN, D., PAVLOU, P. A. and ROSE, G. M. (2002) Encouraging citizen adoption of e-government by building trust. *Electronic markets,* 12 (3), pp. 157-162.

WARNER, J. (2011) Understanding cyber-crime in Ghana: A view from below. *The International Journal of Cyber Criminology, 5,* pp. 736-749.

WARREN, S.D. and BRANDEIS, L.D. (1890) The right to privacy. *Harvard Law Review,* pp. 193-220.

WEERAKKODY, V. et al. (2012) E-government implementation strategies in developed and transition economies: A comparative study. *International Journal of Information Management,* 32 (1), pp. 66-74.

WEERAKKODY, V., EL-HADDADEH, R. and AL-SHAFI, S. (2011) Exploring the complexities of e-government implementation and diffusion in a developing country: Some lessons from the State of Qatar. *Journal of Enterprise Information Management,* 24 (2), pp. 172-196.

WEITZMAN, E.A. (2000) Software and qualitative research. *Handbook of Qualitative Research,* 2, pp. 803-820.

WELCH, E.W., HINNANT, C.C. and MOON, M.J. (2005) Linking citizen satisfaction with e-government and trust in government. *Journal of Public Administration Research and Theory,* 15 (3), pp. 371-391.

WELSH, E. (2002) Dealing with data: Using NVivo in the qualitative data analysis process. In: *Forum Qualitative Sozialforschung/Forum: Qualitative Social Research.*

WERRO, F. (2009) "The Right to Inform v. The Right to be Forgotten: A Transatlantic Clash." In *Liability in the Third Millennium,* eds. CIACCHI, A.C., GODT, C. and ROTT, P. and SMITH, L.J. (Baden-Baden, Germany: Georgetown Public Law Research Paper No. 2).

WESCOTT, C. (2003) E* government to combat corruption in the Asia Pacific Region. In: *Prepared for the 11th international anti-corruption conference. Seoul, Republic of Korea.*

WEST, D.M. (2005) Equity and accessibility in e-Government: A policy perspective. *Journal of e-Government,* 1 (2), pp. 31-43.

WESTIN, A. F. (1970) *Privacy and Freedom.* Bodley Head, London WESTIN, A.F. (1967) Privacy and freedom.

WILKES, J. (2011) *Peel Police Arrest Six in Identity Theft Operation Allegedly Linked To Ghana.* [Online] Available from: http://www.thestar.com/news/crime/2011/05/25/peel_police_arrest_six_in_identit y_theft_operation_allegedly_linked_to_ghana.html [Accessed 19/01/14].

WILLIAMS, I., GYAASE, P.O. and FALCH, M. (2012) Enhancing rural connectivity through an extended internet cafés business models.

WOLCOTT, H.F. (2008) *Ethnography: a way of seeing.* Lanham, MD: Altamira Press.

WORLD BANK (2012) *Data - Ghana.* [Online] Available from: http://data.worldbank.org/country/ghana. [Accessed 15/09/13].

WORLD BANK. (2011) *Definition of E-Government.* [Online] Available from: http://web.worldbank.org/WBSITE/EXTERNAL/TOPICS/EXTINFORMATIONAND COMMUNICATIONANDTECHNOLOGIES/EXTEGOVERNMENT/0,,contentMDK: 20507153~menuPK:702592~pagePK:148956~piPK:216618~theSitePK:702586,00.html. [Accessed 20/01/13].

WORLD STATS (2014). *Internet World Stats - Africa.* [Online] Available from: http://www.internetworldstats.com/africa.htm#gh [Accessed 20/09/14].

WRIGHT, D. (2010) Structuring stakeholder e-inclusion needs. *Journal of Information, Communication and Ethics in Society,* 8 (2), pp. 178-205.

YILDIZ, M. (2007) E-government research: Reviewing the literature, limitations, and ways forward. *Government Information Quarterly,* 24 (3), pp. 646-665.

YIN, R.K. (2009) *Case study research: design and methods.* Los Angeles, Calif.: Sage Publications.

YIN, R.K. (2013) *Case Study Research: Design and Methods.* Los Angeles, Calif. [u.a.]: Sage Publ.

ZAKARIA, M.R. (2013) Personalized E-government System: Towards an Adaptive Maturity Model. *International Journal of Business Information and Technology (IJBIT),* 2 (1).

ZALLER, J.R. (1996) "The Myth of Massive Media Impact Revived." In *Political Persuasion and Attitude Change*, edited by MUTZ, D.C., SNIDERMAN, P.M. and BRODY R.A. Michigan: University of Michigan Press, 1996 pp.17-78.

ZHAO, F. (2011) Impact of national culture on e-government development: a global study. *Internet Research,* 21 (3), pp. 362-380.

ZMIJEWSKA, A. and LAWRENCE, E. (2005) Reshaping the Framework for Analysing Success of Mobile Payment Solutions, *IADIS International Conference on E-Commerce*, Porto, Portugal.

Appendix A: Research interview consent form

Date: .....November 2010

Research Title: Empirical Investigation of the Role of Privacy and Data Protection in the Implementation of Electronic Government in Ghana

Name of Researcher: Eric Agyei-Bekoe

Instituition: Centre for Computing and Social Responsibilty, De Montfort University, Leicester, UK

Course : PhD Computer Science Research

Supervisors: Prof. Simon Rogerson, Dr. Ben Fairweather and Dr. Richard Howley

The research seeks to evaluate the role of privacy and data protection in the implementation of electronic eovernment in developing countries: Ghana as a case study. The research has been approved by the supervisors. No deception is involved, and it involves no risk to the participants. Participation is voluntary and participants may withdraw from the research at any stage. Should you decide to withdraw from the research, please contact the researcher: Eric Agyei-Bekoe, Centre for Computing and Social Responsibilty, De Montfort University, The Gateway, Leicester, LE1 9BH, UK. Email at Eric.Agyei-Bekoe@email.dmu.ac.uk or by telephone on +44 798 539 1905/+44 116 250 6143. Upon receipt of notification to withdraw all data relating to the organisation or individual will be destroyed.

Participation in the research is by interview and it takes 40-50 minutes. All responses are treated as confidential, and in no case will responses from individual participants be identified. All records relating to the research will be securely locked in a filing cabinet. The researcher, his supervisors and examiners are the only authorised people who will have access to the records.

In undertaking this research, the researcher abides by a strict code of conduct of The Chartered Institute for IT, Social Research Association Ethical Guidelines and Economic and Social Research Council Ethics Framework. These ensure that the research is carried out to the highest ethical standard.

For further information please contact the researcher: Eric Agyei-Bekoe, Centre for Computing and Social Responsibilty, De Montfort University, The Gateway, Leicester, LE1 9BH, UK. Email at Eric.Agyei-Bekoe@email.dmu.ac.uk or by telephone on +44 798 539 1905/+44 116 250 6143.

Please sign below if you understand the statements and freely consent to participate in the research.

Name of Participant: ....

Signature: ....

Date: ....

Appendix B: Consent form for follow-up interview

Date: .....October 2012

Research Title: Empirical Investigation of the Role of Privacy and Data Protection in the Implementation of Electronic Government in Ghana

Name of Researcher: Eric Agyei-Bekoe

Instituition: Centre for Computing and Social Responsibilty, De Montfort University, Leicester, UK

Course : PhD Computer Science Research

Supervisors: Dr. Ben Fairweather, Dr. Richard Howley and Dr. Catherine Flick

The research seeks to evaluate the role of privacy and data protection in the implementation of electronic government in developing countries: Ghana as a case study. The research has been approved by the supervisors and is ***a follow-up to earlier fieldwork which took place in November 2010.*** No deception is involved, and it involves no risk to the participants. Participation is voluntary and participants may withdraw from the research at any stage. Should you decide to withdraw from the research, please contact the researcher: Eric Agyei-Bekoe, Centre for Computing and Social Responsibilty, De Montfort University, The Gateway, Leicester, LE1 9BH, UK. Email at Eric.Agyei-Bekoe@email.dmu.ac.uk or by telephone on +44 798 539 1905/+44 116 250 6143. Upon receipt of notification to withdraw all data relating to the organisation or individual will be destroyed.

Participation in the research is by interview and it takes 40-50 minutes. All responses are treated as confidential, and in no case will responses from individual participants be identified. All records relating to the research will be securely locked in a filing cabinet. The researcher, his supervisors and examiners are the only authorised people who will have access to the records.

In undertaking this research, the researcher abides by a strict code of conduct of The Chartered Institute for IT, Social Research Association Ethical Guidelines and Economic and Social Research Council Ethics Framework. These ensure that the research is carried out to the highest ethical standard.

For further information please contact the researcher: Eric Agyei-Bekoe, Centre for Computing and Social Responsibilty, De Montfort University, The Gateway, Leicester, LE1 9BH, UK. Email at Eric.Agyei-Bekoe@email.dmu.ac.uk or by telephone on +44 798 539 1905/+44 116 250 6143.

Please sign below if you understand the statements and freely consent to participate in the research.

Name of Participant: ....

Signature: ....

Date: ....

Appendix C: Research interview guide

I would like to thank you for agreeing to participate in this interview. As mentioned in the consent form, this research seeks to evaluate the role of privacy and data protection in the implementation of e-government: Ghana as a case study.

The aim of the interview is to collect data which would answer the research questions as outlined in the invitation letter. The major points to be discussed are:

- the interviewee's conception of e-government.
- the stage of e-government implementation in Ghana.
- the main obstacles (i.e. Government commitment, organisational, technological infrastructure, human resources/IT experts, public education etc.) that might impede the successful implementation of e-government in Ghana.
- the interviewee's idea of privacy and data protection.
- the awareness of privacy issues in Ghana.
- the interviewee's perception of the effect of implementation of e-government on personal data of the public.
- interviewee's suggestions of priorities/strategies that should be in place for successful implementation of e-government in Ghana.
- interviewee's suggestions for future implementation of privacy law in Ghana.

Before the interview a consent form would be given to each participant to read and sign. The form among other things specifies:

- The aim of the study
- The duration of the interview
- Confidentiality of participants/interviewees
- Interviewees right to refuse to answer any question
- Interviewees right to withdraw from the interview at any stage

- How the responses/data collected would be protected, secured and stored

Interviewee Profile:

Full Name (Including title)...

Organisation... Position.................................

Qualification..

E-mail address...

Interview Date...Time.......................................

Appendix D: Research interview questions

The purpose of the interview is to gather primary data from the research participants. The data collected when analysed would answer the research questions.

(The interview questions are initially explained to the participants for them to have a fair idea of the whole interview process.)

The purpose of this research is to evaluate the steps towards the implementation of e-government privacy and data protection in Ghana. The contribution that this research will make is recommending to the stakeholders/policy makers as to the need to implement privacy legislation alongside e-government. In other words the research seeks to recommend to the Government of Ghana and other policy makers the importance of privacy legislation in the implementation of e-government.

Would you like me to remind you of the research aims and objectives or go straight to the questions?

If it is alright with you, I will be tape recording our conversation. The purpose of this is that I can get all the details but at the same time be able to carry on an attentive conversation with you. I assure you that all comments will remain confidential. If you agree to this interview and the tape recording, please read and sign this consent form.

E-government Questions

1. I will like to start by having you tell me your position or status in your department. Can you briefly tell me your responsibilities in your department? And if you don't mind, may I please know your educational/professional background?
2. In your own words what is e-government?
3. In your opinion do you think e-government implementation is necessary in Ghana? Why?
4. Can you tell me who or which sector is responsible for the e-government implementation in Ghana?

5. Are you aware of any strategic plan towards the implementation of e-government in Ghana? If yes can you briefly explain it?
6. Are you aware of the stage of the e-government implementation process in Ghana? What have been done so far and what is left to be done?
7. In your opinion what challenges has the government faced so far in the implementation of e-government?
8. Are you aware of any obstacles that are impeding the e-government implementation? If yes, what are they?

   What steps are being taken to address these obstacles?
9. In your opinion what do you think needs to be done for the public to embrace the e-government implementation?
10. The previous government was keen on e-government implementation. In your opinion has there been any change of focus since the current government took over?

Privacy Questions

1. In your own words can you briefly explain to me what is meant by privacy?
2. What about data protection?
3. In your opinion do you think the Government of Ghana should implement privacy legislation alongside e-government? If yes why? If no why?
4. In your opinion do you think the e-government implementation will be successful without any privacy and data protection legislation? Explain
5. In your view what would be the advantages or benefits for implementing privacy legislation in Ghana? What about disadvantages?
6. Are you willing to lose your privacy in order to get e-government services? If yes why? If no why?
7. Is there anything else about e-government implementation in Ghana that you would like to share with me? What about privacy and data protection?

Thank you very much for you time.

Appendix E: Sample of transcribed data

Interviewer: In your own words what is e-government?

Participant 1 (P1): E-government is government trying to implement its services and functions to the public electronically, in other words, digitalising government functions to achieve a better supervision, a better co-ordination and a better governing process.

Interviewer: In your opinion do you think e-government implementation is necessary in Ghana?

Participant 1(P1): Yes, it is.

Interviewer: Why?

Participant 1 (P1): E-government is long overdue and we are really lagging behind as compared to the other western countries. Things are as they are now because we haven't got good e-government system in place.

Interviewer: Can you tell me who or which sector is responsible for the e-government implementation in Ghana?

Participant 1 (P1): I know it is Ministry of Communications.

Interviewer: Are you aware of any strategic plan towards the implementation of e-government in Ghana? If yes can you briefly explain it?

Participant 1 (P1): I am aware of something of that sort and they trying to introduce ICT programmes in the basic schools, that is, the primary and junior secondary schools.

Even that I have a query because they have not tried to develop the human resource base at the universities, that is, training the undergrads to go and teach the Teacher Trainees so that they could also go down and teach the basic schools. We train the training colleges' teachers and the various organisations IT departments' staff. So I was expecting the government to first of all equip all the universities computer science departments with facilities and resources for them to gain the necessary knowledge so that they can also train the trainee teachers and they can also go down to the basic schools, high schools to teach the young ones.

Interviewer: When you say "they" who are you referring to?

Participant 1 (P1): I mean the Ghana government.

Interviewer: Are you aware of the stage of the e-government implementation process in Ghana? What have been done so far and what is left to be done?

Participant 1(P1): Yes. I know that the government policy document is finalised and they have started some e-government implantation projects. They have two teams in place working on this e-government implementation. I know there is a Ghana government website too.

Interviewer: In your opinion what challenges has the government faced so far in the implementation of e-government?

Participant 1 (P1): The challenges that the government is currently facing is human base.

Interviewer: What do you mean by "human base"?

Participant 1 (P1): I mean the IT experts. Even the government gets all the money [funds] to acquire the computers needed for this [e-government] project they still need the human resource, I mean, the technical people to handle and manage them. And these human resources are the people we [university lecturers] are training with minimal resources. So I think this is a challenge the government is going to face in carrying out this e-government project.

You know these young people [university students] that we training with limited resources are the same people who are going to go home and teach their mothers and fathers how to use computers and educating them about these e-government services. Yet these same people don't have the resources for their academic work or expose them to it.

Interviewer: Are you aware of any obstacles that are impeding the e-government implementation? If yes, what are they?

Participant 1 (P1): Yes. As I just mentioned, the resources, both human and the technological know-how.

Interviewer: What steps are being taken to address these obstacles?

Participant 1 (P1): The first thing to do address this problem is to meet all the stakeholders especially the university lectures [academics] to develop the higher level computer science education in the country and then enquire which area the government can support so that we get the best effective computer science departments running in the universities. Then after these students we train would be equipped with the knowledge to move straight to teach IT in the secondary schools or teacher training colleges or at best work in the work in the IT departments of both the public and the private sector.

Interviewer: In your opinion what do you think needs to be done for the public to embrace the e-government implementation?

Participant 1 (P1): We can do a lot of education in the media, radio, TV whatever. But as I mentioned earlier a lot can also come from the youth teaching their parents how to use computers, how to browse the Internet and most importantly how to access e-government services online.

Interviewer: The previous government was keen on e-government implementation. In your opinion has there been any change of focus since the current government took over?

Participant 1 (P1): Well, I don't see any difference.

Interviewer: In your own words can you briefly explain to me what is meant by privacy?

Participant 1 (P1): Privacy is giving your personal data to the appropriate unit and ensuring that the data is kept securely for their use, for the purpose for which they collected it and not to send it to any unauthorised people. So it is like protecting your data from being misused.

In short I will say, privacy is protecting your data from being misuse.

Interviewer: What about data protection?

Participant 1 (P1): I think it's got something to do with the law protecting privacy.

Interviewer: In your opinion do you think the Government of Ghana should implement privacy legislation alongside e-government? If yes why? If no why?

Participant 1 (P1): Yes, privacy legislation is very important. It will ensure the unit that collects our personal data when we use the e-government services protects and secures it.

Interviewer: In your opinion do think the e-government implementation will be successful without any privacy and data protection legislation?

Participant 1 (P1): No, I don't think so. Privacy legislation will let people have confidence in using the e-government services.

Interviewer: In your view what would be the advantages or benefits for implementing privacy legislation in Ghana?

Participant 1 (P1): People will go online and use the services freely once they know that they are protected.

Interviewer: What about disadvantages?

Participant 1 (P1): I can't think of any disadvantages for now. But if there are any disadvantages, obviously, the advantages will outweigh them.

Interviewer: Are you willing to lose your privacy in order to get e-government services?

Participant 1 (P1): No way.

Interviewer: Why?

Participant 1 (P1): I won't put my personal data online and find out later that it's being misused.

Interviewer: Since you are computer science lecturer can I ask you whether you teach your students "Privacy and Data Protection" as a module.

Participant 1 (P1): No, we don't. But we do teach data security, network security and aspects of data authentication, authorisation and anonymity. So we teach our computer science students some of these things and it more about security than privacy.

Interviewer: Is there anything else about e-government implementation in Ghana that you would like to share with me?

Participant 1 (P1): Basically if you are using e-government services, your personal data will be collected and if you don't know what is going to happen to it, you will get worried - so personal data must be protected.

Even if you are sending an email you don't know who is accessing it so there must be some sort of privacy law to safeguard it.

Interviewer: Anything else?

Participant 1 (P1): We as academics train these students to become IT professionals and computer science teachers but we are not briefed much about this e-government implementation. We are not aware of what is going on or what is happening out there.

Interviewer: Thank you very much for your time.

INDEX

www.ingramcontent.com/pod-product-compliance
Ingram Content Group UK Ltd.
Pitfield, Milton Keynes, MK11 3LW, UK
UKHW021328190726
13845UKWH00004B/69

9 789349 964068